Himalayan Challenge

Also by the same author:

Reset: Regaining India's Economic Legacy

Himalayan Challenge

*India, China and the
Quest for Peace*

SUBRAMANIAN SWAMY

RUPA

Published by
Rupa Publications India Pvt. Ltd 2020
7/16, Ansari Road, Daryaganj
New Delhi 110002

Sales Centres:
Allahabad Bengaluru Chennai
Hyderabad Jaipur Kathmandu
Kolkata Mumbai

Copyright © Subramanian Swamy 2020

Map not to scale. While all efforts have been made to make the images of the map accurate, the publisher and the author are in no way liable for the correctness or authenticity of the same. Any errors or omissions brought to our attention will be remedied in future editions.

The views and opinions expressed in this book are the author's own and the facts are as reported by him which have been verified to the extent possible, and the publishers are not in any way liable for the same.

All rights reserved.
No part of this publication may be reproduced, transmitted, or stored in a retrieval system, in any form or by any means, electronic, mechanical, photocopying, recording or otherwise, without the prior permission of the publisher.

ISBN: 978-93-90356-19-5

Second impression 2021

10 9 8 7 6 5 4 3 2

Printed at Parksons Graphics Pvt. Ltd, Mumbai

The moral right of the author has been asserted.

This book is sold subject to the condition that it shall not, by way of trade or otherwise, be lent, resold, hired out, or otherwise circulated, without the publisher's prior consent, in any form of binding or cover other than that in which it is published.

*Dedicated to my former Harvard University colleagues,
to whom I owe my interest and knowledge of China in
my formative years—
Merle Goldman, Roderick MacFarquhar, Dwight Perkins,
Henry Rosovsky and John Fairbank*

CONTENTS

Preface ix

1. The Discovery of China 1
2. India's Tibet Policy: Between the Dragon and the Snow Lion 22
3. A Phantom Called McMahon Line 44
4. 1962: 'A Stab from the Front' 72
5. An Uneasy Coexistence 103
6. Strategic Choices: Containment or Engagement? 126

Bibliography 171

Appendix I: Home Minister Vallabhbhai Patel's Note to the Prime Minister 174

Appendix II: Prime Minister Jawaharlal Nehru's Note on China and Tibet 183

Appendix III: 'We Face Common Problems': Deng Xiaoping in a Meeting with Dr Subramanian Swamy in Beijing on 8 April 1981 (As published in India Today) 191

Appendix IV:	India's Voting Record on Issues Relating to China in the United Nations	202
Appendix V:	Declassified CIA Papers: The Sino-Indian Border Dispute	204
Appendix VI:	Extracts from a Soviet Document Dated 2 October 1959 Accessed From the Woodrow Wilson Cold War Archives	214
Index		229

PREFACE

Today, India's perspective on China is that of an aggressive and expansionist threat at one end, and that of it being an ancient sister civilization at the other extreme. Most Indians, however, carry in their minds both caricatures. This causes wild and erratic mood swings in the Indian public perception, fuelled further by media reports of Chinese 'unfriendliness' or alternatively of superficial 'warm gestures', such as Chairman Mao's famous smile at an official May Day reception in Beijing in 1970. This causes the cyclic movements in policy towards China that we have seen over the last five decades, and has sown confusion in China and the world about India's stance on a China policy, as well as destabilized our relations with that country. Further, India–China relations have been frequently destabilized by extraneous forces, which have only exacerbated these irrational wild swings.

This can be corrected only if we have a consultative committee of genuine Chinese studies scholars, current and retired military personnel, retired civil servants and senior journalists, all cleared by security agencies. The findings of this committee should be debated in elite institutions such as the International Institute for Strategic Studies in the United Kingdom (UK), or foreign relations bodies as in the United States of America (US). China has to be decoded by such a body, and not by currently serving civil servants-dominated committees in the government.

In a world that has dramatically changed for India from 1962 (the year of the humiliating border conflict between India and China) to the diabolical terrorist and religion-driven events in the US of 2001, India has yet to live down the loss of its global status caused by China since 1962. The ideal 'cooperative competitiveness' in world affairs vis-à-vis China has eluded India, and thus our nation has been robbed of its due place in the global structure of realpolitik. India has been denied the veto-holding, permanent seat in the United Nations Security Council (UNSC), which is its due, and it has remained excluded from the Group of Seven Nations (G7) despite being a durable and stable democracy.

Now, in 2020, India again risks losing further stature internationally, because the Chinese People's Liberation Army (PLA) has clandestinely and illegally occupied Indian territory by taking undue advantage of the coronavirus pandemic and crossed beyond the mutually agreed upon Line of Actual Control (LAC). As of now, India has held firm its ground, but the Chinese troops have not pulled back to their side of the LAC. The events, as published in the Indian print media in July 2020, of euphoria seem eerily similar to what was published in the same print media in July 1962. However, sadly on 20 October 1962, Indian people were shocked to find that the PLA had invaded Ladakh and Arunachal Pradesh (then known as the North East Frontier Agency [NEFA]) in a synchronized move. India's so-called reputation of the 1950s parity with China was in dust.

China's negative perception of India's capability is rooted even today in the 1962 armed conflict. China officially holds that the conflict was the result of Indian unreasonableness, its desire to inherit the ill-gotten concessions obtained by British imperialists from a then weak China, and India not being reconciled to the situation in Tibet (notwithstanding, India recognized Tibet as a part of Chinese sovereignty and affirmed it as a region of China by two formal treaties signed by two different party's prime ministers (PMs): Jawaharlal Nehru and Atal Bihari Vajpayee—first in 1954 and then in 2003, respectively). China periodically charges India with seeking domination of South Asia, deliberately reusing the Chinese threat. India, China alleges, seeks to find a pretext for its nuclear pursuit in defiance of the established international order on disarmament. China also alleges that India is dreaming instead of becoming a global power with the patronage of the US, which, in turn, as the sole global military power perceives China as a growing challenge to it. China believes that India is one possibility that the US is increasingly turning to in order to develop alternative options to contain China.

Catching Up with China

In the new millennium of the twenty-first century, even though there is a substantial economic gap between China and India, it is coverable by India. If India were to concentrate on a significantly accelerated growth in agriculture, information technology (IT) services and exports during the next decade, post 2021 the gap with China can be quickly bridged, fuelled by the plateauing of Chinese growth rates and the West's growing disenchantment with its perceived aggressiveness. To begin closing the India–China economic gap, clearly, India will have to make strenuous efforts fiscally to raise its investment rate to reach or exceed 36 per cent of the gross domestic product (GDP). This task, of course, is within reach and it is a target for which Indian people would be willing to make a sacrifice. My earlier book *Reset*[1] describes how this can be done. Catching up with China is a worthwhile slogan for India's new millennium, along with a national commitment to achieve an annual GDP growth rate of 10 per cent. Both goals are feasible and attainable within India's grasp, and at a striking distance. The only question is whether or not the present policymakers are up for it.

India's rise as a global power in the twenty-first century depends on India alone. For that to happen, it would require a combination of political sagacity, rapid economic growth, social cohesion as one people, credible and self-reliant military capability and a shrewd diplomacy, without the inferiority complex inherited from our history of the last two centuries. Nobody can then deny India global status. However, by the same token, no power is going to confer that high status on India until then. Thus, if in the years ahead, India fails to attain global status, it will be due to its own domestic and diplomatic failures and not due to any international perfidy or lack of international support.

Such a global status, I believe, would have a multiplier effect if India is able to harmonize its interests with China, perhaps after a leadership change in that country, much like the transition from Chairman Mao Zedong to Chairman Deng Xiaoping did for India and China to live in peace. Such a harmonization, however, cannot be achieved by India appeasing China.

The time has come to reset our China policy with clear short- and long-term objectives and priorities, backed by a strategic and tactical doctrine, and financing the defence budget accordingly.

With the help of adequate historical material, I have in this book shown that for centuries, till 1959, India's relations with China were remarkably free from conflict and one of friendly

---

[1] Subramanian Swamy, *Reset: Regaining India's Economic Legacy*, Rupa Publications, New Delhi, 2019.

cultural borrowing—something unprecedented in world history. One has to study the history of Europe or West Asia to see the contrast. Indian and Chinese people have, at one level, internalized their mutual respect for each other's civilization. This internalized sentiment has to surface and be the cementing force in future relations, free from the deception of the recent past.

Therefore, I argue that the first requirement for an effective Indian policy towards China is to build a national consensus on how we define our complex interests vis-à-vis China. India has to define its perspective on China with clarity and transparency, and must choose either to have a compact with China in the twenty-first century (Option A) or participate in the presently growing prospects to contain China (Option B). There is also a distant, third alternative (Option C)—of a global triumvirate of India, China and the US—that could be possible only from 2050 onwards. This third option cannot be achieved by bilateral summits of the leaders of the two nations. It is a lasting lesson for us that the bonhomie between Nehru and Zhou Enlai ended in war. Now in the last six years, despite 18 summit meetings of PM Narendra Modi with Chinese president Xi Jinping, India–China relations have ended in another military confrontation and possibly, war. Media spin in both cases of Nehru's and Modi's tenure has landed India in difficulty.

A China–India compact will comprise nearly 36 per cent of the world's population, the countries being first and second in the world with a population of nearly 1.3 billion each. China's population is higher than India's, but China's is growing at a slower rate. This compact would not only alter the strategic map of the world, but also offer unique economic opportunities for joint ventures under the World Trade Organization (WTO) disciplines, especially in textiles, services, IT, space research and innovations in Asian and African nations. China–India joint supervision with Indonesia of the Strait of Malacca would impact nearly 75 per cent of the world's commercial sea traffic. Such a compact between China and India thus has multidimensional possibilities. However, it depends on the leadership of the two nations to be able to understand, accommodate and calibrate their perspectives, without of course, causing alarm in the world's present-day sole superpower, the US. Today, China's lifetime President Xi Jinping has made it clear that he wants to demonstrate that India is just a regional power, and perhaps a junior partner of the US, which in turn, is no more the sole superpower. China is, Xi holds, now an alternative to the US in military and economic power. For India, it is easy to blame China, but the real test will be the ongoing face-off between India and China on the Indian territory of Ladakh across the LAC, where China has made major incursions. The outcome of this conflict will decide whether India is a third player in the global power status.

This would then lead to a gradual transit towards a strategic and tactical adjustment for world peace. In other words, I commend an India, China and US triangular relationship for a lasting and long-term new world order. That would require a joint leadership that can contain the xenophobic sections in all three nations and recognize that each nation has its own limitations in this fragile world, as reinforced by the recent coronavirus pandemic. The eschewing of the status quo by action is the basis for a new enlightenment in the twenty-first century.

I have academically specialized in the study of China, with special attention to the economy and its comparison with India. I was initiated into the field in 1964 by the doyen of Chinese studies at Harvard University—Professor of History, John Fairbank. Later, three other Harvard professors had partnered in teaching courses or jointly addressed seminars at Harvard over the period of 1964 to 2011., viz., Prof. Dwight Perkins, Prof. Henry Rosovsky and

Prof. Roderick MacFarquhar, who also wrote a foreword to my book titled *India's China Perspective* (Konark, 2001). My recent book, *India's China Strategic Perspectives* (Haranand, 2019), has been overtaken by events since 5 May 2020, and hence, it has become necessary to write the present book to reflect the changed perspective.

I thank my wife Dr Roxna Swamy, who dared me to learn Chinese Mandarin language when we first met at Harvard, in 1964, for assisting me in writing this book.

It is also appropriate that I thank my publisher, Rupa Publications, for the excellent and patient editorial contribution in bringing out this book.

1

THE DISCOVERY OF CHINA

There is no doubt that the Sino–Indian civilized contact of 2,500 years or more has been friendly for long, continuous periods, and culturally unidirectional from India to China. The legacy of the past 25 centuries of historical contacts between India and China is that of peaceful coexistence and mutual exchange of material and spiritual progress. It is generally accepted that contacts between India and China began as early as 500 BC. Trade and commerce as well as cultural contacts flourished between the two countries via the Silk Road for centuries thereafter.

In 1949, we should have charted a course of mutually beneficial relations based on these centuries-old contacts, and not allowed the relatively more recently formed nations, such as the US, and the now defunct Union of Soviet Socialist Republics (USSR), to mould our thinking to serve their strategic interests and to disrupt this historic Asian compact.

In both countries, a lack of correct perception of its past history was further clouded by 150 years of Western exploitative presence. The disinformation that their scholars propagated led to the present misunderstanding between these two giant, ancient Asian nations. It is no mystery then as to why these two nations did not go to war for centuries till 1962. The contrast with Europe, where every nation went to war with its neighbour almost annually for centuries till after World War II, is but obvious.

It would thus be appropriate to first understand the sequence and depth of Sino-Indian relations in the historical perspective. Few scholars in India have attempted that so far. For all his other faults, K.M. Panikkar, India's first ambassador to China, is the only one I know who understood the reality of the hoary Sino-Indian history, even if he fumbled on the Communist Chinese intentions on Tibet and on the Sino-Indian border question. I have here, therefore, co-opted and relied on his seminal works in the field, and as scholars we are grateful for the same.

The most significant aspect of the ancient contacts between India and China was the establishment of Buddhism in China. The Chinese had responded with great enthusiasm to the arrival of Buddhist missionaries, and thereafter, they took the initiative to bring Indian Buddhist monks and scholars to help teach, explain and establish Buddhism firmly in China.

During the fourth and fifth centuries AD, a second wave of Indian Buddhist monks travelling to China as missionaries created a counterwave of Chinese Buddhists coming to India for advanced training. Kumarajiva and Bodhidharma, who went from India to China, and Fa-Hsien and Yuan Chuang, who came from China to India, are familiar names who greatly enriched the knowledge and understanding of their countries of origin to their hosts.

The Sanskritization of China

Sociologists use the term 'Sanskritization' to mean the acceptance and assimilation by society of ideas, institution and morals that were originally articulated in Sanskrit literature in India, i.e., the 'cultural borrowing' of the whole complex of interrelationship of man with himself, his family and the rest of the world, as well as the concept of the soul and reincarnation.

For over 2,000 years, China was 'Sanskritized', and admitted by Chinese scholars such as Dr Hu Shih, former president of Peking University and a renowned poet. However, considering that modern China has emerged out of a Communist revolution and today is a proud, globally influential power, it should surprise no one that it wishes to underplay its past 'Sanskritization' in order to, ultimately, make it a forgotten nonsubject. Dr Hu Shih looked down on this 'cultural borrowing' from India as being nothing more than a retrograde domination. In his address to Harvard University in 1936, he said: 'With the new aids of modern science and technology, and of the new social and historical sciences, we are confident that we may yet achieve a rapid liberation from the two thousand years of cultural domination (by India).'[1]

In order to understand the extent of past Sanskritization of China, we need to be clear about two things. First, it was Mahayana Buddhism that went to China, whose basic doctrines and principles were in Sanskrit, and not in Pali of the earlier Hinayana Buddhism. Second, the date of Buddha's Nirvana is not 483 BC as Western writers claim, and the date Indian historians are prone to recycle, but was much earlier. Judging by Tibetan records, it could probably be as old as 1800 BC.

It is interesting that Indian historians seem completely oblivious of Fa-Hsien's account on the subject, particularly on the question of when Buddhism first reached China. The Fa-Hsien version records: 'The monks asked Fa-Hsien [after they

---

[1] Page 2471 of the Tri Centennial Commemoration Volumes, Harvard University Press, 1936.

had crossed the Indus] if he knew when the law of Buddha first travelled to the East.'

Fa-Hsien replied:

> I asked various people [of those eastern countries] and they all agree that it was introduced long ago. After Maitreya's [Bodhisattva] image was set up by them, Indian *sramanas* continuously crossed this river bringing scriptures and disciplines. The image was set up about 300 years after Buddha attained Nirvana, during the time of King Ping of the Zhou Dynasty. So, we may say that the spread of the Great Religion dates from the time of that image.

From this statement of Fa-Hsien, we may derive two historical statements of fundamental importance. First, Buddha attained nirvana about 300 years prior to the reign of King Ping of the Zhou dynasty. Even by Western chronology of Chinese historical events, King Ping's reign is stated by Western scholars to be between 770 BC and 720 BC. Therefore, taking 750 BC as the date of Maitreya's image places Buddha's Nirvana at about 1050 BC, i.e., 300 years earlier. However, Ping's reign could well be earlier. The dates in vogue today have been assigned by Western historians, and they could have got the chronology of Chinese history as wrong as that of Indian history. Second, going by Fa-Hsien's account, Buddhism entered China much earlier than we had thought, i.e., sometime before 750 BC.

There is thus much scope for further research here, especially with regard to the relation between Asoka and the Chinese kings. Also, on the basis of Fa-Hsien's account, we can now reject the theory that Confucius and Buddha were contemporaries. My own research concludes the date of Buddha's Nirvana as around 1800 BC, much before Confucius. This is based on Tibetan sources, according to which, the Lhasa Temple had a rope that was knotted for every year after the Nirvana of Buddha.

It is also interesting to see how Western historians have reacted to Fa-Hsien's account. For example, Friedrich Max Müller, who hugely erred in Indian chronology, placed Buddha's Nirvana at around 500 BC in *Buddhism and Buddhist Pilgrims: A Review of M. Stanislas Julien's 'Voyages Des Pèlerins Boudhistes'*[2]:

> As King Ping's reign lasted from BC 750 to 719, this would place the death of Buddha in the eleventh century BC... But if Rhys David be correct, as I think he is, in fixing the date of Buddha's death within a few years of 412 BC, not to speak of Westergaard's still lower date, then the Buddha was very considerably the junior of Confucius.[3]

What is surprising is that Max Müller makes almost no mention of Fa-Hsien in this regard in his entire article.

Fa-Hsien's account was translated into French and English. The semi-official Chinese translation by Li Yung-hsi, which was done in Beijing in 1957, suffers in being quite stylized and reflects the modern Chinese desire to underplay the extent of Sanskritization of China. For instance, the title of Fa-Hsien's work is translated by Li Yung-hsi as *A Record of Buddhist Countries,* whereas the original reads as *Incidents of Travels in India, by the Sramana of the Eastern Tsin, Fa-Hsien, recorded by himself.* 'Sramana' is a Sanskrit word meaning 'holy priest'. The original account describes Fa-Hsien as being distressed by the lack of understanding in China of Buddhist principles, and so he decided to go to India to obtain documents to further the understanding of Mahayana Buddhism in China.

---

[2] *The (London) Times,* 17 and 20 April 1857.
[3] *A Record of Buddhistic Kingdoms Being an Account by the Chinese Monk Fâ-Hien of His Travels in India and Ceylon* (AD 399–414) *in Search of the Buddhist Books of Discipline,* Clarendon Press, Oxford, 1886. Also available at: http://www.buddhanet.net/pdf_file/rbddh10.pdf, last accessed on 9 September 2020.

Li Yung-hsi's translation says, 'Fa-Hsien was distressed to observe that not all the canons of the Monastic Rules were obtainable in China.' For this reason, the translation insists that 'Fa-Hsien and his friends went to India to obtain these rules and regulations'. That is, Fa-Hsien did not go to attain better spiritual understanding, but to obtain documents, just as one would go to a library. Such underplaying by Indian scholars is understandable especially since even modern Indians find Prof. Hu Shih's perception incredible. This is because they have never been exposed to the earlier tradition, but influenced by Western scholars, who had been their mentors and benefactors.

During the last 50 years, Western writers on Sino-Indian history have sought to develop the two views on Fa-Hsien, perhaps to discredit him. First, they hold that Fa-Hsien may have been a devout monk, but that his historical sense was poor. To support this thesis, they point out that Fa-Hsien does not even once mention Vikramaditya or Chandragupta II. Given that Vikramaditya represents the peak of Hindu revival, during whose time Fa-Hsien was reportedly in India, should he not have mentioned him even once? There is a rebuttal for this. According to India's *de-falsified* history, Chandragupta II of the Gupta dynasty was a contemporary of the Greek envoy Megasthenes, whom Western scholars place at around 300 BC. That Fa-Hsien did not make a single mention of Chandragupta II is easy to understand because Chandragupta, to put it simply, did not live at that time. Western historians such as Sir William Jones have wrongly and falsely determined Chandragupta II's reign circa AD 400, on the arbitrary assumption that the Sandrocottus mentioned in Megasthenes's *Indika* is Chandragupta Maurya. However, this arbitrary determination of Western historians is rejected by modern, liberated Indian historians familiar with the Puranas. The Western view is wrong because

Megasthenes's Sandrocottus was actually Chandragupta Gupta, *not Maurya*.

Second, Western scholars hold that when Fa-Hsien says it was 300 years after Buddha's Nirvana that Maitreya's image was built, 'it does not mean much since Fa-Hsien was very vague on other matters'! It could just as well be three years! These arguments, however, do not hold water, because Fa-Hsien's account is full of accurate description of topography and the hospitality of the people. It merely points out that such Western historians have not read Fa-Hsien, who is quite precise as the following passage in his narration shows:

> While in this world, he (Buddha) spent 45 years expounding the law, teaching and edifying the people, those without peace he gave peace, those without salvation he gave salvation. When he fulfilled his mission, he attained nirvana. Since his nirvana 1497 years ago, the Eye of the World has been closed and all the living creatures have never ceased to grieve.

European scholars were of the view that the first contact between India and its great neighbour China was not before the establishment of the Qin dynasty (or Ch'in dynasty) by Qin Shi Huangdi, the first emperor, in 221 BC. However, Fa-Hsien's account proves that this is not well founded. Though, at present, no specific date can be given for the discovery of China by India, it is probably true that India was in contact with the south-western regions of China from the earliest period of history. After the establishment of the Qin dynasty and the unification of China,[4] the contact between India and China became much deeper and closer, especially when the north-west of China and the Gandhara region, and the Kushans and a number of

---

[4]Unification of China was led by Qin Shi Huang (formerly Qin Shi Huangdí) to unify all that was ancient China and fortify his rule.

'Indianized' kingdoms developed relations that sustained for over a thousand years.

Transcending Geographies

This centuries-old contact was deepened around three main lines of communication between India and China across Central Asia: via Bamiyan and Bactria; via Kashgar across the Tarim Valley; and via Kashmir, Gilgit and Yasin across the Pamir Mountains. These routes became important after the second century BC and continued to be the most important highways of communication till the middle of the ninth century AD, when Islam interposed an effective barrier.

At the centre of the Gobi Desert, there is an oasis known as Yumen (Jade Gate) on the border of the former Chinese empire, near a valley sheltered by hills on all sides, known now to the world as Dunghuan. There, on the sides of the hills, are hundreds of excavated caves beautified by mural paintings and sculptures of very high quality that depict scenes from the life of Buddha and from the Jataka stories. These caves house a great international monastery.

Dunghuan was the last stage of the journey, a sort of resting place or pit stop for scholars, missionaries and other travellers arriving from India, the Indianized kingdoms of Central Asia and other areas of the Buddhist civilization to the great empire of China. It was also the first stage for those undertaking the strenuous journey across the snows of the Pamirs and the desert lands of Central Asia, to visit the holy places of Buddhism in India. It was the great clearinghouse for all travellers to China from the north-west, and the monastery with its temples, caves for meditation and large collection of books provided an ideal resting place.

At Dunghuan, the three northern routes from India converged. Of the three routes, the first lay through Afghanistan, with stages at Jalalabad, then known as Nagarahara, and at Bamiyan. French archaeologists have shown us what a great centre of Indian culture Bamiyan was in the first millennium of the Christian era. From there, through Bactria, the area of Samarkand, the route went eastwards over the passes of the Tian Shan Mountains. A second route, which was shorter but more difficult, lay through Kashmir and Gilgit to Kashgar and from there to Tokhai. A third was directly to Kashgar and from there along the Tarim basin to Dunghuan.

All along these routes flourished kingdoms, great and small, the population of which professed Buddhism, spoke Sanskrit and had accepted Indian culture, till Islamic forays destroyed it all, and laid it in ruins. A large number of manuscripts have now been discovered in this region and most of them are in the Indian script of the Kushan and Gupta periods. Some of the dynasties, which ruled in these areas, were also of Indian origin. In fact, up to the very borders of China on its north-west side, kingdoms which had imbibed the spirit of Indian culture were in existence at least from the first century AD till the emergence of the Qing dynasty in China, and the onslaught of Islam in India. Thus, India, China and Zoroastrian Iran were the pivots on which turned the cultural dynamics of most of Asia.

The route across Tibet, it should be noted, developed at a later period, and was never important from a commercial point of view. It however endured. The earliest route via Assam and Burma never fell into actual disuse, though it lost much of its importance for India as a whole after the growth of traffic across Central Asia.

Another important route to China was by sea. The maritime routes to the Pacific Ocean were known to the coastal peoples of India from the earliest periods of history. In fact, sea communications grew continuously in importance, especially in South India, and were of the highest importance to Sino-Indian relations till the blockade of the Chinese coast by the Portuguese.

As during the first century of the Christian era, we have allusions in Chinese records to the existence of Hinduized kingdoms, in what was known as Indo-China, where the Chinese had also penetrated. The two civilizations may be said to have confronted and fused with each other there at least from that time. There was a continuous interaction between the ports of India and these Hinduized states and also directly between the Indian ports and South China.

Because of the sea route, the trade with South India developed separately. Diplomatic relations were also established between the South Indian courts and the Chinese empire. According to Panikkar, a Chinese writer, Pan Ku, who lived at the end of the first century, mentioned that during the reign of Han emperors, the Chola kings had sent emissaries to China. The route given by Pan Ku as well as the name of the state concerned indicates that the kingdom ought to be that of the Cholas in Kanchipuram.

It is also stated that Wang Mang, the ruler in first century AD and founder of the short-lived Xin dynasty, sent presents to the king of Kanchipuram. Pan Ku adds that the exports from South India were 'shining pearls, rare gems and strange products', which the Chinese received in exchange for silk and gold. Pan Ku also makes it clear that these were brought to China on Indian ships. The Chola kingdom was a great naval power. As Panikkar points out, the territories of the Srivijaya Empire included both the Malay Peninsula and Sumatra and, in the day of its glory, also a major portion of Java. For over 700 years, this Chola state in the Hindu tradition of *Shashtrata* (persuasion by argument) controlled communications between the Indian Ocean and the

Pacific, and was the intermediary in the cultural and commercial traffic between India and China.

In South Indian literature of the thirteenth and fourteenth centuries, junks and sampans—both types of ships—are frequently mentioned. From Quilon (Kollam) in Kerala on the west coast, ships sailed regularly to the ports of South China. The last visit of Cheng Ho's armada to the port of South India was in AD 1424.

Prof. Hu Shih had, in fact, told Panikkar that the earliest contacts of Buddhism with China were through the southern route. Later, no doubt, with the more extensive relations established through the Indo-Buddhist kingdoms of Central Asia, the southern influence seems to have become less important. However, obviously, it did not at any time cease because of the existence of Sanskrit inscriptions in Szechuan and the continuing influence of Tantric worship in south-western China.

With the arrival of the Portuguese in AD 1498, the sea route was closed to Chinese vessels. Over the next four centuries, India's connections with China were through the Europeans. In the early nineteenth century, Indian merchants reappeared in China, but this time under the British flag. The great Parsis (Zoroastrians whose ancestors escaped to India from the Islamic slaughter of Persia) of Bombay (present-day Mumbai), especially the Camas and Chinoys, participated in Chinese trade. Small Indian trading communities came to be established at Canton, Shanghai and Tientsin, as well as other treaty ports. As merely subsidiary to British trade, they could not however be said to have materially contributed to the relations between China and India.

Propagators of Indian Thought

Paradoxically, as Panikkar regretfully notes, today every school-going child in India knows the names of Fa-Hsien, Yuan Chuang and Yijing, but does not know anything of the great number of very distinguished Indian scholars who spent their lives in China, translating Indian books, teaching in monasteries and generally propagating Indian thought. Apart from the development of religion and philosophy, Indian monks also promoted the advancement of phonology, astronomy, medicine, chemistry and physical exercise in China.

The earliest known Indian scholar to travel to China in AD 65 was Kashyapa Matanga, who had with Dharmaratna reached Luoyang in Henan Province of central China from today's Madhya Pradesh. One of the best remembered and most notable Indian scholars was Kumarajiva (end of fourth century). Between the time of Kashyapa Matanga and Kumarajiva, Indian culture had penetrated into China, both from the north and from the south of India.

Kumarajiva, the son of an Indian scholar from Kashmir named Kumarayana, who had established himself as a great scholar, was born around AD 343/344. His mother, Jiva, formerly a Buddhist nun, encouraged him in his career as a Buddhist priest. At age nine, she entrusted his schooling to Bandhudatta, a celebrated Sarvastivadin[5]. From him, Kumarajiva had his first training in Buddhist doctrines. Three years later, when he was only 12, he met Buddhayasas at Kashgar and was converted to the Mahayana doctrine. Kumarajiva was a student of the Vedas as well. He had therefore mastered both Hindu and Buddhist learning.

After completing his studies, Kumarajiva returned to Tibet, and achieved an international reputation as a scholar, teacher and expounder of Buddhist doctrines. The Qin emperor was so impressed by Kumarajiva's fame that he sent an envoy, General Lü Kuang, to invite him to the Imperial Court in Beijing, but Kumarajiva was reluctant to go. This was resented by the Chinese

---

[5] A member of the Buddhist school of Sarvastivada.

envoy, who declared war on the local king and, after defeating him in AD 385, abducted the monk to China.

In the meantime, the Emperor of China had been murdered, and therefore the general who had kidnapped Kumarajiva, kept the monk with himself. Though Kumarajiva had already become familiar with Chinese, he now had an opportunity to correct the imperfections of the provincial dialect during his 16-year stay in Gansu as the guest of the general.

In AD 401, when he was nearly 60 years old, Kumarajiva reached Chang'an (now Xi'an), the Imperial Capital of the new Emperor of China. His mastery over classical Sanskrit, a language he had learnt since his childhood, and now Chinese, meant that he was an ideal interpreter of Indian culture to China. Emperor Yao Xing accorded him unusual honours and made him the Rajguru (or Kuo-Shih). For the next 12 years, till his death in AD 413, Kumarajiva was engaged in translating Buddhist texts and correcting earlier translations. A Bureau of Translators was set up under his supervision, with over 800 scholars on the staff. Over 106 works, including most of the Mahayana texts, were translated. Of these, 56 are still available, and waiting for scholars to delve into. His most prominent work was the translation into Chinese of the central texts of the Madhyamika school, which later on became the basic texts of the 'Three Treatise' school of Buddhism.

Kumarajiva, who had begun as a follower of Hinayana Buddhism, had by then become a staunch Mahayana adherent. Till Kumarajiva's time, Chinese Buddhism seems to have been mainly of the Hinayana school. It is Kumarajiva's apostolate in China that established Mahayana as the dominant school of Chinese Buddhism, and consequently, that was responsible for the spread of that school in the Far East. From that point of view alone, Kumarajiva's contribution could well be said to be of the highest historical significance for India's contribution to Buddhist studies in China and East Asia.

Another revolutionary teacher who is still revered in China is Bodhidharma, who belonged to a royal family of Kanchipuram in South India. He preached the doctrine that the only reality is the Buddha Nature (Ultimate Reality) in the heart of man, and the realization of that Buddha Nature can only come from direct experience, and not by learning or asceticism. This represented the first introduction of Hindu mysticism in Buddhist garb into China.

Bodhidharma lived in the Shaolin monastery, and meditated in silence for nine years. There, he taught Wu Shih (probably Kalaripayattu of Malabar), the martial arts of self-defence, which Japan later imported from China. Wu Shih in Chinese is known as Karate in Japanese. Even today, modern India does not know that ancient India gave Karate (Wu Shih) to Japan via China and the world, and not the other way around!

Vajrabodhi, a priest from Kerala, introduced the 'Mantra Sastra' into China. He had attained sufficient eminence in sciences to become the guru of the King of Kanchi. Late in life, he converted to Tantric Buddhism. After some years at Nalanda, he, with his chief disciple, Amoghavajra, left for China by sea, reaching there in 719 CE in his 58th year. The Mantra sect which Vajrabodhi established was tantric esotericism, based on Moola mantras, and on worship of Devi through Yantras or diagrams as practised among the Saktas in India. Its Buddhist counterpart is generally in the Vajrayana form.

Thus, it was not only Buddhism that had penetrated into China. Sankhya, tantra shastra and other Hindu beliefs were also introduced into the thought of that country. How much of Hinduism was included in this export of ideas may be seen from the fact that in the vast collection, which Dr Raghu Vira, one of the greatest civilizational scholar-thinkers and founding member of the

International Academy of Indian Culture in Delhi, brought back from China, there is a third-century summary of the Ramayana.

Another source of Sanskritization was through Tibet. In the middle of the sixth century, Srongtsan Gampo unified the clans of Tibet. His son introduced into Tibet a modified Indian alphabet based on Nagari. It was Srongtsan Gampo who invited numerous Indian scholars to Tibet, notably Shantarakshita, who became his guru. It was at Gampo's suggestion that the great Padmasambhava, also known as Guru Rinpoche, the precious teacher, was invited to Tibet. He was the founder of the Tantric sect of Buddhism in Tibet. Tibet became the land of great monasteries under Guru Rinpoche's inspiration, and Tibetan tantricism secured a great hold on the border nationalities of China. During the Mongolian period, Lamaism became a fashion in the Yuan dynasty, as the emperor himself accepted the creed. The Tibetan monk 'Phags-pa was invited to the Mongol court in 1260 by Kublai Khan, the fifth Khagan of the Mongol Empire and founder of the Yuan dynasty. He was recognized as 'imperial preceptor' and 'state preceptor'. It is 'Phags-pa who invented the alphabetic system for the Mongol language, hence it is called the 'Phags-pa script.

This position of influence continued even under the Manchus or the Qing dynasty. The Buddhism that reached China, Mongolia and other countries through Tibet was of the Tantric variety. Further, it led to a penetration of especially the Saivite cults into China, a subject which has so far not been studied at all. In the collection brought back by Dr Raghu Vira, there is a banner with the Gayatri Mantra written on it in Mongolian characters.

The Buddhist religion, however, did not reach China as a system of elaborate metaphysics and spiritual discipline—as Panikkar has astutely noted—but as a form of popular worship and belief gradually taking root among the people, probably the poorest and the most lowly to whom the Buddhist missionaries, traders and travellers had brought the good tidings of mercy and delivery from pain.

The apparently rapid progress made by Buddhism in the Yangtze Valley and on the southern coast towards the end of the second century seems to indicate that it had a long period of slow but steady permeation among the people. By the third century, when the men of letters began to admire and defend it, Buddhism had already become a powerful religion, not because there was governmental patronage (of which there was but very little), but because of its powerful following among the people. It was the common man's religion and it continued to be so.

However, the general idea that with the downfall of the Tang dynasty Chinese pilgrims ceased to frequent holy places in India or pursue their studies at Indian centres of learning, is false. Analysing the Chinese inscriptions discovered at Bodh Gaya, famous scholar Émmanuel-Édouard Chavannes in *Revue de l'histoire des religions* concluded: 'The Chinese pilgrims who went to India in this period (in the 10th and 11th centuries) were numerous.'

Chinese Influence on India

The dominance of Indian thought in China for a period of over 600 years and the continuance of Buddhism in its naturalized form as one of the principal factors in Chinese life even now, impelled Dr Hu Shih, in his 1936 Harvard discourse titled *The Indianization of China*, to conclude that: 'The long history of Indianization of Chinese institutions, thought, art, and life in general furnishes the most extensive material that can be found for the study of cultural borrowings on the grandest scale.'[6]

---

[6]Hu Shih, *The Indianization of China: A Case Study in Cultural Borrowing*. Paper Delivered at the Harvard Tercentenary Conference of Arts and Sciences, 1936 (published by Harvard University Press, 1937).

Dr Hu Shih's description of the acceptance of Buddhism by the masses of China in the fourth, fifth and sixth centuries is worth quoting in this context:

> Then there came the great religion of the Buddha together with all the Mahayana trimmings of the pre-Buddhist and non-Buddhist religions of India. Never before had China seen a religion so rich in imagery, so beautiful and captivating in ritualism and so bold in cosmological and metaphysical speculations. Like a poor beggar suddenly halting before a magnificent storehouse of precious stones of dazzling brilliancy and splendour, China was overwhelmed, baffled and overjoyed. She begged and borrowed freely from the munificent giver. The first borrowings were chiefly from the religious life of India, in which China's indebtedness to India can never be fully told. India gave China, for example, not only one paradise but tens of paradises; not only Hell but many hells, each varying in severity and horror from the other. The old simple idea of retribution of good and evil was replaced by the idea of the transmigration of the soul and the iron law of karma which runs through all past, present and future existences.
>
> These and thousands of other items of belief and practice have poured from India by land and by sea into China and have been accepted and gradually made into parts of the cultural life of China.[7]

The dominance and firm grip that Buddhism came to acquire in China was, of course, the result of a long-lasting process of considerable interaction and exchange with India spread over centuries, which benefited both countries in many ways. As recent

---

[7]Chih-P'ing Chou (ed. Hu Shih). *English Writings of Hu Shih: Chinese Philosophy and Intellectual History*, Volume 2, China Academic Library, Peking.

excavations in Xinjiang have revealed, the Chinese were responsible for preserving many valuable Sanskrit works of the Gupta and post-Gupta period, by organizing their Chinese translations and printing them for posterity.

Naturally, with such a people as the Chinese, justly proud of their own long-established civilization, with their distinctive attitude towards life and their own philosophies, this wholesale acceptance of what was essentially a foreign religion, with its attendant culture, could not proceed for long without strenuous opposition. The decline of Buddhism in India—as also the rise of Confucian ritualism and Tao School in China—led to a weakening of contacts between China and India.

There was opposition from the Confucian literati, who not only vigorously defended Confucianism, but also counter-attacked Buddhist doctrines, especially the tendency of converts to become monks and to renounce their families and practise celibacy—both directly opposed to the strong familial tradition of Chinese civilization and its emphasis on ancestor worship.

As a result of this organized counter-attack, Indian influence in China had to face four periods of serious and sustained persecution, in AD 446, 574, 845 and 955. As Dr Hu Shih states, 'It is significant to note that all edicts for the persecution of Buddhism emphasized the fact that it was an alien religion introduced from a foreign barbarian country, and that it was a national disaster and a humiliation for the Middle Kingdom [Celestial Empire] to be thus under the influence of aliens.'[8] However, these exhibitions of imperial power and nationalist reaction never had more than temporary success. Indian influence in China had gone too deep and penetrated the masses to such an extent that, whatever the official policy or orders, the Sanskritization movement went on apace.

After the tenth century, however, the religious fervour for

---

[8]ibid.

Buddhism began to decline in India. Thereafter, over the next two centuries, trade and commerce between the two countries also declined on account of a number of economic and political developments, such as Islamic invasion and British colonialism. Thus, eventually, whatever little residual contacts existed faded with the advent of the colonial and imperialist era in Asia.

Dr Hu Shih explained this as being due to the twin processes of domestication and assimilation. 'Look at the faces of the deities in a Buddhist temple in China today,' he stated, 'and trace each to its earliest Indian original and you will realize how this process of domestication has worked... Maitreya, for example, has now become the big-bellied, heartily laughing Chinese monk that greets you as you enter any Buddhist monastery in China. Indeed, all faces of the Buddhist deities have been Sinicized through a long but unconscious process of domestication.'

Indian influence on Chinese sculpture and painting is well known and does not require to be restated here. With regard to drama, scholars trace three stages: first when the technique, the story and its characters were borrowed from India. Slowly, while the story and the characters remained Indian, the technique was suitably altered to meet Chinese requirements. In the third stage, Chinese characters replaced the Indian ones and the story too was suitably modified. A new national Chinese drama thus came into being in which Indian influences can only be noticed by scholars. Even in music, the following quotation from *Chinese Literature*, an official publication of the People's Republic, explains the position:

> As early as the Sui dynasty (AD 581–618), Vedic Indian music was formally recognized by the Chinese government as one of the chief categories of music. Later, during the Tang dynasty (AD 615–907) the tune of a Brahmin Dance which as introduced into China from the North West, became, after a certain amount of modification, the melody of the celebrated

Rainbow and Feather Garment Dance. This melody was so popular with the Chinese of the Tang dynasty that the famous poet, Pai Chu-yi wrote a poem in praise of it. ...It is little wonder that when a Chinese audience today hears Indian music, they feel that while possessing a piquant India flavour it has a remarkable affinity with Chinese music.[9]

The final conclusions of Dr Hu Shih are worth quoting:

> What had happened during these thousand years to bring about such a tremendous difference in the Chinese outlook on life? Nothing but the gradual deepening and intensifying of the Indianization of Chinese thought, life and institutions. Buddhism was fading away, but its cultural content had been domesticated and appropriated by the secular thinkers and had penetrated into Chinese life and institutions far beyond the confines of the monasteries and nunneries of Buddhism.
> ...In these and many other aspects, the great philosophers of esoteric rationalism [in China] were unconsciously acting as the most effective agents for the final Indianisation of China.

So was Sino-Indian relations during the first millennium of the Christian era a one-way traffic, in which India gave and China received, leading so distinguished and objective a scholar as Dr Hu Shih to describe the movement as the 'Indianisation of China'? Scholars, however, recognize that such one-sided influence has an implicit bilateral content. The bilateral contacts were so vigorous and extended over such a long period that it would be absurd to deny the influence of Chinese civilization on India.

The wide prevalence of silk from very earliest times is attested to by literature. As noted by Yuan Chuang, fruits of different kinds, especially pears and peaches, were introduced from China.

---

[9]*Chinese Literature*, Issue no. 4, 1955, p. 164.

Vermilion probably came first from China. In the south of India, the technique of the fishing industry in the backwaters seems to have been introduced from Canton. Also, it is well known that a flourishing porcelain industry was introduced in Kerala by the Chinese. In fact, it is known that a small colony of Chinese existed near Quilon for many centuries. The architecture of many houses in Kerala is distinctly Chinese.

Intimate religious, cultural and social relations existed between the two major civilizations of Asia for a period of nearly 1,500 years. For nearly a thousand years, from the first century BC to the tenth century AD, it was one of the major facts of the world's cultural history. Its importance in shaping the mind of East Asia, including Japan, Korea and Mongolia, is something that cannot be overlooked.

The Asian mind is a community based on ideas, beliefs and traditions, which are the contributions of the close association of the Indian and Chinese peoples over so long a period.

2

INDIA'S TIBET POLICY: BETWEEN THE DRAGON AND THE SNOW LION

The status of Tibet, and India's perception of it, has been one of the destabilizing factors in Sino-Indian relations. Publicly and formally, the Indian government regards Tibet as an integral part of China. However, in popular parlance, and in many of our actions, we do not behave as if Tibet is a part of China. There are two basic questions that need to be answered if we have to have a clear-cut Tibet policy. First, was Tibet an independent country at any point in history? Second, can Tibet be a viable, independent country at some point in the not-very-distant future? While the first question belongs to the realm of historical research, it is the second question which we have to answer before forming our national security policy. A perusal of historical records is, therefore, essential in order to find answers to these contentious questions and remove the public confusion on Tibet.

Although Buddhism was established in Han China several years before Christ, in Tibet, in particular, it arrived much later, in the seventh century AD before the institution of the Dalai Lama. In China, the Yuan dynasty founded by Kublai Khan in AD 1271 vigorously promoted Buddhism. It was Kublai Khan who unified Tibet under the Sagya Sect (Flower Sect). However, before the institution of the Dalai Lama was established, the Nyingma Sect (Red Sect), created under the influence of Padmasambhava, also known as Guru Rinpoche, had flourished in Tibet. The Yuan dynasty ended in the mid-fourteenth century, and in its place came the Ming dynasty. This coincided with the rise of the Gelug Sect (Yellow Sect) of Buddhism founded by Tsongkhapa. The Dalai Lama represents the Yellow Sect of Buddhism in Tibet.

In 1576, the Ming dynasty's Prince Anda (or Altan) Khan of Mongolia invited the then Gelug priest Sonam Gyatso to lecture on Buddhism in the Qinghai province. He then declared him a Rajguru. In 1578, Altan Khan conferred the title 'Dalai Lama' on this priest. The title means 'Ocean of Wisdom'. 'Dalai' in Mongolian (not Tibetan) means 'ocean'. The Sanskrit word for 'lake' is 'dal'. He was also named the Third Dalai Lama. The first and second Dalai Lamas were named posthumously, as they were the earlier 'head priests'.

It was the Fifth Dalai Lama Ngawang Lobsang Gyatso who formalized Tibet's confederation with ancient China. He sought the intervention of the Qing dynasty, which replaced the Ming dynasty in 1644, to stabilize himself in Tibet. Emperor Shunzhi not only despatched troops to consolidate the Dalai Lama's power, but also gave him a gold seal denoting Beijing's recognition.

In 1720, with the help of the Chinese emperor Kangxi, the then King of Tibet was deposed and the Ninth Dalai Lama was made the political head of Tibet. Since then, all succeeding Dalai Lamas (including the present one in India) made it the established practice to obtain Beijing's seal of approval to ensure legitimacy as the Dalai Lama. Monarchy came to an end in China in 1911, but the government in Beijing continued its role in Lhasa as a protector.

Understanding Chinese Suzerainty

This Chinese 'suzerainty' over Tibet has been an accepted fact even by governments hostile to China. However, it was Lord Curzon, the Imperial Viceroy of India, who first raised the question of Tibet's total independence. He regarded the idea of suzerainty as a 'constitutional fiction'. Curzon also directed Lieutenant Colonel Sir Francis Younghusband to go to Lhasa in 1903–04 to investigate if there was any Russian perfidy in Tibet. As a sequel to Younghusband's expedition, the Anglo-Tibetan Convention, also known as the Treaty of Lhasa, was signed in Lhasa in September 1904. The high points of this convention were that Tibet would deal directly with India instead of via China, and that Chumbi Valley on the Sikkim border would be given to India for 75 years.

The British government in London rejected Curzon's move, and ordered that the Anglo-Chinese Convention be called to prepare a draft agreement to supersede the Anglo-Tibetan Convention. Curzon resisted this by delaying tactics. Finally, London recalled Curzon and sent Lord Minto in his place. Later, the Convention between Great Britain and China Respecting Tibet was signed in April 1906 in Beijing, by which the Chumbi Valley was returned to Tibet on payment of a mere ₹2.5 million (₹25 lakh), in 1908. However, it has been with India since 1936. Article 2 of the Convention reaffirmed Chinese suzerainty over Tibet.

To further confirm this, Britain and Russia signed the Anglo-Russian Entente in St. Petersburg on 31 August 1907, in which Article 2 stated: 'In conformity with the admitted principle of suzerainty of China over Tibet, Great Britain and Russia engage not to enter into negotiations with Tibet except through the intermediary of the Chinese government.' In other words, the British government reasserted its consistent stand formalized in 1890 when the Convention between Great Britain and China relating to Sikkim and Tibet was signed in Calcutta (present-day Kolkata) guaranteeing Chinese suzerainty over Tibet. Thus, the then principal parties—China, British India and Russia—had accepted Chinese overlordship in Tibet.

However, this course of history was disturbed for a short duration when on one occasion, in 1913, Tibet rebelled. Dr Sun Yat-sen, the leader of the Chinese Nationalist Party, had toppled the Qing dynasty in Beijing, following which the Thirteenth Dalai Lama (predecessor to the present Dalai Lama) declared Tibet as an independent country. However, this was not for long. By 1929, under the same Dalai Lama, Tibet once again began to accept Chinese suzerainty. Incidentally, the Chinese always considered suzerainty to mean 'Chinese sovereignty with Tibetan autonomy', and hence, the province is called Tibet Autonomous Region (TAR). Suzerainty essentially meant autonomy of Tibet, subject to Chinese directions in defence and foreign affairs.

It is argued sometimes that this suzerainty was forced on Tibet by foreign powers. The argument, which is advanced by some Tibetans in Delhi, is rather thin because even the institution of the Dalai Lama had taken root with Chinese military patronage. Throughout the history of Tibet, the Dalai Lama sought and obtained the Chinese emperor's umbrella. Even the Dalai Lama as the unquestioned religious-cum-temporal leader of Tibet was made possible by the intervention of the Chinese emperor. Thus, when on 22 February 1940, the present Fourteenth Dalai Lama was anointed, a representative of the Chiang Kai-shek-led Kuomintang (KMT) government was especially despatched to Lhasa, and he officiated at the inauguration ceremony. Hence, to say that before 1951 Tibet was independent of China is not historically correct.

However, it was the year 1950 that changed Tibetan history drastically. In January that year, the Chinese government in Beijing, led by Mao Zedong, sent a note to Tibet asking the Tibetans to 'reunite with the motherland'. Then in October 1950, a year after the founding of the People's Republic of China (PRC), Chairman Mao ordered Chinese troops to enter Tibet. The Chinese army crossed Chin-sha River from the Szechuan province and liberated Chamdo, about 500 kilometres east of Lhasa.

Upon learning that China had marched its troops to the borders of Tibet, Deputy PM and Home Minister Sardar Vallabhbhai Patel, in a letter dated 7 November 1950, enquired of the PM and External Affairs Minister Jawaharlal Nehru as to what action the government was proposing to take to protect Tibet.[10] Sardar Patel listed 'Ten Points'—problems which, in his opinion, required early solution and around which India would have to build her 'administrative or military policies'. These included the policy regarding the McMahon Line and blocking Communist China's entry to the United Nations (UN) by voting against replacing the deposed Kuomintang China (now reduced to Taiwan). Earlier, without conferring with Sardar Patel, Nehru had declined the US offer of the UNSC veto-holding seat vacated by the KMT government after Chairman Mao dislodged it, to India.[11] All that Sardar Patel had wanted from Nehru was a recognition that since China may soon repudiate all treaties that Tibet was then presumed to have signed with India, calling it 'imperialism imposed', on the undefined state of the frontier, this called for a

---

[10] Avtar Singh Bhasin (ed.). *India–China Relations 1947–2000: A Documentary Study*, Vol. I, Geetika Publishers, New Delhi, pp 441–47.
[11] See Dr Anton Harder, 'Not at the Cost of China: New Evidence Regarding US Proposals to Nehru for Joining the United Nations Security Council,' Woodrow Wilson International Center for Scholars, Washington DC, USA, Working Paper, No. 76, March 2015. Also, for the same offer made by Soviet Union in 1955, see *The Hindu*, 28 September 2005.

'policy in regard to McMahon Line'. Sardar Patel also suggested that *before recognizing* the government of the PRC, India 'might have a discussion in the Cabinet'.

On receipt of this sound advice, Nehru was obviously irritated. Instead of a point-by-point reply, which a deputy PM was by right entitled to, Sardar Patel got a lecture on 'perspectives' from Nehru, who perhaps thought he had divine wisdom on foreign policy. This was reflected in his nominal reply to Sardar Patel on 18 November 1950, when instead of a letter to a colleague, Nehru sent him a Note that he had prepared without a covering letter. He wrote back rather patronizingly: 'If we lose our sense of perspective and world strategy and give way to unreasoning fears, then any policy that we might have is likely to fail.' He admitted that:

> We cannot save Tibet, as we should have liked to do, and our very attempt to save it might well bring greater trouble to it. It would be unfair to Tibet for us to bring this trouble upon her without having the capacity to help her effectively. It may be possible, however, that we might be able to help Tibet to retain a large measure of her autonomy.

Nehru further added—the significance of which is relevant even today—the following: 'It must be remembered that neither the UK, nor the USA, nor indeed any other power is particularly interested in Tibet or in the future of that country. What they are interested in is embarrassing China.' Further, Nehru added that a Cabinet discussion would not be useful because 'most members of the Cabinet have hardly followed these intricate conversations and consultations'.

Disappointed by Nehru's attitude (after Sardar Patel had passed away on 15 December 1950), an authorized Tibetan delegation went to Beijing from Lhasa in April 1951 and signed the 17-Point

Agreement on the merger of Tibet with China on 23 May 1951. The Tibetan leadership, without any friendly nation ready to help, capitulated to Beijing. After the Tibetan government headed by the Dalai Lama had surrendered, the Chinese army was welcomed to Lhasa with fervour and rejoicing on 26 October 1951, as per the 17-Point Agreement signed between the two governments. It is thus technically wrong to say that the Chinese army overran Tibet. This was the culmination of events that ended with a complete military takeover of Tibet while Nehru's government watched.

Thereafter, Nehru recognized the Chinese sovereignty over Tibet region, when on 29 April 1954 he signed Panchsheel, or the Five Principles of Peaceful Coexistence, which was first formally enunciated in the Agreement on Trade and Intercourse between the Tibet Region of China and India. This when all along he had said that India would not go beyond recognizing the 'suzerainty' of China. Nehru blundered in not obtaining a settlement on the India–China border while agreeing to this 1954 Treaty on Tibet. Nehru was also wrong when in the late 1950s, he yielded to pressure from the USSR, which was upset with a Communist rebel and ingrate China, to train Khampas and Tibetans to regularly ambush Chinese military convoys inside Tibet. We got the blame without having a fall-back position. This sowed the seed of mistrust between China and India, leading to the useless war of 1962.

Later, on one occasion in the late 1950s, in Answer to a Question in parliament, Nehru told Nath Pai, Member of Parliament (MP), that the Chinese language did not distinguish between 'sovereignty and suzerainty', and therefore, in the translation of the Indian note into Chinese language, an error had crept in: that is, 'suzerainty' was translated as 'sovereignty'.[12] This is entirely false. According

---

[12]Subramanian Swamy, *India's China Perspective*, Konark Publishers Pvt. Ltd, New Delhi, 2001, p. 47.

to my knowledge of Mandarin Chinese (now labelled Gwoyeu—the national language), for centuries, the Chinese have used the term *tzong jwu chuan* to describe 'suzerainty', and *jwu chuan* to denote 'sovereignty'. Unfortunately, nobody then in parliament knew the Chinese language to expose Nehru's ignorance, if not a deliberate lie. Such arrogance blended with ignorance of facts ultimately led to the 1962 War and the discrediting of Nehru. He began to look humbled, albeit sick. He died on 27 May 1964 of an undisclosed ailment (his death certificate has been classified as a 'national secret').

Tibet had unravelled into a disaster in India–China relations. It is not the border dispute that is at the core of the unsettled and cyclically rocky India–China relations; it is the convoluted and often unarticulated Indian approach to the status of Tibet and the misperception of India's vague and opaque goals which fuels Chinese misunderstanding of India's intentions. When the Chinese leaders repeatedly stated that the border dispute can be set aside till 'other issues are sorted out', they are actually indicating that if Tibet's status as a province of China is genuinely accepted by India, then (I infer) China would consider discussing the border on India's terms, but not before.

Suspicions and Hopes

Tibetans in India today, however, denounce the 17-Point Agreement, saying it was done at gunpoint. That may be the case, but during their visit to India in 1956, both the Dalai Lama and the Panchen Lama did not oppose this agreement. They were dissuaded by Nehru from doing so. At that point, no Chinese gun was held to their head in New Delhi. However, they had relied on Nehru's advice 'to lump it'.

The Chinese government had kept to the 17-Point Agreement

till 1958. In that year, under the Great Leap Forward programme launched by Mao Zedong, in the name of democratic reforms, the central Chinese government began to forcibly change the political and economic system in Tibet. This was in violation of the 17-Point Agreement, which expressly stated (Point 4) that 'The central authorities will not alter the existing political system. The central authorities also will not alter the established status, functions and powers of the Dalai Lama. Officials of various ranks shall hold office as usual.' Similarly, it was expressly stated (Point 11) that, 'there will be no compulsion for carrying out reforms on the part of the central authorities'. Seeing these developments and fearing arrest and imprisonment, the Dalai Lama and nearly 100,000 Tibetans escaped to safety in India in 1959, where they were given political asylum.

Later, during the period of the Cultural Revolution (1966–76), the 17-Point Agreement was torn to shreds by the Red Guards—groups of militant university and high-school students formed into paramilitary units. The Panchen Lama, who had gone to Beijing in 1964, could not return to Lhasa till 1983 for this reason. Of the 1,600 major monasteries in Tibet, 1,400 were destroyed by the Red Guards running amock. It was deeply distressing for me to read about how the religious Tibetans were sent to political slaughter. From 1959 to 1977, the Chinese government functioned in Tibet in breach of the 17-Point Agreement. This continued till the Four Modernizations programme of Chairman Deng Xiaoping was announced in 1980.

After Deng Xiaoping took charge, the Chinese Communist Party (CCP)[13] General Secretary Hu Yaobang and Deputy PM Wan Li paid a visit to Tibet in 1980. Hu formally acknowledged 'error and regret' for the tortures inflicted on the Tibetans during

---

[13]The Chinese Communist Party (CCP) is also known as the Communist Party of China (CPC).

the earlier periods. That same year, the CCP issued new directives on Tibet. The Chinese government officials also declared the need for preserving the 'autonomy of Tibet', and new policies to that effect were announced. On 15 December 1982, *Beijing Review*, the authoritative national weekly, published an editorial piece titled 'Policy towards the Dalai Lama', which stated: 'The Dalai Lama and his followers are welcome to return to China. Upon their return, the government will make appropriate political and personal arrangements for them.'

Till date, the question thus remains whether the conditions are ripe for the return of the Dalai Lama and whether His Holiness wants to return. If indeed the Indian government is genuinely committed to its stated policy of regarding 'Tibet as a part of China'—stated not once (in 1954) but twice (in 2003 too), leaving no hope whatsoever of an independent, sovereign Tibet, then it should constantly be in search of opportunities whereby the Dalai Lama himself feels that it is safe to go back to Lhasa. Otherwise, His Holiness cannot be forced to go back and he is welcome to continue living in India as a venerated Holiness of Buddhism.

The Dalai Lama himself appears to be in two minds about his return. Some years ago, in an interview to the *Far Eastern Economic Review*, he said: 'During the last 20 years, we have stood for independence not because we hated the Chinese or their ideology, but only because of the sufferings of our people. But circumstances change and we cannot hold on to the past.' Subsequently, he declared that he would visit Tibet. However, it appears that some Tibetan refugees in India are averse to the Dalai Lama even paying a visit to Lhasa. Naturally, all refugees dread what will happen to them when they return if the circumstances have not changed.

However, the continued presence of the Dalai Lama in India serves as a festering reminder that all is not well between India and China because of the continuing acceptance by the Indian government of the émigré government of independent Tibet with a full-fledged Cabinet in Dharamshala, Himachal Pradesh, complete with a PM and Ministers. No doubt, the Dalai Lama is a revered spiritual leader and a scholar of Buddhist and Hindu theology, and in that capacity, we are privileged that he chose to live in our country. Till the question of the Dalai Lama is satisfactorily resolved, the relation between India and China cannot be properly called 'normal'. And the only satisfactory resolution of this contentious question, given the treaties of 1954 and 2003, is the Dalai Lama's safe return to his honoured position of centuries and a guarantee of his physical survival when he returns to Tibet.

While the veneration of the Dalai Lama inside Tibet even 61 years after his escape to India in 1959 is astounding, it can by no means be taken for granted given the cultural policy of the PRC and new generations graduating from Chinese educational institutes. Even among monasteries in Tibet, there are pro- and anti-Dalai Lama factions today. While the younger generation still respects the Dalai Lama, they reject the socio-economic order that existed earlier. The rest of Tibet is in no mood for the kind of revolt which would pave the way for the triumphant return of the Dalai Lama as the temporal head of independent Tibet.

Dithering Voices

Like Tibet, in India, too, there were divergent views on the return of His Holiness and the larger question of Tibetan independence. In the period 1977–78, the Janata Party government led by Morarji Desai reconsidered the question of Tibet in the light of the support given to Tibetan independence by two ministers, Raj Narain and George Fernandes. External Affairs Minister Atal Bihari Vajpayee (who earlier used to vociferously support Tibetan independence), while answering in the Lok Sabha Starred Question No. 247 on 8 March 1979, on behalf of the government, stated the following:

> We regard Tibet as a region of China. That was done in 1954 under an agreement between India and China. But we would be happy if the Dalai Lama and Tibetans go back if they think that conditions are suitable for them to return to their country.

Later, both Morarji Desai and Charan Singh told me that Vajpayee never cleared this statement [to parliament] with them.

In other words, the Janata Party government had also concluded that Tibet was to be regarded as a part of China, and the government's endeavour was that when conditions become ripe and the Dalai Lama himself feels that it is safe to return to Lhasa, the Indian government will see him off with honour. That is, New Delhi would neither ask the Dalai Lama to leave, nor ask him to stay. The decision will be that of the Dalai Lama.

However, while the Indian government's position was seemingly clear on the Tibet issue, with no room for a second interpretation, there is nevertheless enough indication that in private, its Ministers took stands inconsistent with their own government's declaration in parliament.

For example, Union Minister for Industries George Fernandes as the Janata government's 'Minister-in-waiting' protocol representative for the visiting Soviet PM Alexei Kosygin in March 1979, four days after the foreign minister's authoritative reiteration on the floor of parliament, argued with the visiting Soviet leader that USSR should declare its support for independent Tibet. His plea was in complete violation of the Janata government's commitment in parliament, and reflected more on the status of Fernandes as an adherent of the Free Tibet lobby campaign, rather than as a member of the Cabinet.

Excerpted below is the declassified transcript, prepared by the Research and Analysis Wing (RAW) of the Cabinet Secretariat, of the conversation between Fernandes and Soviet Premier Kosygin en route from Delhi to Anand-Baroda-Bangalore-Delhi, on 11–13 March 1979. On 12 March, while travelling from Anand to Baroda by car, the following exchange took place (interpreter's notes):

(George Fernandes–GF): Will you be prepared to take a stand recognizing independence of Tibet? The past governments (of India) made a mistake in not doing so.

(Alexei Kosygin–K): I did not know that. Mrs Indira Gandhi when she came to Moscow told us that India was opposed to China's seizure of Tibet, regarded it as illegal, and that is why her government was giving refuge to the Dalai Lama. It is your (Janata) government which supports the Chinese position. I heard it for the first time from your Foreign Minister (Vajpayee) four days ago.

GF: I and other like-minded persons always supported Tibet's right to freedom, and always criticized the Indian government's failure to do so. The Janata government should undo what the previous governments had done.

K: It is question for the Indian government. The Soviet government never suggested even in the fifties that China might conquer Tibet.

GF: Don't you think then a fresh statement is necessary about Tibet's independence? From a mighty power like the USSR, it would be a great encouragement.

K: Tibet is far from the Soviet Union and Soviet Union regards Tibet in India's exclusive sphere of influence. It is for India to take a stand. Anyway, is there much of Tibet left? They have massacred them and forcibly married them.

GF: I draw great inspiration from your statement. Lovers (*sic*) of Tibet freedom could count on the Soviet government's support if and when India takes a firm stand.

K: You are right.

This discussion between Kosygin and Fernandes also shows that when Mrs Gandhi was in power, prior to 1977, she had privately told the Russians one thing (that Tibet is an independent country forcibly occupied by China), and the Indian parliament another thing (that Tibet is a part of China).

Several years later, in December 1998, as Defence Minister, Fernandes penned a foreword for the Penguin edition of D.R. Mankekar's book, *The Guilty Men of 1962*, in which he gave vent to his openly held commitment to the anti-Chinese, pro-Tibet independence lobby. He called Mankekar's book, a 'masterpiece' and added: 'The well-fostered myth that the danger to India's security comes from Pakistan has now been exploded, and a new realism of India's threat perception has begun to take root in its place.' That new 'realism', of course, was to perceive China—and not Pakistan—as a danger to India, when in fact, both these nations are in a compact to threaten India's integrity.

In March 1983, while speaking in the Lok Sabha on the foreign affairs debate, I had pointedly asked the following question: 'Does the Government of India (GoI) regard Tibet as a part of China or not?' On 31 March 1983, the then foreign minister, P.V. Narasimha Rao, in reply, stated that the Congress government did indeed regard Tibet as a part of China.

This declaration, however, did not square with other developments. In March 1983, 70 Congress MPs signed a Memorandum and sent it to PM Indira Gandhi, requesting her to give a Tibetan rebel delegation observer status in the seventh Non-Aligned Summit in New Delhi. Could Congress MPs dare to sign such a Memorandum in a party which was in the iron grip of Mrs Gandhi without some guidance from above?

Notwithstanding these differing voices, the question of Tibetan independence was asked and answered in 1950 by the then Congress government and again by the Janata Party government in 1977–78 in parliament. On both occasions, the two governments of the Congress and the Janata Party, respectively, gave the answer in the negative, that is, 'Tibet could *not* be sustained as an independent country.'

This was reinforced several years later in the joint press communique issued on 23 December 1988, at the end of PM Rajiv Gandhi's visit to China. The Indian government had reiterated its policy regarding Tibet, an autonomous region of China, and that anti-China political activities by Tibetan elements would not be permitted on Indian soil. These statements were repeated during the subsequent exchange of visits by the PMs of India and China in 1993 and 1996, respectively.

A Realpolitik Approach

Most Indians are sentimental about the status of Tibet vis-à-vis China. There is an undercurrent of Pan-Hinduism which is responsible for this sentiment. However, there are national security consequences of executing policy based on such a sentiment. If India promotes Tibetan independence, can China not promote Kashmiri, Uttarakhand (as per a new political map recently endorsed by Nepal's Cabinet), Assamese, Naga and Punjabi secession? Of course, this is already happening.

International affairs are based on *realpolitik* and the Chinese are past masters in that realpolitik. While we were singing 'Hindi Chini Bhai Bhai' (India and China are brothers), the Chinese were building roads through what we had claimed as our ancestral property. Now they are sitting on that property, but recently the government said that no one (Chinese) ever came across to our side of the LAC in May–June 2020.

Another question is that if India supports the independence of Tibet and succeeds in it, can India sustain Tibet's defence and security? Earlier, Tibet, which is more or less the 'outer Tibet' idea of Foreign Secretary Sir Henry McMahon of British India, was 1.3 million sq. km in area, i.e., one-third the size of India. Today's Tibet province of China is only about a quarter of what has historically been Tibet, and which is inhabited by just one-third of the original population of Tibetans. It can only nominally be called Tibet Region of China. The other areas, including Amdo in the Qinghai province, Kham in Sichuan, Yunnan and Gansu, have been amalgamated after PM Vajpayee travelled to Beijing in 2003 and affirmed by a joint declaration that the residual Tibet is the 'original' Tibet Region of China (as per the language of the 1954 Treaty). The other portions are dissolved in the four other provinces of China, and assimilated. The full import of Vajpayee as the Prime Minister of India selling out on Tibet is paradoxically even further than Nehru's, and without any demonstrable gain to India. It has to be termed as gross appeasement to cool the Chinese anger over Vajpayee's letter to US President Bill Clinton in May 1998, citing the nuclear threat from China as the reason for India testing its nuclear devices in May 1998 (which China had taken as a gross insult). The Chinese government thereafter froze all contacts and dealings with the Vajpayee government till 2003, when according to an article published in *The Japan Times* of 8 July that year, PM Vajpayee went to Beijing to 'kowtow'(on bended knees) to the Chinese, and 'to sell out' Tibet to China to cool Chinese anger.[14] The 2003 Treaty has not been widely

---

[14] Brahma Chellaney, 'Vajpayee Kowtows to China,' *Japan Times*, 8 July 2003. Available at: https://www.japantimes.co.jp/opinion/2003/07/08/commentary/

publicized to the Indian public. Except for publishing statements of a few intellectuals, hardly any media coverage was given for the sell-out of Tibetan interests by the Vajpayee government in 2003.

So, can 1.3 million sq. km of the most hazardous territory be defended by 2 million Tibetan people without external assistance from the US and Russia? Even at the height of the 1959 Tibetan rebellion, the US State Department spokesman had stated: 'The United States never regarded Tibet as an independent state.' We shall have to await the result of the November 2020 Presidential Election to know if the past US 'strategic relationship' with China will continue or be formally cold storaged. And if the Democratic Party nominee is elected US President this November, even the acrimony on the coronavirus controversy between the two countries will abate. Thus, it is most unlikely that the US will ever support Tibetan independence, especially after it has quit Afghanistan due to exhaustion.

As for Russia, even when as the USSR it was several times larger than it is today and that too at the height of its anti-China phobia (when Kosygin visited India in 1979), it did not go beyond stating that Tibet was 'in the exclusive sphere of India' and that too in conversation with George Fernandes. Over the last five years, Russia has become more and more a 'junior partner' of China. More about this development later in this book. Today, the residual Russia with its economic dependence on China is busy negotiating pacts with China. Russian President Vladimir Putin has been to Beijing in 2019 to discuss a formal compact with China. The Indian people should be forewarned about this.

In other words, if at all we are inclined, it will be only India that is left with the mantle of achieving Tibetan independence and sustaining it. Are we prepared to take on this responsibility? Once Tibet becomes independent with Indian help, can India prevent

---

vajpayee-kowtows-to-china/, last accessed on 26 October 2020.

the US or the politically disguised Russians from establishing a better rapport with Tibetans than India has? Was India able to prevent Bangladesh from getting closer to the US, China and Saudi Arabia, let alone protecting the hapless Bangladeshi Hindus from frequently being dispossessed of their land and being killed by mobs—this even though it was the Indian army that had liberated Bangladesh? Ironically, all these three countries to which Bangladesh is today cosying up to, had opposed its emergence in 1971.

In my opinion, it is wasteful and harmful to talk of Tibet's independence unless we Indians change our mindset on international affairs. The present coy mindset of India is best reflected by the Bharatiya Janata Party (BJP) government's refusal to send troops to Afghanistan to fill the gap left by the proposed US plan to withdraw from that country and thereby create a vacuum. The US was willing to provide all the military hardware India required if India took over this responsibility. Instead, India's prima donna ministers gave lectures to the US about not interfering in other countries' internal affairs. So now a Pakistan-aided Taliban, overseen by the US, has filled the vacuum.

As things stand, either Tibet has to be part of China or it has to be a protectorate of India. India, at present, has no military reach and substance to sustain Tibet's independence even if we have the inclination. Since the latter is not possible, India should accept the first reality (Chinese sovereignty, which now is the status quo of a largely amputated former Tibet since 2003).

This is not to suggest that the Chinese government is blameless in its handling of Tibetan affairs. Moreover, whenever a semi-free Tibet looked southward politically, Tibet took aggressive postures towards Indian interests. Throughout the nineteenth and twentieth centuries, independent Tibetan governments had laid claims to Sikkim, Bhutan and Arunachal (which the Chinese today are articulating in various border talks with India). Tawang in Arunachal has always been considered by Tibetan Lamas as a seat of Tibetan authority. In 1902, Tibetan troops actually invaded Sikkim to capture the area. Lord Curzon ordered a large contingent of the army to go and repulse the Tibetan invasion. Thus, those who argue for Tibet's independence should also be prepared—for historical consistency—that Sikkim, Bhutan and Arunachal Pradesh could come under threat from Tibet itself. If Nepal can somersault, why not Tibet? Is our nation, ready for that contingency? Will India accept and be prepared for these consequential claims of an independent Tibet?

In India's strategic interest, it is essential to befriend, or at the very least, have normal relations with China, provided our military strength is matching and commensurate with the benefit that accrues to India. According to my understanding of the situation, this means squarely resolving the contradictions between our legitimate claims on the border and consequently our concerns in and about Tibet. That, however, would be circumscribed by our voluntarily made clear commitments in writing regarding Tibet in the two treaties signed by the highest political authority of the two respective party governments of India—first in 1954 by PM Nehru and second in 2003 by PM Vajpayee—to recognize China's sovereignty over the Tibet Autonomous Region (TAR) of China. Some Indian intellectuals who study China have largely condemned these treaties as a betrayal of India's national interests, as a one-sided surrender to China, of the hoary commitments made to Tibet and to Buddhism. That should show us as a weak nation or as a nation having a weak leadership and covering it up with media spin. The Chinese must have chuckled and hoped that in the future too Indian governments would behave similarly. They are not far from wrong at the moment.

If the Narendra Modi-led government has no intention of

disowning the 2003 treaty signed by Vajpayee, then it is the responsibility of the GoI to lay bare to the Indian public that we no more have any right to raise Tibetan freedom issues, except those that come within the charter of the UN.

If our past two treaty commitments in Tibet are made transparent to the Indian public, and our government's actions are consistent and demonstrably in keeping with the commitments—implicit and explicit—about the above two treaties, one of the main hurdles of ambivalence in our relations with China will vanish. However, this places us in a highly embarrassing predicament, since the GoI's permission to set up an émigré government of independent Tibet in Dharamshala (Himachal Pradesh) will have to be withdrawn. No doubt, India has a special responsibility to host His Holiness the Dalai Lama as a revered religious leader. He is welcome in India as a spiritual leader, 'but not as a spiritual and nominal head' of an 'exile' government in Dharamshala.

The treatment extended to the Dalai Lama also reveals this ambivalence in our attitude towards Tibet. The government says that India has only extended political asylum to the Dalai Lama, because his life would be in danger if he returns to Tibet. However, the Bureau of His Holiness the Dalai Lama is quite active in New Delhi propagating the thesis that Tibet is an independent country. If the Indian government sincerely believed that Tibet is a part of China, then the activities of the Bureau of His Holiness the Dalai Lama should be considered as no less repugnant than the activities of the Khalistan movement in the UK or Canada.

Given these two treaties, it is an act of bad faith to have permitted this émigré government on Indian soil. It should now be converted into a Tibet Human Rights Centre, which is within the rights of nations under the UN Charter and Resolutions. Thereafter, expressing our concerns to the government in Beijing, in bilateral meetings and in UN fora, on matters of human rights including religious freedoms in Tibet, would not only *not* be misunderstood, but China could be forced to accommodate these concerns as international commitments under the UN Charter.

The Indian mind also needs to be purged of the inherited British imperialist duplicity on Tibet, which was to keep Tibetan status nebulous in everyone's mind by concocting a feudal concept of 'suzerainty'. This resulted in Tibet being neither independent nor a part of China, i.e., in a Trishanku state. This purging of the imperialist perfidy was the responsibility of the Indian government, which should have made it clear to the people in 1954 itself. We could have listened to Sardar Patel when the Chinese army overran Tibet and annexed it by a written agreement on the border. However, Nehru was contemptuous of Sardar Patel's advice and the people were made to chant 'Hindi Chini Bhai Bhai' without understanding the implications of that slogan. However, because of this confusion on facts, the government has been hamstrung by the pro-independent Tibet lobby, even within Modi's government and earlier in Morarji's Janata Party government. The crux of the matter is that China–India relations can never become a friendly and warm partnership unless public confusion on all such issues is removed. However, clearing the confusion will come at a cost, which the Indian people must be willing to bear.

If our intentions on the Tibetan question are consistent, then for transparent diplomacy, it is necessary that these intentions are understood as such by China. Alternatively, if we believe Tibet to be an independent country, and want to liberate it, then an entirely different course in our diplomacy and military strategy is called for.

Today, we are getting the worst of both positions. We accept Tibet as a part of China, and yet we allow the seeds of doubt to germinate in the mind of our neighbour about our intentions. However, sadly, India does not have easy options on Tibet. It can err in two opposite directions. On the one hand, under Chinese pressure, the government may be tempted to make Tibetans feel unwelcome, and even force them to leave. On the other, it can support the freedom for Tibet as demanded by the Dalai Lama's Bureau. Both these options are not in India's interest.

India–China relations thus suffer from this ambivalence. It is, however, a fact that throughout centuries Tibet had behaved as if its future lay within the overall framework of China. Never in its history did it side with India, not even on the legitimacy of the McMahon Line in 1914. Therefore, those who advocate the independence of Tibet do not and cannot argue on the basis of history. Their advocacy can only be to further political mischief, or to enlarge themselves at the nation's cost. India–China relations should, therefore, not be derailed by misconceptions and misplaced adventurism, whereby all that happens is that our valiant soldiers die for a nebulous cause, and are forgotten soon after.

3

A PHANTOM CALLED MCMAHON LINE

The exploitation and domination by imperialist and colonial powers that India and China experienced in common, and their struggles against them, did not however bring the two countries together, even though both became free of the different degrees of imperialist colonization around the same time: in 1947, India won her freedom from the British, and in 1949, the Communist Party of China (CPC) had won the civil war against a clique patronized by European colonial nations. Thus came to power the newly proclaimed Republic of India and the People's Republic of China (PRC) in a free world in which India awoke 'to life and freedom' and 'Chinese people have now stood up', as Chairman Mao declared.

However, the two ancient nations were already sharply divided into two ideologically opposed formations: China was part of the tightly knit socialist communist bloc led by the USSR, and India was conceptually a part of democratic anti-Communist alliances post-World War II, which were inspired by the US. So, while the PRC was unambiguously aligned with the former USSR, Nehru, independent democratic India's first PM and a socialist inspired by the USSR, was troubled by the emerging bipolar world order, and thus he equivocated in the early years of the post-World War II period. Nehru ultimately chose to tilt towards the former USSR on issues that became explicit in the crucial hours of the serial global moral emergencies, beginning with the Korean War of 1950, followed by the Suez Crisis of 1956, the Hungarian Revolution of 1956 and the Soviet-led invasion of Czechoslovakia in 1968.

These ideological differences aside, the two new governments that came into existence post the end of World War II faced an unfinished task: how to convert their undelineated frontiers into demarcated legal boundaries. A 'boundary' is first agreed to as a line marked on an agreed map in diplomatic negotiations (called delineation). Later, it is jointly marked out on the ground (called demarcation). It is then visualized exactly on a map (called cartography) and thereafter, it is formalized as an agreement between two sovereign governments (called treaty), in which each nation recognizes both its own limits on a map and the limits of its neighbour's territory on that map, after which it becomes a recognized boundary.

The focal point of the Sino-Indian border dispute is whether the boundary, which stretches along for about 3,488 km, had ever been formally demarcated or even delineated. The Chinese stand on the question has been that the Sino-Indian border had never been formally demarcated, and the claimed delineation is disputed. India, on the other hand, had contended till 1988, that the Sino-Indian border had been delineated through age-old customs, traditions and later in agreements such as the McMahon Line on the eastern end of the Indo-Tibet border, which British-controlled India had proposed in 1914 (and 'which was accepted by the then independent Government of Tibet'). Hence, India claims, without substantial basis, that the McMahon Line cannot be disputed under international law.

Bordering 14 countries, China had claims of lost territories against most of its neighbours. Thus in the 1950s, Beijing faced the possibility of disputes with many of its neighbours, particularly with the erstwhile Soviet Union, which was the inheritor of vast far eastern tracts of Chinese imperial territory annexed by Tsarist Russia under imposed treaties. China negotiated and concluded boundary treaties turn by turn with Burma (Myanmar), Nepal, Pakistan, Afghanistan, Mongolia, Korea, Laos and Vietnam. In the case of Vietnam, under Deng Xiaoping's leadership, China used a minor boundary dispute concerning distances of no more than a few hundred metres to attack Vietnam in order to 'teach it a lesson'. However, with Vietnam, too, the disputes have now been resolved.

In the case of the Sino-Soviet border, Moscow had initially refused to renegotiate the nineteenth-century treaties by which the Tsars had annexed great tracts of the Qing empire, which became Siberia and the Maritime Province. It suspected that Beijing's insistence on negotiation was with the intention of reclaiming that territory. However, China's insistence led to armed conflicts, first in 1969, and thereafter till 1979 on the Ussuri River banks. The threat of a nuclear war had then loomed on the frontier. In 1987, under President Mikhail Gorbachev, the USSR, however, agreed to renegotiate the Sino-Soviet borders. In 1997, the heads of state of Russia and China met in Beijing and proclaimed their border settlement as a model for resolving problems left over by history through negotiations based on 'equality, mutual understanding and concessions'. The Central Asian successor states of the USSR have also followed suit and have now reached a settlement on their boundaries with Beijing.

In comparison to the magnitude of China's overall border problems, the task facing independent India when it emerged from British rule in 1947 was trivial. Of the seven countries with whom India shared official boundaries, the outstanding issues with six were settled at the threshold of freedom (five when the British handed over power to India and the sixth in 1972 after Bangladesh was formed). Only the border with the then independent Tibet had not been demarcated in 1947–50. Even though the attempts of the British governments in London and India to reach an agreement with China about demarcating the Indo-Tibet boundaries had failed in 1914, these efforts were not revived thereafter for as long as the British remained in India. A perusal of the record of the Sino-Indian border dispute therefore raises an important question: Did a legal India–China border ever exist on any date?

Unearthing British Perfidy

Britain had taken the initiative to mark a border; and hence in 1913, it convened a tripartite conference in Simla including a Tibetan delegate, a representative of the Chinese government and Britain's representatives, the ostensible purpose of which was primarily to regulate relations between Lhasa and Beijing, by demarcating a line to divide 'inner' and 'outer' Tibet as spheres of influence of China and Britain, respectively.

Thus, the British approach to the border was that of an imperial power, and not that of one defending the Indian nation state. The British, of course, never had considered or admitted that India was ever a nation. This ruling British view, most famously expressed by John Strachey, a British colonial administrator, in his book *India (1888)* was that:

> [The] first and the most essential thing to learn about India is that there is not, and never was an India, or even any country of India, possessing, according to European ideas, any sort of

unity, physical, political, social or religious, no Indian nation, no people of India, of which we hear so much.[15]

In March 1914, the then foreign secretary of the British Indian government, Sir Henry McMahon, arranged secret and bilateral negotiations in Delhi with Lhasa, in which the Tibetan representative, Lonchen Shatra, was induced to accept a new border line, which came to be named after the foreign secretary. This McMahon Line was drawn on a map on a scale of eight miles to the inch, covering the sector from just short of Laos on the Burma border with Bhutan (through Burma), which the British had then included as part of their 'Indian empire'.

On 13 June 1914, about three weeks before McMahon initialled the Simla Convention with Tibet's plenipotentiary Lonchen Shatra, Sun Pao-chi, China's foreign minister, handed over a memorandum to the British ambassador to Beijing protesting, *inter alia*, the McMahon Line (then called the Red Line because it was marked by McMahon in red pencil). On 16 June 1914, the British ambassador Sir John Newell Jordan communicated on Sun Pao-chi's memorandum to Sir Edward Grey, British foreign secretary in London, in the following words:

> I have the honour to forward translation of the memorandum handed to me by Mr Sun Pao-chi, Minister for Foreign Affairs, on the 13th instant, together with copy of a map showing the boundaries of inner and outer Tibet as proposed by Sir Henry McMahon (red and blue), as now proposed by the Chinese government between inner and outer Tibet, as first put by the Chinese at conference (yellow).

Therefore, the Chinese objection was not merely the boundary between inner and outer Tibet, but boundaries of outer Tibet

---

[15]John Strachey, *India (1888)*, Kessinger Publishing, LLC, 2008.

(red line) as well, which included the so-called McMahon Line.

On 1 July 1914, just two days prior to the signing of the Simla Convention, the Secretary of State for India, Robert Crewe-Milnes, sent a telegram to Viceroy Charles Hardinge, as follows:

> Conference regarding Tibet. Please refer to your telegram dated the 29th ultimo. A final meeting of the conference should be summoned by Sir H. McMahon on 3rd July. If the Chinese plenipotentiary then refuses to sign, negotiations should definitely be terminated by Sir Henry. He should express to the Tibetan representative great regret at failure to arrive at a settlement and should also assure Lonchen Shatra that Tibet may depend on diplomatic support of His Majesty's government and on any assistance in the way of munitions of war which we can give them, if aggression on part of China continues.

Just in case Viceroy Hardinge had still remained in doubt, Crewe-Milnes sent another telegram on 3 July 1914:

> With reference to your telegram of the 2nd instant, separate signature with Tibet cannot be authorized by His Majesty's government. Sir H. McMahon should proceed in the manner laid down in my telegrams dated, respectively, the 1st and 2nd July, if the Chinese delegate refuses to sign.

Thus, McMahon was not authorized to sign any agreement with Tibet in the absence of Chinese concurrence. However, disregarding these instructions, he went ahead and initialled an 11-Article Convention on 3 July 1914 with the Tibetans. The initialling of the Simla Convention maps by McMahon and Lonchen Shatra was in violation of the Anglo-Russian Convention of 1907, by which Britain had agreed not to deal with Tibet except through the intermediary of China.

Viceroy Hardinge, however, had been indulgent with McMahon. In telegrams to Crewe-Milnes, he frequently referred to the fact that by being tough with the Chinese, the Russians were getting their way in Mongolia.

However, even he had to say the following while forwarding McMahon's memorandum to London on 23 July 1914:

> ...We recognize that a consideration of the eastern or Indo-Chinese portion of the north-eastern frontier did not form part of the functions of the conference, and we would therefore request that the views and proposals put forward may be regarded as personal to Sir Henry McMahon, and not at present carrying the endorsement of the government of India.

Sir Henry McMahon was able to get away from being cashiered from services for flouting instructions, by using the age-old bureaucratic device of finding contradictions in instructions from London and 'not having time for references'. He recorded in his Memorandum regarding the progress of negotiations from 1 May to 8 July 1914 that:

> I was somewhat uncertain however as to the exact intention of His Majesty's government in regard to final action... There was no time for a further reference to London, and I accordingly decided that if the Chinese plenipotentiary refused to cooperate at the last moment, I would not sign with Tibet, but would initial the amended Convention and map in concert with my Tibetan colleague.

Therefore, the so-called McMahon Line has no legal validity arising from any agreement or convention that is binding on the Government of China.

So why did the British authorities not implement McMahon's 'agreement' reached with Tibet's representative? One reason was that for a few inches of Indian territories on a map, Britain did not want to jeopardize its commercial interests in China. The Chinese Revolution or the 1911 Xinhai Revolution led by Sun Yat-sen overthrew the Qing (or Manchu) dynasty, and on 11 December 1915, Yuan Shih-kai became the first president of the new Chinese Republic. President Yuan was being wooed by the British, and they did not want to annoy him. Besides, in negotiating with the Tibetans, McMahon was flouting instructions from London, and was going beyond his brief, which was considered a 'monumental crime' in British bureaucracy ethics.

Incidentally, it is quite significant that all the three plenipotentiaries at the Simla Convention—of India, Tibet and China—were sent home in disgrace by their respective governments soon after the conference.

The Tibetan government in Lhasa disowned its representative, who was also sent into obscurity because of his signing away Tawang to Sir Henry McMahon. After the authorities in Lhasa repudiated their representative's unauthorized action, the Chinese government, suspecting what had gone on behind its representative's back, declared that any agreement reached between Britain and the Tibetan authorities would be 'illegitimate and null'. The Chinese representative, Chen I-fen (also called Ivan Chen), was disgraced because he had initialled the maps without his government's sanction. The Chinese government promptly disowned it. In fact, Chen was suspected of being a British lackey, if not actually an agent. In a secret telegram sent on 20 August 1911, Sir John Jordan, the British ambassador to Beijing, stated: 'It is a decided gain to have a man like Ivan Chen on the frontier.'

In his report to London, the then Viceroy in India, Charles Hardinge, also disowned McMahon's dealings with the Tibetans.

McMahon's actions at Simla were thus held by Whitehall in London as having exceeded his authority. Ironically, the man who did the most for British India, Sir Henry McMahon, was immediately transferred to Egypt as Ambassador, which was the British bureaucracy's way of expressing displeasure. This was in sharp contrast to the lionizing he was privy to in London after McMahon's earlier venture in Afghanistan.

Britain refused even to acknowledge the existence of his maps thereafter. Further, between 1914 and 1933, the British government did not change its stand. In fact, three years after the Simla Convention, the Survey of India published Official Maps in 1917, in which the McMahon Line, was *not* shown. Instead, the 'traditional' border along the Assam Himalayan foothills below the Tawang tract and well below the McMahon Line was shown. In 1929, the *Encyclopædia Britannica* published its fourteenth edition, where the map of the Indo-Tibet border was also published. Volume 24 shows the same 'traditional' boundary—below Tawang—and not the line determined 15 years earlier by McMahon.

The British government refused to acknowledge the existence of the McMahon Line till 1936. However, in 1933, the Thirteenth Dalai Lama attained heaven. The KMT government despatched General Huang Mu-sung with a high-powered delegation to Lhasa to mourn his death. The delegation carried enough gold to bribe the whole of Tibet, and it stayed in Lhasa for six months. This scared the British in India. General Huang also obtained a reaffirmation from the Tibetans of Chinese 'suzerainty' over Tibet.

In 1935, British botanist Francis Kingdon-Ward was arrested by the Tibetans because he had entered Lhasa via Tawang. They argued that he needed Tibetan-authorized papers even to pass through the Tawang tract. The Foreign and Political Department of the British Indian government (forerunner of the Ministry of External Affairs or MEA) was entrusted with the case of Kingdon-Ward's release. Deputy Secretary Olaf K. Caroe (later knighted) therefore called for the files. A perusal of the files enabled Caroe to stumble on the McMahon-Shatra Agreement on the McMahon Line, which had made the Tawang tract Indian territory. Years later, Sir Olaf Caroe recorded in a journal article the following: 'The McMahon Line was drawn just before World War I, and then forgotten and I know all about this because it was I who discovered that it had been forgotten.'

To bolster their case against the arrest of Kingdon-Ward, the British Indian government, on the prodding of a deputy secretary, decided to pursue with His Majesty's Government in London the need to accord official sanction to the McMahon Line, and with retrospective effect!

In those days, official public sanction of treaties, maps, etc., was given by a publication called *A Collection of Treaties Engagements and Sanads: Relating to India and Neighbouring Countries*, under the editorship of Sir C.U. Aitchison, and published under the authority of the Foreign and Political Department, British Indian government. These Aitchison volumes had been appearing at 15 years' intervals, but without any reference to the McMahon Line. Thus in 1929, Volume XIV of the Aitchison Treaties made no reference to the McMahon Line, but it did contain a paragraph about the Simla Convention of 1914, and the attempt to settle boundaries of inner Tibet, i.e., the Sino-Tibetan frontier (but not outer Tibet, i.e., the Indo-Tibetan border). It also records the Chinese government's refusal to sign the convention.

Naturally, Caroe's attention moved from the files to the Aitchison volumes, with the object of obtaining official recognition to the 'forgotten' convention. So, Caroe wrote to the India Office in London seeking permission to make public the 1914 Simla Convention and incorporate the maps in the Aitchison Treaties.

In his letter dated 19 April 1936, addressed to the Assistant Under-Secretary of State for India, John Walton, Caroe argued:

> ...The Government of India think there would be advantage in inserting in their public records copies of the 1914 Convention. Their absence from such a publication as 'Aitchison's Treaties,' if it became known to the Chinese government, might well be used by them in support of the argument that no ratified agreement between India and Tibet is in existence.

On 4 June 1936, Walton recorded an India Office minute, in which he cited the 'risk of attracting unwelcoming Chinese notice' as the reason for non-publication of the 1914 papers and maps. Then, in a subsequent India Office Minute dated 9 September 1936, Walton recorded:

> The juridical position in regard to the north-east frontiers is not perfectly secure, because the agreements of 1914 on the subject were concluded only with Tibet and not with China, and China has an acknowledged claim to suzerainty over Tibet.

However, other pressures to publish the 1914 maps emerged. The Government of India Act of 1935 required a precise delineation of tribal Assam. Similarly, the impending separation of Burma from British India required precise descriptions of the boundary. Caroe used this pressure to press his arguments. He wrote:

> While the Burma government were informed of the location of this frontier (i.e. the McMahon line), the Assam government apparently were forgotten and seem to have had no intimation up to this day.

Caroe won his point, but the British government urged him to include the 1914 Convention documents in the Aitchison Treaties 'unobtrusively' and with 'minimum publicity'. London also wanted the GoI to bring out a revised edition of the Aitchison Treaties, and withdraw and call back the earlier editions that were in circulation.

All this suited Caroe very well. He quietly ordered the withdrawal of the old set of Aitchison Treaties and reprinted a fresh set in 1938, 'but fraudulently with a 1929 dateline'. This was entirely unethical, but Caroe went even further. He replaced the short factual paragraph about the 1914 Convention with a long, embellished three-paragraph set. He also included as many favourable references for British India as was synoptically feasible. This act was not only immoral, but a crime of forgery under the Indian Penal Code (IPC).

The reprinted fraudulent copy then 'unobtrusively' replaced the original Aitchison Treaties all over the world (there were only 62 copies that were originally circulated).[16] In three places, however, the original copy remained—one in Caroe's office (to become the MEA later), the second in the India Office Library in London and the third in the Harvard University Widener Library. Harvard, my alma mater, just refused to part with the original. I got easy access to it in the 1985–86 academic year, when I returned as Visiting Professor to teach economics. (See Table 1.)

---

[16]C.U. Aitchison, *A Collection of Treaties, Engagements and Sanads*, Published under the Authority of the Foreign and Political Department, Government of India, Vol. XIV, 1929.

TABLE 1: Original and Reprinted Versions of the Aitchison Treaties

(1929) Published original (available in Widener Library, Harvard University, US)	(1936) Reprinted and Forged (with the Ministry of External Affairs, New Delhi)
In 1913, a conference of Tibetan, Chinese and British Plenipotentiaries met in India to try and bring about a settlement in regard to matters on the Sino-Tibetan frontier, and a tripartite Convention was drawn up [and] initialled in 1914. The Chinese government, however, refused to permit their Plenipotentiary to proceed with the full signature.	In 1913, a conference of British, Chinese and Tibetan Plenipotentiaries was convened in Simla in an attempt to negotiate an agreement as to the relations of the three Governments and to the frontier of Tibet, both with China and India. After prolonged negotiations, the conference, under the presidency of Sir Henry McMahon drew up a tripartite Convention between Great Britain, China and Tibet, which was initialled in Simla in 1914 by the representatives of the three parties. The Chinese government, however, refused to ratify the agreement, by their refusal depriving themselves of the benefits which they were to obtain thereunder, among which were a definite recognition that Tibet was under Chinese suzerainty, and an agreement to permit a Chinese official with a suitable escort not exceeding 300 men to be maintained in Lhasa. The Convention was, however, ratified by Great Britain and Tibet, by means of a declaration accepting its terms as binding between themselves. The Convention included a definite territory.

Source: Author's original research

Thus in reality, the McMahon Line was a non-starter for 22 years till 1936, when in a fraud on history committed by the British Indian government, it became a useful tool; hence its sudden appearance in new official maps of the British Indian government. Thereafter, the British government began propagating that the McMahon Line was indeed India's legal boundary, claiming that it was legitimized by a formal assent of Tibet and China, for which Caroe arranged a forgery to support the false assertion: that the boundary had been agreed to at the 1914 Simla Convention.

Thereafter, the Surveyor General of India was ordered to change the Survey of India maps to incorporate the McMahon Line. In 1938, he did so, after pointing out numerous geographic anomalies in this boundary. Later, until 1954, the Survey of India maps showed the McMahon Line as 'undemarcated', and the Aksai Chin area as 'boundary undefined'. Consequently, in the 1940s, some British maps began showing the McMahon Line as the boundary, qualified only with the word: 'undemarcated' (that is, still awaiting agreement on its exact alignment and marking out on the ground, by joint inspection process of the two neighbours).

However, this was not all. British imperialists also ensured that the status of Aksai Chin on the Kashmir frontier in the west remains unclear and disputed.

In 1841, Maharaja Gulab Singh led the Sikhs to Tibet and his General Zorawar Singh captured the Tibet-Kailash-Mansarovar area. Tibetans with Chinese help, counter-attacked in Leh (Ladakh). However, the fierce Sikhs from India were victorious. In 1842, a treaty was signed between Kashmir, Tibet and China, known as the Dogra-Tibet Treaty of 1842. By that, even if the descriptions are vague, Aksai Chin was ceded to India. However, the British mutilated that treaty in 1848, after taking over following the Anglo-Sikh war of 1845–46. Since then the status of Aksai Chin became unclear.

On 10 June 1873, Trelawney Saunders, a cartographer at the India office, prepared a map for the British Foreign Office, which roughly followed the Karakoram range as the boundary. This was favoured by every viceroy till 1899. On 14 March 1899, Sir Claude MacDonald, the British Minister in Peking (Beijing), delivered a note to the Chinese Foreign Office proposing a new line 'for the sake of avoiding any dispute or uncertainty in the future'. It acknowledged that the boundaries of Hunza (in the Northern Areas under Pakistan's control) with China 'have never been clearly defined' and suggested that in that sector both sides should relinquish their claims on each other. (This is precisely what the Sino-Pak agreement of 2 March 1963 is based on.) The note proceeded to define the boundary eastwards from the Karakoram Pass down to 'the eastern boundary of Ladakh a little east of 80 degrees east longitude'. By this line, Aksai Chin became Tibetan.

Thus emerged the Macartney–MacDonald Line. The Macartney in the hyphenated duo was Sir George Macartney, the British representative in Kashgar, whose reports to London prodded the scrapping of Maharaja Gulab Singh's achievements of 1842. Peking, however, did not respond to the offer of 1899. London, therefore, reverted to a more ambitious Ardagh Line of 1 January 1897, with various modifications. The long and short of it was that the boundary remained undemarcated.

During World War II and immediately after it, the Chinese KMT government protested to the interim Indian government. In early 1947, and even as late as in 1949, the KMT government, although on the way out by then, delivered to New Delhi a formal note repudiating all documents emanating from the Indian government.

Historical evidence clearly points to the fact that the entire land border between India and China was never legally delineated, much less demarcated. This fact had been withheld from the Indian people for a long time, and thus they continued to erroneously believe that China was a party to the 1914 Simla Convention and that it had later welched on it.

Flip-Flops on Tibet

We paid a price for this error in 1962, just like we continue to suffer due to Nehru's dilly-dallying attitude on Tibet. During the first four decades of the twentieth century, Tibet was seen by British imperialists as a buffer state. From 1946 to 1951, Nehru had, in fact, de facto pursued the same policy as the British did towards Tibet. The two main features of this policy included treating Tibet as an autonomous buffer state between India and China; and recognizing Chinese suzerainty but not sovereignty over Tibet, i.e., recognize Tibet's autonomy even for treaty-making powers, especially in relation to India. In March–April 1947, despite protest from the KMT Chinese delegates, a Tibetan delegation was invited to the Asian Relations Conference (ARC) in New Delhi by Nehru, in his capacity as the 'interim' PM of the British Indian government. After independence, the Indian government wrote to the Lhasa government in September 1947, stating that all the previous treaty commitments (e.g., the Anglo-Tibetan treaties/conventions) would be respected as before. But on 16 October 1947, the Government of Tibet, claiming to be free and independent, sent a note to New Delhi demanding the return of vast tracts of land from Ladakh to Assam. In 1949, an Indian army officer was sent to Lhasa as an adviser to the Tibetan government. While this inherited policy was pursued by Nehru casually, from the day the PRC was established, Chairman Mao pursued China's strategic objectives in Tibet with clear determination and brutal clarity.

Unaware of this, Nehru brazenly proclaimed to parliament on 20 November 1950 that the McMahon Line was indeed India's border with Tibet in the north-west, reiterating that it had been 'fixed by the Simla Convention of 1914'. Nehru then went on to say that 'map or no map, the McMahon Line was India's boundary and we will not allow anybody to come across [it]'. Further, in the Ladakh area, Nehru had maintained that the India–China boundary was delineated by the Treaty of 1842 signed by the Maharaja of Kashmir, Tibet and China, and that in 1847 'the Chinese government admitted that this boundary was sufficiently and distinctly fixed'. Furthermore, Nehru told parliament that this area 'now claimed by China has always been depicted as part of India on official maps, has been surveyed by Indian officials, and even a Chinese map of 1893 shows it as Indian territory'. There is no substance to any of these claims of Nehru.

While Nehru was discoursing in parliament on the fixity of the McMahon Line, the Survey of India, the GoI's official cartographer, published in the same year a map titled, 'India Showing Political Divisions in the New Republic' (see map on page 61) showing the border along the McMahon Line as 'undemarcated', and the Aksai Chin area as 'boundary undefined'. Obviously, the Home Ministry, in which the Survey of India's office was housed, was unaware of the MEA's stand, and in turn the PM was in the dark about his own government's maps.

In February 1951, the Nehru government took control of Tawang, thereby affirming McMahon, who had drawn his line to bring Tawang into India. Lhasa, as capital of the as-yet-free Tibet, then vigorously protested India's seizure of Tawang, and again made clear that Tibet regarded the McMahon Line as without validity. And yet the Indian government, ostrich-like, began to pretend that there was no dispute on the border, and that there was nothing to discuss about it with China.

Nehru changed his outlook on Tibet by unfavourably diluting his earlier stand further, when in May 1951 the PLA took full

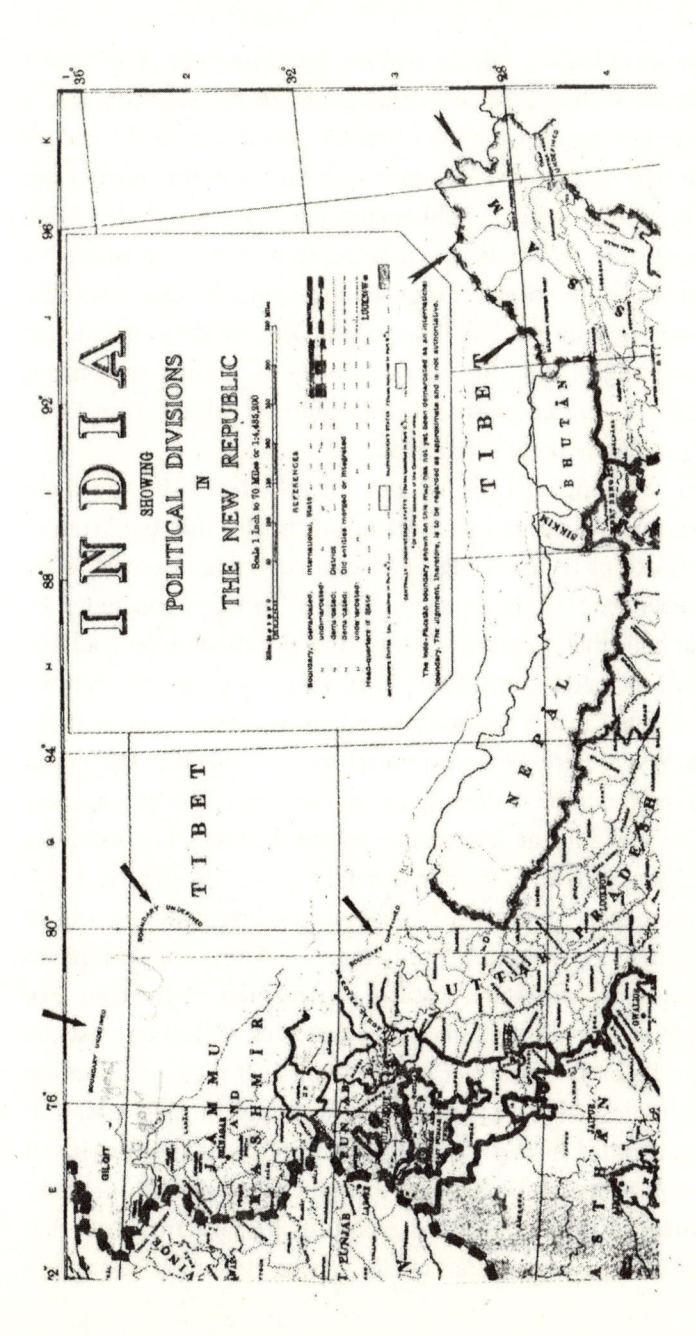

India Showing Political Divisions in the New Republic published by the **Survey of India (1950)**. On this map, the Sino-Indian boundary in the Eastern Sector is drawn generally in accordance with the McMahon Line, but it is marked as boundary undemarcated (↓). No boundary is drawn at all in the western and middle sectors, there are only the words boundary undefined (↓). This way of delineation was consistently followed by official Indian maps prior to 1954.

command of Tibet, which Beijing legitimized by a 17-Point Agreement with the Dalai Lama's government. Tibet became a province of China—which is what 'sovereignty' implied—and all the treaties and agreements signed by the Government of Tibet with India and other neighbouring countries stood dissolved, because China repudiated them as an imperialist imposition.

Amongst these treaties that were scrapped by China was the one incorporating the McMahon Line. One could have stretched the initialling of the 1914 Convention as a binding agreement, but the day we accepted the sovereignty of China over Tibet, even that flimsy basis evaporated.

The US and Britain showed scant interest in the 1914 Convention. Nehru told parliament much later that the Western nations, except to use Tibet to 'embarrass China', cared little for its independence and sovereignty. He had perhaps concluded by circular logic that there was nothing, therefore, that India could do militarily to dislodge the PLA, which was by now (after November 1962) situated firmly in the trans-Himalayan plateau of Tibet.

However, there were sane voices in the 1950s that had urged Nehru to raise the border question with the Chinese because then India would at least know where it stood. For example, Girija Shankar Bajpai, former secretary general to the MEA and then thereafter governor of the Bombay Presidency, wrote to Nehru in 1953, cautioning him that for China the McMahon Line might be one of those 'scars left by Britain in the course of her aggression against China [who] may seek to heal or erase the scar on the basis of frontier rectifications that may not be either to our [India's] liking or interest'. Nehru's reply to Bajpai was: 'It is not in India's interest to raise the question of the McMahon Line. And if the Chinese raised the issue, we can take our stand that there is nothing to discuss about it.' Bajpai wrote back that the Chinese have 'no intention of raising it until it suits their convenience.' Such sound advice fell on deaf ears.

A little earlier in 1952, Nehru wrote to Sheikh Abdullah, then titled 'Prime Minister' of Jammu and Kashmir, stating:

> We need not raise the question of our frontier...but if we find that the Chinese maps continue to indicate that part of our territory is on their side, then we shall have to point this out to the Chinese Government. We need not do this immediately, but we should not put up with this for long and the matter has to be taken up.

Nehru should have known that the Chinese coyness on the border question was not an oversight at all. On 16 June 1952, Nehru had wired the then India's ambassador to China, K.M. Panikkar, stating:

> We think it is rather odd that in discussing Tibet with you (on 14 June) Chou En-lai did not refer at all to our frontier. For our part, we attach more importance to this than to other matters. We are interested, as you know, not only in our direct Frontier but also in Frontiers of Nepal, Bhutan and Sikkim, and we have made it perfectly clear in Parliament that these frontiers must remain. There is perhaps some advantage in our not ourselves raising this issue. On the other hand, I do not quite like Chou En-lai's silence about it when discussing even minor matters.

In fact, it was Panikkar who persuaded Nehru not to press the border issue. Even though he was India's ambassador to China, he often acted like Mao's envoy rather than Nehru's, invariably defending the Chinese acts of omission and commission. Even when the Chinese were caught napping with their wrong, aggressive foot forward, Panikkar would defend them. 'The Chinese attitude about these issues has all along been that these arise from unequal treaties and are "scars left behind" by the British,' he would say. Even when the PLA was busy disrupting and distorting the Tibetan way of life, Panikkar would send a note back home, saying: 'Not much news has been appearing about Tibet of late and it is expected that the work of re-organisation there will naturally take time and will be handled with tact and care by the Chinese authorities.'

By his long epistles, Panikkar managed to get Nehru to reply: 'In view of what you say, it will be desirable not to raise the question of our frontier at this stage'. Panikkar was not accountable to the people, but Nehru was. He should have taken the nation into confidence on the true state of the border.

Nehru however remained confused. In a note to his foreign secretary (on 25 July 1952), he wrote:

> I appreciate the reasons which Panikkar advanced. But I am beginning to feel that our attempt at being clever might overreach itself (sic.). I think it is better to be absolutely straight and frank.

On 6 September 1952, Nehru again wrote to the foreign secretary, affirming that: 'On reconsideration, I accept Shri Panikkar's advice that we should not make specific mention about the frontiers.'

As to what made Nehru somersault and become ostrich-like, few have a clue even today. Two years later, Nehru thought that instead of fruitlessly antagonizing Beijing by maintaining the old policy on Tibet, Delhi should befriend the 'new China'.

Hindi Chini Bye Bye?

The new-found friendship drive was reinforced when India and China signed the Agreement on Trade and Intercourse between Tibet Region of China and India on 29 April 1954 in Beijing. The preamble to this agreement indicates the wider purposes of the treaty. The Five Principles of Peaceful Coexistence, or Panchsheel, was embodied in it for the first time. One of the five principles of the treaty was 'mutual respect for each other's territorial integrity and sovereignty', which clearly implied that the borders of each party to the treaty were known to the other. Had China believed that there was a territorial dispute of any size about the entire Sino-Indian boundary *that* was the time to raise the question, when the two countries were solemnly pledging to respect mutually the 'territorial integrity' of the other. Though it was an agreement on trade and intercourse, it was concluded to settle all outstanding issues and to consolidate the friendly relations between the two countries. The Government of China did not reveal their territorial claims, even when the two countries negotiated and signed this agreement on Tibet.

Even as India formally recognized Tibet as a part of China, the Sino-Indian border was not delineated. No mention whatsoever was made in the treaty on the finality of the so-called McMahon Line. Nehru failed to heed Sarder Patel's warning that because the Government of China had in 1914 refused to agree to be a signatory to the Simla Convention, therefore Nehru should have demanded a price for agreeing to recognize the sovereignty of China over Tibet. He should have asked the Chinese leadership to clarify its position on the McMahon Line. If the Chinese can accept the McMahon Line *in toto* with Burma, then provided we had negotiated with our eyes open, why not with India?

Despite the direct nexus of the recognition of Tibet as a province of China with this border question, India had failed to press for a solution simultaneously. Even today, China's claims on the border are primarily based on Tibetan documents.

Chinese Premier Zhou Enlai wrote to the Asian and African

leaders about the Sino-Indian boundary question on 15 November 1962. He cited the Tibetan documents to support China's claims. The names of rivers, passes and other places in the Eastern Sector (NEFA; now Arunachal Pradesh) were all in the Tibetan language. Zhou based China's claims over the Aksai Chin by declaring that it used to be a part of Xinjiang and the Ngari district of Tibet. In short, China's claims on the border with India are based on Tibetan documents and other Tibetan evidences. Of course, Nehru could have countered that by claiming that the Kashmir maharaja Lalitaditya Muktapida of the Karkota dynasty (724 CE–760 CE) had conquered Xinjiang, but he knew little about ancient India. For him, India was a discovery.

Indeed, most of the 245 items of evidence presented by the Chinese side at the 1960 India–China official meetings between Nehru and Zhou Enlai were Tibetan official documents. And yet, India missed a vital opportunity—and the moment of her maximum bargaining position—by failing to raise the border question in 1954, when the sovereignty of China over Tibet was affirmed by treaty.

Under the Agreement, the GoI had unilaterally handed over all of India's extra-territorial rights in Tibet, acquired in 1914, to China. The argument put forth by Nehru was that these rights were acquired by the British through imperialism. Then, was not the McMahon Line a product of the same imperialism? The Indian case on the border became riddled with such contradictions that it made its case look ridiculous in any international forum.

Nehru's assertion in parliament about the McMahon Line thus made no legal sense. If by our own admission, Tibet ceased to be independent and a subsequent India–China treaty affirmed the same in 1954, then how is an earlier commitment (Simla 1914) with a merged or 'gifted' state (Tibet) still valid if the inheritor state (China) had already disowned the commitments? In fact, the commitment itself was never owned, let alone it being disowned or not.

How could any government take the view that on the one hand the McMahon Line was the absolute official boundary because of the 1914 Simla Convention, which China itself as an invited third party had rejected, and on the other accept that Tibet is and was a province of China? The irony of the Indian contention is that the 'treaties and agreements' which India had entered into with independent Tibet were held to be valid, even after Tibet was no longer considered independent and had merged with China, and despite the consequent Chinese repudiation of any 'imposed' treaty which India failed to get clarified. This irony was reinforced by His Holiness the Dalai Lama in his address to the Indian Council of World Affairs (ICWA), New Delhi, on 7 September 1959, where he said:

> The government of India contends that the boundary between Tibet and India has been finally settled according to the McMahon Line, but this boundary was laid down by the Simla convention. And this convention was valid and binding only as between Tibet and the British government. If Tibet had no international status at the time of conclusion of the convention, it had no authority to enter into such an agreement. Therefore, it is abundantly clear that if you deny the sovereign status of Tibet, you deny the validity of the McMahon line.

Clearly, this elementary logic escaped Nehru till he was rudely awakened to it by later events.

Much later, on 8 November 1962 when Nehru moved a resolution in parliament (the resolution became famous because MPs had stood up to take an oath 'to drive the aggressors out'), he misinformed the Lok Sabha even on the true position of the

1914 Convention. On that occasion, he said in the House:

> Even if the Chinese did not accept it [the McMahon line]—and I would like to say that the objection they raised in 1914 was not based on their objection to the McMahon line—it was based on their objection to another part of the treaty which divided inner Tibet and outer Tibet. The McMahon line did not come in that.

This statement of Nehru was false on the following two grounds. First, the Chinese *did* object to all the boundary lines drawn by Sir Henry McMahon. Second, if indeed Britain had taken the Simla Convention of 1914 as final, why did the imperial power then refrain from publishing these maps for 22 years, till 1936?

It is because of these unstated and unarticulated approaches that since 1949 the history of the Sino-Indian border dispute has been that of Nehru's unforgivable contradictions in public posture and private persuasion, which was passed off as the Indian government's policy. Even worse, he stuck to these contradictory stances on the border dispute throughout his tenure as the PM, as is evident from his ill-famed Forward Policy. This policy was not the outcome or a reaction to the Chinese incursions of 1959–60, as is commonly assumed, but rather a premeditated design of Nehru as early as 1954. In a minute of 12 May that year, just after signing the India–China Agreement in Tibet, Nehru wrote: 'I agree also that we should establish checkposts at all disputed points, wherever they might be, and our administration should be right up to these borders.' That it proved to be counterproductive later is another matter.

Here, a few further dates warrant recalling to provide the comprehensive context. On 18 June 1954, Nehru sent a 'Note on Tibet and China' to the secretary general, the foreign secretary and joint secretary of the MEA, which stated:

> No country can ultimately rely upon the permanent goodwill or bonafides of another country, even though they might be in close friendship with each other. It is not inconceivable that China and the Soviet Union may not continue to be as friendly as they are now. Certainly it is conceivable that our relations with China might worsen, though there is no immediate likelihood of that. Adequate precautions have to be taken. If we come to an agreement with China in regard to Tibet, that is not a permanent guarantee but that itself is one major step to help us in the present and in the foreseeable future in various ways.

Nehru further added:

> Of course, both the Soviet Union and China are expansive. They are expansive for evils other than communism, although communism may be made a tool for the purpose. Chinese expansionism has been evident during various periods of Asian history for a thousand years or so. We are perhaps facing a new period of such expansionism.

On 1 July 1954, Nehru further despatched a 17-para Memorandum to his officials, which contained an important directive to publish new maps. Paras 7 to 10 of this memorandum enlist it all:

> 7. All our old maps dealing with this frontier should be carefully examined and, where necessary, withdrawn. New maps should be printed showing our Northern and North Eastern frontier without any reference to any 'line'. These new maps should also not state there is any undemarcated territory. The new maps should be sent to our Embassies abroad, should be introduced to the public generally and be used in our schools, colleges, etc.

8. Both as flowing from our policy and as consequence of our Agreement with China, this frontier should be considered [as] firm and definite, one which is not open to discussion with anybody. There may be very minor points of discussion. Even these should not be raised by us. It is necessary that the system of checkposts should be spread along this entire frontier. More especially, we should have checkposts in such places as might be considered disputed areas.

9. Our frontier has been finalized not only by implication in this Agreement but the specific passes mentioned are direct recognitions of our frontier there. Checkposts are necessary not only to control traffic, prevent unauthorized infiltration but as symbols of India's frontier. As Demchok is considered by the Chinese as a [disputed] territory, we should have checkposts there. So also at Tsang-Chokla.

10. In particular, we should have proper checkposts along the Tibet border and on the passes etc. leading to Joshimath, Badrinath, etc.

Thus, it is highly puzzling that Nehru publicly postured to befriend China, but his confidential minutes, notes and memos were postured on aggressive intentions which were, paradoxically, not matched by commitment to military preparedness and adequate defence expenditure.

In 1954, a pragmatic policy would have been to incorporate a negotiated border settlement with the trade agreement as a price for giving up the rights India had acquired in Tibet through the 1914 Convention—a price India had failed to extract earlier: first at the time of recognition of the PRC (in 1950), and second, while proposing that China replace Taiwan in the UNSC and General Assembly (in 1951).

Instead, the GoI took the matter to a ludicrous limit by secretly revising the 1950 Survey of India map in 1954, and arbitrarily drawing the Kashmir (Aksai Chin sector) and NEFA borders as if it had already been defined and demarcated. Thus, through a bureaucratic sleight of hand—first in 1914, then in 1936 and finally in 1954—the GoI defined a Sino-Indian border without the other side's concurrence. Such a 'definition' of a border is unparalleled in the history of modern nations.

The Sino-Indian Agreement of 1954 was thus honed in the basic contradiction in India–China relations: the unresolved boundary dispute with a resolved Tibetan status. However, after its signing, each nation drew its own silent conclusions to suit its respective interests and rapidly moved to establish its respective claims in the disputed or ill-defined territories.

4

1962: 'A STAB FROM THE FRONT'*

The territorial dispute that the 1954 Agreement swept under the carpet was later activated during 1959–62 by domestic events in China, in particular in Tibet, and by the reactions to it in India, the consequences in public opinion, which neither of the two countries could control.

In October 1954, PM Nehru visited China. It was the first visit by a non-communist head of state since the creation of the PRC. Nehru mentioned to the Chinese leaders that he had seen a few maps published in China which showed a wrong boundary between the two countries. He also added that he was not worried about it, as the boundaries of India were 'quite clear' and not a matter of argument. The Chinese PM had replied that these maps were 'reproductions of old maps drawn before 1949' and that they had had no time to revise them. Later, in a letter to Zhou (dated 14 December 1958), Nehru reminded him that he had raised with him the question of 'wrong maps' published in

---

*'A Stab from the Front' as written by M.J. Akbar in his book *Nehru: The Making of India*, Penguin Books (first published in 1989).

China, and according to Nehru, Zhou had told him that 'these maps are reproductions of old pre-liberation maps and [China] had no time to revise them.' Again, in 1956, when Zhou visited India, Nehru referred to the wrong Chinese maps, especially in relation to the Eastern Sector. Zhou then had said that he had accepted the McMahon Line as the border between China and Burma, and he would accept this border with India also. Or Nehru believed he said so. However, factually what Zhou told Nehru was correct. Formally, China signed a border agreement with Burma in 1960, accepting the McMahon Line as the international boundary. Hence, I hold that India should be firm with China on the Arunachal–Tibet border as drawn by the same McMahon Line.

Playing Poker—The Chinese Way

So, was there a deeper purpose in the minds of the two countries' leadership for not resolving the conflict by negotiation? Did the PMs of China and India, Zhou and Nehru, respectively, communicate on the issue honestly and transparently to minimize the danger of an armed conflict? Obviously, Zhou and Nehru were playing poker—the Chinese way. Nehru was the novice, Zhou the consummate inscrutable artiste, who could wriggle out of every commitment earlier made, as we saw later in 1959.

This was proved beyond doubt when China published the completion of a motorable road across Aksai Chin, linking Xinjiang with western Tibet in the July 1957 issue of *China Pictorial*. Depicted on a map, it described that 'notable engineering feat' in an article on the achievements of their first five-year plan. The map also included in Chinese territory four of the five administrative divisions of NEFA, some areas in Uttar Pradesh (UP) in the Middle Sector and large areas in Ladakh. There was an uproar in the Indian parliament which evaporated Nehru's favourite slogan—'Hindi Chini Bhai Bhai'. The opposition parties altered the slogan to 'Hindi Chini Bye Bye'.

The India–China border dispute was thus formally notified by this map and the subsequent Indian reactions to it. Thereafter, the relations founded on Panchsheel steadily tumbled for the worse, culminating in a border war between the two giant Asian nations in 1962.

In the summer of 1958, an Indian patrol in the area was detained by the Chinese and in reply to the protest, the Chinese referred to their frontier guards as having detained the Indian patrol because they were in 'Chinese territory'. The following year, a Chinese PLA force came to Khurnak Fort in Ladakh, and arrested an Indian patrol party in Aksai Chin.

The GoI then drew the attention of the Chinese authorities to this map. It was also pointed out that as the Chinese Communist government had been in power for nearly nine years, 'corrections' in Chinese maps were overdue. In his letter to Zhou dated 21 August 1958, Nehru recalled that such cartographic contradictions had been raised in discussion with Zhou when Nehru had visited China in 1954, but that he had been reassured that 'current Chinese maps were based on old maps' and that the People's Republic 'had had no time to correct them'. The letter concluded with an offer, which seems deliberatively offensive, to send a free copy of the latest Indian official map to guide Beijing's cartographers. The sting in Nehru's letter lay in the concluding sentence: 'There can be no question of these large parts of India [shown as within China on Chinese maps] being anything but India and there is no dispute about them.'

Then in his letter to Zhou on 14 December 1958, Nehru revealed that:

> I remember your telling me that you did not approve of this border being called the McMahon line... You told me

then that you had accepted this McMahon line border with Burma and, whatever might have happened long ago, in view of the friendly relations which existed between China and India, you propose to recognise this border with India also.'

Nehru then goes on to add: 'I had thought then of writing to you on this subject, but I decided not to trouble you over such a petty matter.'

'Petty matter' it was not! Nehru's failure to write a formal letter to Zhou in 1956 was a costly error, but the latter also failed to record in writing his government's stand at that time despite knowing of the 1954 Survey of India maps. Thus, even when India had raised the matter of these wrong maps, the Chinese did not even suggest that the boundary was in any manner under dispute. These lapses then built up the atmosphere of distrust.

However, an amazing admission was to come from Zhou in his 23 January 1959 letter to Nehru, admitting that it was 'true that the border question was not raised in 1954 when negotiations were being held between Chinese and Indian sides for the Agreement on Trade and Intercourse between Tibet region of China and India. This was because conditions were not yet ripe for its settlement'. Then why did the time become ripe in 1959 for the dispute to be raised? That is something Premier Zhou did not clarify in the letter. This admission clearly means that Zhou led Nehru up the garden path, and Nehru, too, was naive enough to tread that path. He further made an official claim that the McMahon Line was illegal and invalid, and claimed that the international boundary was below the mountains. In summary, his points were:

i. The Sino-Indian boundary had never been formally delimited. That is, no treaty or agreement on the boundary had even been concluded between the Chinese central government and the Indian government.

ii. Border disputes (did) exist between China and India and, therefore, it was unavoidable that there would be discrepancies between their respective maps.
iii. The Aksai Chin area was China's and had always been under Chinese jurisdiction.
iv. The McMahon Line had no legitimacy as an international boundary, but China was likely to accept that alignment at the appropriate time and in the appropriate circumstances, *as it was doing in the negotiations with Burma.*

For China, the issue was not about border or tracts of land, but of India's perceived goals in Tibet, which had been inflamed by Nehru's ambiguity, and the growing Indian opposition led by Ram Manohar Lohia and his disciples. Lohia was clear in his stance, albeit a bit impractical. Nehru may have had an instinctively practical attitude to Tibet, but it was dented by ambiguity, deception and doubt, as exhibited in his letter of 22 March 1959 to Zhou, in which he wrote:

> Contrary to what has been reported to you, this line [McMahon Line] was, in fact, drawn at a Tripartite Conference held at Simla in 1913–14 between the Plenipotentiaries of the Governments of China, Tibet and India. At the time of acceptance of the delineation of this frontier, Lonchen Shatra, the Tibetan Plenipotentiary, in letters exchanged, stated explicitly that he had received orders from Lhasa to agree to the boundary as marked on the map appended to the Convention. The line was drawn after full discussion and was confirmed subsequently by a formal exchange of letters; and there is nothing to indicate that the Tibetan authorities were in any way dissatisfied with the agreed boundary. Moreover, although the Chinese Plenipotentiary at the Conference objected to the boundaries between Inner and Outer Tibet

and between Tibet and China, there is no mention of any Chinese reservation in respect of the India-Tibet frontier either during the discussions or at the time of their initialling the Convention. In our previous discussions and particularly during your visit to India in January 1957, we were gratified to note that you were prepared to accept this new line as representing the frontier between China and India in this region and I hope that we shall reach an understanding on this basis.

This was clearly a false understanding of the records on the GoI's position, and the falsity Nehru ought to have known. It is difficult to believe that officials such as Girija Shankar Bajpai, former foreign secretary, would, after Independence, not have at least orally briefed Nehru about the fraud on maps committed by Sir Olaf K. Caroe during British rule in 1936. It is thus not possible to give Nehru the benefit of the doubt on this matter.

Exactly 12 years after making declarations in parliament on the fixity of the McMahon Line, Nehru would learn later, to his cost, that he was wrong on two counts. The McMahon Line was not a definitive border at all, and he was not militarily prepared to stop the Chinese from crossing it.

On 25 August 1959, Chinese troops crossed the McMahon Line in the NEFA area (now Arunachal Pradesh) and exchanged fire with Indian troops already stationed at Longju. India reported one soldier as killed and a dozen wounded. Although the Indian and Chinese versions of the Longju incident differed, it was clear that this incident soured relations between the two nations. Almost two months later, on 21 October, Chinese troops further penetrated into Ladakh and opened fire on an Indian patrol near the Kongka Pass, a strategic military outpost, killing nine Indian soldiers and 10 others were taken into custody. Both sides suffered casualties. China had thus, by that year, already begun to resort to force unqualified by any adjective—defensive or offensive. The question is: why?

The India–China friendship was further severely wounded in the autumn of 1959. Zhou made specific territorial claims to an estimated 40,000 sq. miles of territory in Ladakh and NEFA. In his letter to Nehru dated 8 September 1959, Zhou wrote,

> Nevertheless, since China and India have not delimited their mutual boundary through friendly negotiations and joint surveys, China has not asked India to revise its maps. In 1954, I explained to your Excellency for the same reason that it would be inappropriate for the Chinese Government to revise the old map right now.

The question was not raised earlier even though the GoI had made public declarations affirming the 'established boundaries' of India, and published maps in 1954 accordingly. While Nehru can be faulted for not raising the border question earlier, Zhou should have by then known of the new 1954 Survey of India map. This was not an old map of India, but a freshly revised one. Why did Zhou not raise a protest with Nehru?

Thereafter, on 26 September 1959, Nehru wrote back to Zhou expressing his great 'surprise and distress' over the latter's letter. Referring to the McMahon Line as the boundary in the eastern area of the frontier, Nehru stated:

> When I discussed this with you, I thought we were confronted with the problem of reaching an agreement on where exactly the so-called McMahon Line in the eastern section of the boundary lay. Even when I received your letter of 23 January 1959, I had no idea that the People's Republic of China would lay claim to about 40,000 square miles of what in our view has been indisputably Indian territory for decades and in some sectors for over a century.

Nehru added:

> We did not release to the public the information which we had about the various border intrusions into our territory by various Chinese personnel since 1954, the construction of a road across Indian territory in Ladakh, and the arrest of our personnel in the Aksai Chin area in 1958 and their detention. We did not give publicity to this in hope that peaceful solutions of the disputes could be furthered.

There cannot be an admission of a PM that is so self-condemnatory. Seeing these developments, Nikita Khrushchev, the first secretary of the Communist Party of the Soviet Union (CPSU), invited Chairman Mao and his senior colleagues to Moscow. The heated discussion that took place on 2 October 1959 between the two leaders, with interventions from their colleagues, is in Appendix VI.

Zhou wrote again to Nehru on 7 November 1959, reiterating his earlier suggestions for maintaining the status quo on the border. He further suggested that both sides should withdraw their armed forces 20 km from the LAC, the demarcation that separates India-controlled territory from China-controlled territory.

On 5 February 1960, the Indian PM wrote to Zhou, suggesting a meeting between the two. Zhou came to India in April 1960, at its weakest moment since 1949, while China was in the middle of its worst internal crisis since 1949 because of i) the failure of the Great Leap Forward, ii) the worst drought of the century that claimed 16 to 32 million lives in famine, iii) the near collapse of the industrial system due to the sudden pull-out of Soviet engineers with their blueprints from 160 major industrial projects under turnkey collaboration agreements. This resulted in the sacking of Defence Minister Peng Dehuai and the rise of the more moderate Liu Shaoqi as the new President of China, challenging Chairman

Mao after succeeding him as head of state, and Deng Xiaoping emerging as Party Secretary General.

Following six days of talks between the two premiers, Zhou in a press conference made six points, which were:

i. That the two sides accept that there is a dispute;
ii. There is an LAC up to which both sides exercise jurisdiction;
iii. In determining boundaries, geographical principles like watersheds ought to be applicable on all sectors;
iv. A settlement of the boundary ought to take into account the national feelings of the people of the two countries to the Himalayas and Karakorams;
v. Pending settlement, both sides should recognize the LAC and not put forward territorial claims as preconditions, but individual adjustments can be made; and
vi. In order to ensure peace and tranquillity, both sides should refrain from patrolling all sectors of the boundary.

This Six-Point Agreement of the PMs confirmed the serious differences between the two nations with regard to the understanding of basic facts about the border issue even after a decade of interaction between them. Nehru by now had been forced by his Cabinet colleagues on the defensive. So, he asked Zhou to individually meet his hardliner Cabinet colleagues. In an unprecedented move, Zhou called on the senior ministers of the Nehru government to explain China's point of view, but received a cold reception of heated words from them in the meeting.

The PMs, therefore, agreed that in the near future, officials of the two governments should meet and examine relevant documents and make a joint report, and that, in the meantime, every effort should be made to avoid friction and clashes on the border.

The GoI, after the officials' meet, published the *Report of the Officials of the Governments of India and the People's Republic of China on the Boundary Question* (in February 1961), and the Government of China published it in April 1962. The *Officials' Report* is a unique document—one of its kind—and serves even today as the basic source material on the border dispute between China and India.

Mao's Art of War

It was clear that Nehru had erred on China, not on the score of appeasement but because of his attitude of self-righteousness, by treating India as if it were his family silver. However, the Chinese were better and smarter in the art of deception. In 1962, Nehru paid for his folly. India lost its artificial international status because Nehru was exposed as a 'paper tiger' by the Chinese. This comes out clearly in the heated exchanges between senior politburo members of the USSR and of China in their respective communist parties (see Appendix VI).

Nehru's belief that the Chinese leadership would not take any extreme military steps against India and his confidence in the ability of the Indian army, accompanied by doctored reports, encouraged his decision to not make concessions, and to go ahead with an active Forward Policy. The policy entailed patrolling and establishing positions in territories claimed by China as well as showing a presence and preventing a creeping take-over by Chinese forces of territories claimed as Indian. 'This Forward Policy shall be carried out,' Nehru told his aides 'without getting involved in a clash with the Chinese, unless this becomes necessary in self-defence'. Later, in October 1962, Nehru even went so far as 'to instruct the Indian army to evict Chinese forces that crossed the McMahon Line.'

Various events reinforced Nehru's myopic conviction that he had assessed the situation correctly. By 1960, the international situation had also changed. China had broken with the USSR; and due to the brazen and unnotified building of a road through Aksai Chin in 1957 by the Chinese government, Indians manifested a growing disenchantment with China.

This was enhanced following the escape of His Holiness the Dalai Lama and his entourage from Tibet to India. Although the GoI had repeatedly assured China that the Dalai Lama was in India only as a religious leader, a 'government in exile' under the Dalai Lama became active in India (see Appendix VI). India then began to be encouraged by both the US and USSR to take on China.

Another myopic conviction of Nehru arose from the Indian army's success in taking over Goa in 1961, in which it had challenged a US North Atlantic Treaty Organization (NATO) ally and a 'power' such as Portugal. That this action did not provoke the US and the NATO was proof of the army's efficiency. And thus Nehru thought that India's well-established status in the international arena protected it from the danger of any future massive retaliation from the Chinese.

The Forward Policy seemed to be successful as a calculated risk (as Nehru put it in parliament): 'We have taken the risk and we have moved forward, and we have stopped effectively their further march.' The reliability of the deterrent effect of the army and China's political and military weakness seemed thus proven.

This misperception about China was bolstered by a number of bilateral confrontations in which Chinese forces retreated or did not retaliate, the most prominent of them being in July 1962 in the Galwan Valley in the Western Sector. In Galwan Valley, the Chinese army had surrounded an Indian position, but retreated when the Indian forces stood firm, threatening to retaliate against other Chinese positions in the Western Sector.

In Nehru's view, the Forward Policy was 'defensive'. It was designed, Nehru stated, to contain Chinese territorial 'expansionism', based on the belief that if the Chinese could establish posts in the disputed territory, so could India. Nevertheless, the policy did have an offensive component, too.

In the summer of 1962, India's Forward Policy took on a new dimension. The Indian armed forces, taking advantage of the stoppage of patrolling on the Chinese side—perhaps because of internal developments in China—set up a series of checkposts in deep and remote areas of north-east Kashmir and Arunachal Pradesh, and even in those areas where the Chinese had already established their posts. Indian troops also began establishing new checkposts in those areas that had been vacated by the Chinese during the preceding winter, and had not returned because the snow had not yet melted. In February 1962, the Indian government decided to set up as many checkposts as possible along the McMahon Line in the NEFA area; one of the new ones being Dhola in the Thagla area. This checkpost was provocative for two reasons. First, the Dhola post was located in an area where the Chinese had questioned the exact demarcation of the McMahon Line, and where India really could not lay a firm claim. Second, this post was located close to the Chinese base and thus could symbolize a threat to the Chinese position in Tibet. Indian troops and paramilitary forces began infiltrating behind Chinese checkpoints in Ladakh. By the end of July that year, India had thus recovered control of about 5,000 sq. km of territory in the Ladakh area that Nehru had cartographically laid claim to by publishing new maps.

India's Forward Policy was thus being devised to excite direct provocation by China. The forward probes behind Chinese positions in Ladakh and the NEFA area was interpreted by China as a sign of India's determination to assert its territorial claims by force. The success of the Forward Policy was, however, dependent on China refraining from open warfare. Unfortunately on this, Nehru had miscalculated and misjudged China. India's forward moves that summer of 1962 proved counterproductive, since it enabled China to take notice and be ready for a counteroffensive in October the same year. China prepared for the war, while India walked into it, as revealed by our military preparedness.

At the end of 1961, in the Western Sector, instead of the five regular battalions that were required, there was only one regular infantry battalion and two battalions of the J&K militia with almost no artillery deployed. As a result, in the summer of 1962, the Indian army maintained a series of military posts and positions in the Western Sector that for the most part, except in the Demchuk area, did not even reach the border line claimed by the Chinese.

On the other hand, the Chinese had a network of roads and a military force the size of a division in the Western Sector, including armoured components. Therefore, in a letter dated April 1961 to the minister of defence, the Indian Army Chief, General Kodendera Subayya Thimayya, wrote: 'As things stand today, it has to be accepted that should the Chinese wish to carry out strong incursions into our territory at selected points, we are not in a position to prevent them from doing so.' Along the northern border, the ratio of forces was five to one in favour of the Chinese, whose units were concentrated, while those of the Indian army were scattered over a wide area, with hardly any communications or manageable supply routes between them.

There were units which could receive supplies only from the air and were dependent on the weather and the pilot's ability to make their airdrops accurate; ground conditions made the retrieval of inaccurately dropped supplies almost impossible. The

Air Force was thus under constant pressure to overstretch its transport capacity.

Field officers in the Eastern Command suggested concentrating Indian forces at potential invasion points in the Eastern Sector. This would have solved a large number of the logistical problems and would have forced the Chinese to fight where India chose. Moreover, sitting on the McMahon Line itself allowed only backward manoeuvers, unless India had wished to invade Tibet. However, this suggestion, which was both tactically and strategically wise, had become impossible politically. New Delhi thought it essential to demonstrate a military presence in the entire area.

From a logistical point of view, the army was unable to supply its soldiers with suitable personnel equipment and provisions for Himalayan conditions. For example, in 1962, the Indian soldier was issued a weapon dating back to World War II. The army was short of 60,000 automatic rifles, 700 anti-tank weapons, at least 2,000 light mortars, artillery ammunition, 5,000 communication sets, 36,000 radio batteries and 2,000 light trucks. Two tank regiments were paralysed due to lack of spare parts, and aircrafts were grounded for the same reason. However, the Chief of General Staff (CGS), Lieutenant General B.M. Kaul, a distant relative of Nehru, rejected any criticism of the Indian soldier's equipment and decided that even though 'it did not reach the level of that of NATO soldiers, it definitely fulfilled requirements'.

The level of training and the morale of the Indian troops were also in a deplorable state. The Indian army was, by and large, a plain's army, trained and equipped accordingly. Its past conventional warfare had been in the north-west frontier of Punjab. As early as the beginning of the 1950s, army commanders thought that they should prepare for the possibility of an attack from the north and the east. Contigency plans were made to issue a Document dealing with tactics, strategies, organization and equipment of the Chinese infantry.

Nehru, however, shelved the idea for fear of provoking China. At the end of the 1950s, the army chief who had visited Switzerland to observe the training procedures, organization and equipment of the Alpine army divisions, proposed the establishment of a number of mountain divisions to be supported by a motorized force, whose regular base would be at the foot of the Himalayas. Nehru rejected this suggestion on the grounds that India could not take on unjustified expenditures. There were few officers trained in mountain combat, a position that remained so till the end of 1962.

Nehru had never been to the disputed area, and was dazzled and impressed by the maps shown to him by sycophantic senior army men, on which dozens of new established positions were marked as part of the Forward Policy. However, on the map, the terrain did not look as forbidding as it was in reality. On a map, distances are measured in kilometres, but in the mountains, they are measured in days. It is no wonder that subsequently in late 1962, Nehru fell victim to his own illusions.

In parliament and other forums, Nehru insisted that there was no need for worry. 'The army was improving its performance and capabilities,' he told parliament in July 1962, much as the Modi government is doing today. While we are well placed today in Ladakh, much more needs to be done in the Northeast. Nehru was proud of the extent of road-building, especially in the Eastern Sector, which was more defensible and secure. In August 1962, he declared in parliament that 'over the previous two years, the balance of power had been changing in India's favour'.

On that subject, Nehru received regular pleasing information from the then minister of defence V.K. Krishna Menon, who, according to his biographer T.J.S. George, 'was such a votary of self-reliance that he refused to import defence equipment and turned the military factories into production lines for hairclips and pressure-cookers'[17]. M.J. Akbar takes the story forward when he writes in *Nehru: The Making of India:*

> The Army was convinced that Menon was more concerned about promoting himself than defending his country at home... Even Nehru was perturbed at Menon's foreign tours. When the Chinese advanced into Ladakh in 1959, the Defence Minister was in New York and showed no desire to return till Nehru rebuked him.

Shockingly, Menon had allowed a Chinese military mission to tour India's major defence establishments as late as in 1958.

Nehru was especially pleased with the growth in the logistic capabilities of the Indian Air Force. In October 1960, 10 helicopters, 24 IL-14 planes and eight AN-12 cargo planes were purchased. In 1961, another 13 Bell Helicopters were purchased. At the beginning of 1962, eight additional AN-12 and 16 Mi-4 helicopters were ordered despite the dissatisfaction of the Air Force with the performance of the Soviet helicopters in the Himalayan heights (17,000 ft.). In June 1962, 29 American Fairchild cargo planes were acquired and in October an agreement was signed with the USSR, in which the supply of two MiG squadrons and the establishment of an Indian aircraft industry to produce Soviet MiGs were promised.

In the summer of 1962, as India began implementing the Forward Policy's provocative offensive, Beijing warned India that if it did not withdraw its aggressive forward posts and stop the provocations, Chinese frontier guards would be compelled to act in self-defence. On 20 June, Nehru stated in parliament that India

---

[17] Utpal Kumar, 'Nehru's India Helped China Conquer Tibet,' *Sunday Guardian*, 24 November 2018. Available at: https://www.sundayguardianlive.com/news/nehrus-india-helped-china-conquer-tibet, last accessed on 20 October 2020.

had set up a few new patrolling checkposts in the Ladakh area, west of the Xinjiang-Aksai Chin-Tibet Road, challenging Chinese checkposts. Nehru further stated that India's position had thus improved on the ground, and would become even better in the future. Defence Minister Menon openly declared that India would use military means to settle the boundary question with China, unmindful of our defence preparedness and gross misreading of Chinese capacities.

In July 1962, in a new turning point, Chinese troops encircled an Indian post in the Galwan Valley, Ladakh, and an exchange of fire ensued. But then suddenly, the Chinese troops withdrew, which led to a false sense of complacency in New Delhi that China was reluctant to fight.

In the meantime, in the same month, China had secretly agreed to reopen talks with the US at Warsaw, Poland. In these talks, China offered to soften its stance on Taiwan and also to the US's presence in Korea and Japan. US President John F. Kennedy then proposed further secret talks to normalize relations with China. Nehru was obviously not aware of all this. The stage was thus set for China to engage in hostilities on the border, confident that the US would be moderate in its response to help India in the war. Perhaps China was also confident that the USSR would become embroiled in what came to be known as the Cuban Missile Crisis of October 1962.

On 17 July 1962, three months before China launched its offensive, its ambassador to New Delhi, Pan Zili, sent a note to Beijing highlighting stalemate in negotiations with India, and also expressing his concern about its impact on ties between the two neighbours. This note was among documents from 1949 to 1965, which were declassified by the Chinese Ministry of Foreign Affairs Archives in Beijing. India has never so far agreed to release the documents in the commissioned report written by the Lieutenant

General Henderson Brooks (and Brigadier P.S. Bhagat).

The Chinese government then followed Ambassador Pan's note and arranged two 'last-ditch' meetings in Geneva between its vice foreign minister Zhang Hanfu and R.K. Nehru, MEA secretary general, and also between Foreign Minister Chen Yi, a former PLA general, and India's defence minister, Menon.

In a 20 July 1962 note, the Chinese foreign ministry appeared to arrive at the conclusion that the meeting with R.K. Nehru was futile. 'He did not put forward new issues,' the note said. 'Our side emphasized that the border issue was serious and if India did not withdraw troops, it should bear all the results.' Fifty-eight years later, in September 2020, these were the exact words of the Chinese defence minister Wei Fenghi to India's defence minister Rajnath Singh in a face-to-face meeting in Moscow on the sidelines of the Shanghai Cooperation Organisation (SCO) conference.

Three days later, on 23 July, Chen Yi met Menon in Geneva over breakfast. In the note of the meeting, the Chinese foreign ministry said Chen had complained of India's continuing 'advancements' in the west. Chen suggested both sides issue a joint communique, stating India and China would agree to negotiate on the border issue to avoid conflict. However, Menon, afraid by now of domestic ire and a feeling of betrayal amongst Indian people, flatly said no.

The two meetings left the Chinese convinced that negotiations on a new border according to Chinese perception would be a waste of time.[18] On 24 August 1962, Ambassador Pan sent another note to Beijing attacking Nehru for 'overestimating his own cunningness'. He suggested to Beijing that the government's effort should be to make clear its position more widely. 'Our aim must be to make the Indian masses and middle classes know that

---

[18]See Appendix V.

it is actually China that desired to negotiate and ease the tension, and that Nehru did not have sincerity for negotiations,' Pan said.

Twelve days before China launched its offensive, Zhou Enlai disclosed about the imminent military action in a meeting with the ambassador of the Soviet Union to Beijing. Without offering any evidence, he claimed that 'India will launch an attack, and that China will definitely defend ourselves'.

In a 13 November 1962 letter to the military ruler and President of Pakistan, Ayub Khan, Premier Zhou, after routing the ill-prepared Indian army, wrote: 'This serious Sino-Indian border is completely caused by the Indian government's long-term deliberate attempt.'[19]

Thus, today we in India are back to the same script with Defence Minister Rajnath Singh. Again, the meeting with Indian ministers is being used to justify Chinese invasions of India's border.

Of course, the Indian army is much stronger and well equipped today and PM Modi is not Nehru. However, the atmospherics are the same: China stringing Indian leaders by photo ops and idle discussions till the climate becomes opportune to attack the Indian forces. What else can explain the waste of time resulting from one-to-one meetings between Modi and Xi Jinping over six years, and that too 18 times? Even now, futile meetings of BRICS, and those arranged by Russia of the two nations' defence ministers, external affairs ministers and national security advisors have been held with no result, except China making sure that India is rendered falsely complacent.

Only a White Paper can clarify—unless the long-tucked-away-as 'secret', Henderson Brooks Report on the 1962 debate is

---

[19] Ananth Krishnan, 'A Last Opportunity, Missed,' *The Hindu*, 26 October 2012. Available at: https://www.thehindu.com/opinion/op-ed/a-last-opportunity-missed/article4031762.ece, last accessed on 26 October 2020.

declassified. Otherwise, India will not benefit from knowing the past follies and will have to repeat it again and again.

Nevertheless, on 26 July 1962, the GoI informed the Chinese government that India was prepared to enter into discussions on the basis of the Officials' Report. While notes on preliminary discussions to ease the tension were being exchanged, the Chinese troops, on 8 September 1962, marched across in the Eastern Sector, viz., the McMahon Line. They began a forceful push in the Dhola-Thagla area in NEFA, encircling a key Indian post at Dhola. The Indian troops were first ordered to stay firm, but the next day, were ordered to make immediate preparations to move forward within 48 hours and deal with the Chinese.

The Chinese saw it as an Indian decision to use force to evict them from the Dhola-Thagla area. This time, China was not as conciliatory as in the 1959–61 period. On 26 September 1962, Nehru declared at a press conference at Lagos (Nigeria) that India would deal with the Chinese 'by using force'. The decision to 'evict' China from Indian territory by force was officially stated on 12 October 1962 when Nehru announced at a press conference at New Delhi's Palam Airport that he had ordered the Indian army to drive the Chinese out of NEFA. That declaration was seen as India's ultimatum to China. Confirming this, on 14 October, Menon told a meeting of Congress workers at Bangalore that the government had come to a final decision to 'drive out the Chinese'. He declared that the Indian army was determined to fight the Chinese to the last man. *India almost did*!

In the face of increasing tension on the Sino-Indian border, the Chinese foreign ministry sent notes to the Indian embassy in Beijing on 4 August, 13 September and 3 October in 1962, and proposed to the Indian government that the two sides should meet immediately, without any precondition, to ease tension. However, all the proposals were rejected by India, now on a high horse of its ill-fated Forward Policy. This set the course for open warfare, but China was ready and prepared. India was not. The *People's Daily* (of 14 October 1962) advised Nehru to 'pull back from the brink of the precipice', an ominous warning that Nehru ignored.

On 18 October, Chairman Mao said at an enlarged meeting of the CCP's Polit Bureau:

> For many years, we have taken a number of measures to seek a peaceful resolution of the boundary issue but India rejected all of them. They intentionally provoked even more violent armed clashes. They are bullying others too much. Now that Nehru is determined to fight with us, we have no way out but to keep him company. However, our counterattack is only meant to serve a warning to Nehru and the Government of India that the boundary question cannot be resolved by military means.[20]

Thus, inexorably, China and India went to war, a limited one but of long-term consequence, which has even now yet to fully unwind. The war was clearly the logical outcome of the state of opaque diplomacy between the PMs of the two countries, who hid from each other their respective real agendas. 'A stab in the back,' as Nehru would put it with sorrow, but as M.J. Akbar stated in his book on Nehru, there is evidence that it was 'a stab from the front'.

A Zero-Sum Game

On 20 October 1962, there was a massive onslaught by China in both the Western and Eastern Sectors of the border, overwhelming the Indian forward posts. The Chinese army marched, even by

---

[20]Major General Lei Yingfu, *My Days as a Military Staff in the Supreme Command*, Beijing, 1997.

Chinese maps, well into the Indian territory, leading to a full-fledged border war. China with two to three divisions and equipped with modern weapons fell upon the Indian troops, human wave upon wave, in all three sectors of the border, but with the main thrust in the NEFA and Ladakh areas. India was taken by surprise, and was not at all prepared for such contingency of a massive wave of Chinese armed personnel across the Himalayas, despite its Forward Policy adventurism. China's rapid advance, supported by a well-established line of supplies and communications, give further credence to the thesis that China was fully prepared, and had chosen its own moment to strike. It was China that first launched the offensive, with infantry and artillery.

India's retaliation to the Chinese offensive was weak, uncoordinated and poorly planned. It proved disastrous. Like ninepins, post after post of the Indian army collapsed into Chinese hands. Almost everywhere Indian troops, wholly unprepared for mountain warfare, outnumbered and outsmarted, were demoralized. Within less than four weeks, China gained occupation of all the territories which it claimed in the Ladakh and NEFA areas, leaving the Indian army in tatters.

Why India did not stake its advantage in the air theatre is a mystery. Had the Indian Air Force been pressed into action then, the course of the 1962 Sino-Indian War could have been different. In fact, at the time, C. Rajagopalachari, independent India's first governor general, had advocated the deployment of the Indian Air Force to destroy the supply lines of the Chinese army, which were long into Tibet and threatened by the imminent severe winter on the Himalayan peaks and Tibetan plateau. This folly can only be attributed to Nehru's loss of nerve, and his reaping of the consequences of Menon's encouragement of sycophancy in army promotions. His chosen commanders, such as Lt Gen B.M. Kaul, had fled the battlefield pleading a 'cold'.

On 24 October, Premier Zhou put forward his three-point proposal for ceasefire and disengagement. India made a counter-proposal, that the status quo on the border, as of 8 September 1962, be restored, and thereafter, the two countries should enter into discussions.

The Chinese rejected that but then, dramatically, on 21 November, they halted their remarkable advance and declared a unilateral ceasefire and withdrawal from Indian territory. In the history of the modern world, China may be the only country to declare a unilateral ceasefire, especially after such a rapid and substantial advance into a foreign territory. And in an equally unprecedented move, China, soon thereafter, vacated the occupied territories and returned to their original pre-conflict position. Accordingly, the Chinese forces withdrew 20 km behind the McMahon Line, which they called 'the 1959 Line of Actual Control (LAC)' in the Eastern Sector, and also 20 km behind the line of their latest position in Ladakh, which they further identified with the so-called '1959 LAC' in the Western Sector. China, however, warned of a return if Indian forces attempted to reoccupy the vacated areas.

The question remains: why did China withdraw after such a successful advance? It clearly points to the possibility that having shown the world that it was not down and out after the internal events of 1959–61, having achieved its political aim of humbling India in the eyes of non-aligned and third-world countries, China had no use for territories it could not defend when the snows fell on the Himalayas in the bitter winter. Further, having obtained its military objectives, China saw no further advantage in continuing the offensive. A further advance into Indian plains would have compromised its military position because its supply lines through the high and snowy mountains would become indefensible. India, on the other hand, could have recovered from the shock and deployed its conventionally trained army to better advantage, and perhaps engage its relative superiority in air power.

Other reasons for Chinese de-induction could have been the anger and unity displayed by the Indian people against China, the fear of US intervention and the risk of Russia's open support to India. Thus, the strategic disadvantages of a continued war over the Himalayan mountains during the winter and the lack of any advantage in expanding its limited territorial claims in India, combined to convince China to stop its advance and declare the unilateral ceasefire.

After the war, a grieving PM Nehru wrote to Premier Zhou and said:

> Nothing in my long political career has hurt and grieved me more than the fact that the hopes and aspirations for peaceful and friendly neighbourly relations, which we entertained and to promote which my colleagues in the Government of India and myself worked so hard ever since the establishment of the People's Republic of China, should have been shattered by the hostile and unfriendly twist given on India–China relations during the past two years.

There was no need for Nehru, albeit 'hurt and grieved' to cry on the Chinese PM's shoulder because he had gone out of his way not only to befriend China, but also to plead the cause of China in the councils of the world. He had advocated its admission to the UN and surrendered to China the vacant veto-holding seat in the UNSC offered to India by the US, and had all along opposed the military pacts which were set up to isolate China. Clearly, Nehru's India–China perspective was based on adhocism and a *noblesse oblige* psychology, and not on realpolitik. Nehru's reputation as a world leader was in a shambles, and China may have also been smug with the psychic satisfaction that the Tibetans wanting independence could not hope anymore that India's military could liberate Tibet for a long time to come.

The war left the Chinese in possession of 14,500 sq. miles of territory in Ladakh. India declined to accept these unilateral terms, but stated that it would not disturb the ceasefire. At the same time, India asked for restoration of the status quo ante of 8 September 1962 in all sectors of the boundary, as a condition precedent for a mutually agreed ceasefire. A stalemate resulted, that in effect remains so even today.

On 26 May 1963, Beijing's New China News Agency (NCNA) International Service (now Xinhua News Agency) reported: 'The Chinese side had handed over to India all the 3,942 Indian military personnel captured while attacking the Chinese frontier guards during the Sino-Indian border conflict in October and November 1962 and the bodies and ashes of 26 captured Indian military personnel who died.'

On 21 November 1963, on the occasion of the anniversary of the ceasefire, *Renmin Ribao* (Chinese: *People's Daily*), the official news daily, carried an editorial announcing that the Chinese government was still awaiting negotiations with the Indian government on the border issue. It stated: 'As far as China is concerned, the door is wide open for reopening Sino-Indian negotiations and for a peaceful settlement of the boundary question. China has patience. If it is not possible to open negotiations this year, we will wait until next year; if it is not possible next year, then the year after next.'

In his last speech to the Bombay session of the All India Congress Committee (AICC) on 17 May 1964, 10 days before his demise, Nehru said that India was prepared to negotiate with China if the Chinese government agreed to remove its posts in Ladakh. He added that the initiative lay with China and that it was now for the Chinese 'to take steps or say nothing'.

On 19 May, Xinhua dismissed Nehru's call as another 'precondition' and as an 'obstacle' raised by India to the holding of negotiations. The official agency went further and claimed that the 20 km demilitarized area had always been Chinese territory, and that there was no question of China withdrawing is posts in its own territory.

Towards the end of December, Zhou, speaking to the National People's Congress in Beijing, decisively and finally rejected the idea of holding talks between the two countries on the basis of 'no posts either side' in the demilitarized zone in Ladakh. He called the suggestion an unreasonable Indian precondition and declared that China would never dismantle its posts from this area. He also reminded India that China had not relinquished its claim to 90,000 sq. km of India territory south of the McMahon Line. This territorial demand was in addition to the 23,200 sq. km of territory in Ladakh already with China by then.

Between 1960 and 1985, the Chinese negotiation position was that of trading off their claim in the East with the Indian claim in the West. This was, in reality, to ratify the status quo: India with Arunachal, and China with Aksai Chin and plus.

One of the tragic verdicts of research on the Sino-Indian border dispute is that the 1962 armed conflict between the two nations was totally unnecessary and bereft of any legal basis fit for presentation in any world forum. The Indians called the war as Chinese aggression and perfidy, and the Chinese called it a fit reply to Indian expansionism and a lesson taught to India. It was of course neither!

It was, in fact, a war of folly that made two giant neighbours, with no fundamental strategic conflict nor any history of hostility, fight a war that had few worthwhile territorial gains of strategic value. At that stage, the strategic gainers were the US and the USSR, with India left all alone. Thereafter, India totally titled into the Soviet camp.

It is a tribute to the Indian people that they rose as one to sacrifice for their nation's defence. Many parted with their gold and savings for the National Defence Fund. This had a huge impact on China because it had thought that India will dismember and not actually unite with fervour, setting aside all internal differences.

The War was, however, not simply an outcome of a border dispute; it emerged fundamentally from the problem of Tibet. China had liberated Tibet by force in 1950, and later had put down a rebellion in 1959. However, the possibility of India providing the psychological syndrome for the Tibetan rebels to continue their struggle loomed large after the Dalai Lama had been given political asylum with great fanfare in India.

To a significant extent, too, the 1962 offensive can be attributed to the Sino-Soviet dispute. China seemed to have believed that a strike against India would test that country's friendship with the Soviet Union, expose the 'ideological error' of revisionist USSR's support to 'bourgeois' India, and thus emerge as the true adherent to Communism.

In September 1959, TASS, the official Russian news agency, had put out a statement on the August 1959 Longju incident. TASS advised India and China to resolve the border conflict by peaceful means. This equation of a Socialist state (China) with a bourgeois one (India) by another Socialist state (USSR), and implied equivocation on the issue, enraged the Chinese leadership. On 13 September 1959, the Central Committee of the CPC in a stiff letter to its counterpart in the Soviet Union (the CPSU) accused the latter of 'exposing the family secret' of the Sino-Soviet rift on the border dispute of China with India, thus betraying the Communist cause, which brought glee and jubilation among the Indian bourgeoisie.[21]

It was not only the TASS's reaction to the Longju incident that

---

[21]See Appendix VI.

triggered the Chinese ire. Ever since the 'paternal' CPSU started demanding proof of acceptance by China of junior partner status by the CCP (e.g., by agreeing to place Chinese naval ports under Soviet supervision), the Soviet refusal to hand over a sample atom bomb and technical data since China 'did not need the bomb' etc., the Chinese began to suspect that the Soviet Union might, in the future, collaborate with China's enemies, such as the US and India, to cap China's growth.

A draft report dated 18 December 1959 to the CPSU Politburo's Mikhail A. Suslov, the leading member responsible for CPSU's relations with foreign political parties, berated the CCP's leadership in the edit page article in *Renmin Ribao*, in May 1959, titled 'The Revolution in Tibet and Nehru's Philosophy'.

Suslov commented that 'Nehru had behaved with reserve on the Tibet issue, and that the present foreign policy line of the Nehru government is a positive factor in the struggle for strengthening peace'. The term 'present foreign policy' meant Nehru's non-alignment policy with a pro-Soviet tilt. Nehru's acquiescence in the 1956 brutal crushing by the Soviet tanks of the Hungarian revolution had warmed the Soviet hearts.

Suslov also ridiculed the view expressed by Chinese interlocutors that there was a possibility of a downfall of the Nehru government. The Left-led massive central government employees strike in India in 1960 may have made the Chinese think that way, unable to comprehend bourgeois democracy and India's functioning anarchy. They were possibly also misled by the Indian communists' typical linguistic hyperbole on the imminent collapse of capitalism in India.

Subsequent events, such as the withdrawal of Soviet technicians from China, stepping up Soviet assistance to India's Third Five-Year Plan, the patronizing attitude of the CPSU towards the CCP after the failure of the Great Leap Forward and the Camp

David summit of Nikita Khrushchev with US President Dwight D. Eisenhower, convinced the Chinese that a grand alliance against China was emerging, consisting of the US, the USSR and India.

Thus, on 27 October 1962, a week into the border war, the *Renmin Ribao* editorial opined that 'Nehru had become a pawn in the international anti-Chinese campaign. This is the root cause and background of the Sino-Indian boundary dispute.'

Caught in the middle of the Cuban Missile Crisis, the Soviet Union initially pacified the Chinese by making statements supporting China against India. Indeed, the MiG-21 aircraft deal of August 1962 with India was suspended. The USSR declared that the Chinese were their 'brothers' while Indians were merely 'friends'.

However, as soon as the Cuban Crisis was over, the Soviet Union reverted to neutrality on the Sino-Indian dispute. In December 1962, in a major shift reflecting the Sino-Soviet growing rift, Khrushchev's address to the Soviet parliament made that clear. Pravda, the official organ of the CPSU wrote in their editorial of 19 September 1963:

> ... It is significant that, although the People's Republic of China Government strives to put all the blame for the conflict on the Indian Government, the non-aligned Afro-Asian nations deemed it necessary to urge none other than the Chinese Government to withdraw its forces twenty kilometres from the line which they reached as a result of major military operations in the autumn of 1962...
>
> However, the Government of PRC did not avail itself of the good services of these countries when they were offered... No wonder, many people now say that the PRC Government, while extolling in every way the initiative of the non-aligned nations, and declaring that it 'values' and 'pays tributes' to their good services, actually ignores these efforts and does not display any desire to profit by the proposals.

Years later in 1997, Chinese officials permitted the publication of an interesting memoir, *My Days as a Military Staff in the Supreme Command*, of Major General Lei Yingfu, the commander of forces on the Tibet plateau, during the late 1950s and in particular in 1962.[22]

General Lei wrote that Chairman Mao had summoned him on 10 October 1962, 10 days before the major assault by China across the Himalayas. To Chairman Mao's almost rhetorical query as to why Nehru had wanted an armed conflict with China, General Lei had advanced three reasons which found favour with Mao.

First, that Nehru thought China was so weak that it was in no position to respond in the distant south-west. Second, China was surrounded by troops of the US and the USSR on all sides and could not afford to take them on in a Sino-Indian military conflict. Third, the logistics of moving troops was so difficult for China that Nehru thought China could not deploy regular PLA troops to fight the Indian army.

According to General Lei, Chairman Mao then convened an extraordinary meeting of the Politburo of the CCP on 18 October 1962, wherein the General presented his plans for armed deployment and engagement. Premier Zhou strongly advocated counter-attack in defence, positioning himself typically after sensing the mood as hawk-like. In his valedictory remarks, Chairman Mao concluded:

> Perhaps we may not win… The worst result may be that India will occupy Tibet. But Tibet is China's sacred territory, everyone in the world knows this…this can never change. We will someday recover it.

---

[22]Jiangxi Province Government Publishing House, Chinese language edition, 1997.

Years later, in April 1981, Chairman Deng Xiaoping (a participant in the October 1962 Politburo meeting) told me in Beijing that:

> There is the whole Tibetan plateau between us. There is very little oxygen and it is not even possible to deploy a large number of troops. Even if you were to take part of Tibet, that would not be a threat to China. The real threat is from the North (see Appendix III).

In conclusion, the deeper purpose of the border war was for China to expose to the world as vapid and unrealistic the view that India was in a position to intervene militarily in Tibet to liberate it—a prospect that the Dalai Lama and 100,000 Tibetans abroad were propagating. Besides this, China launched its offensive to explode the myth of Nehru as a 'world statesman', supported by the US and the USSR. China made the border claims a convenient excuse to achieve these deeper goals, which it did succeed in full measure by the decisive defeat of India on the ground in 1962.

5

AN UNEASY COEXISTENCE

It is regrettable for the Chinese and Indian peoples, representatives of two giant ancient civilizations with a centuries-old peaceful interaction and cultural borrowing, to have become antagonists in a manner that has never before happened in history. This is a rather pathetic commentary on the myopic vision and quality of leadership on both sides of the Himalayas, however asymmetric or uneven may be the burden of responsibility placed for that folly of 1962 and the continuing distrust today (when we have yet again reached the battlefield in Ladakh, on the border of the two most populous nations).

Sadly, after 1962, India–China bilateral relations froze and came down to its nadir. India withdrew its Consulates from Lhasa and Shanghai, forcing the Chinese (at India's demand) to close down its Calcutta and Mumbai Consulates. Though India's Foreign Secretary put out the first diplomatic feeler on 12 November 1969, for sending back India's ambassador to Beijing, the new ambassador actually arrived in Beijing only in July 1976. The Indian government took six years and eight months to put this decision into action. The pressure of the Soviet Union on India to not proceed had delayed the ambassador's arrival.

The Xinhua News Agency correspondent was also ordered to leave India, and Chinese publications were banned in India. The properties of the Bank of China's branch offices in Calcutta (in which were deposited the royalties from published books of Nehru as author) and Bombay were taken away by the Indian authorities, and overseas Chinese in India were detained in prison.

In 1968, during the brutal suppression of the democratic movement in the then Czechoslovakia, Mrs Gandhi capitulated. Three years later, in 1971, she moved closer to the Soviet Union when she signed the Treaty of Peace, Friendship and Cooperation (a treaty that required India to mutually consult the USSR before reacting to any threat to either signatory, and to render assistance if either's interests were threatened, as it indeed was for India in 1971 during the Bangladesh Liberation War).

However, in the late 1970s and early 1980s, the traumatic and perceived betrayal by China in Indian memory had begun to fade. Mrs Gandhi lost the elections in March 1977, and was succeeded as PM by the victorious Janata Party leader, Morarji Desai. In China, Chairman Deng Xiaoping led his country to an *entente* with the US, and also entered into strategic alliance with the US *against* the USSR. Besides, he reformed China's command economy to a market economy. Politically, China remained authoritarian, while socially, Westernization was permitted.

The Janata Party government initiated normalization by unilaterally announcing the end of the Indo-Soviet Friendship Treaty in the context of the Sino-Soviet hostility over the Zhenbao (Dao) Island in Ussuri River. In 1979, China attacked Soviet ally Vietnam, to 'teach it a lesson'. However, Morarji, who had a clear dislike for the USSR and its Communist ideology, declined to support the USSR despite this being mandated in the Indo-Soviet

Friendship Treaty. He maintained that it was not in our national interest to take sides.

Despite dire warnings from Soviet Premier Alexei Kosygin, Morarji initiated serious political measures through back channels to normalize relations with China. Kosygin in a rage travelled to New Delhi in March 1979. While in Delhi, he made an extraordinary demand. He wanted to warn the Indian people about the Chinese habit to betray, despite the thawing of relations with China, over the Indian government-controlled television channel, Doordarshan. Kosygin was permitted to make the broadcast on 9 March 1979. In his broadcast, he appealed to the Indian people citing China's treacherous nature and warning that a thaw in India's relations with China would bring sorrow to India, as was the case in 1962. However, his exhortation evoked little concern in India. It was none of Soviet Union's business.

Thereafter, for the first time in India since 1950, nationalism became a factor in foreign policy issues. National interest and security became the new parameters for foreign policy determination between India and other nations. There was growing consensus in the country that we *should* befriend China, irrespective of what had happened in 1962, since much documentation that has so far come out in the public domain about the follies of Nehru, Menon and General Kaul in the conduct of our border policy, showed that we had played into China's hands and become sitting ducks. Further, there were sound strategic reasons for this new consensus in 1977.

First, it was the unanimous opinion of India's defence chiefs that defending against a China-Pakistan joint attack at that stage would be nearly impossible for our armed forces at the then level of equipment and maintained manpower. This is a reality that shall remain so for the foreseeable future, too. Therefore, India must strive for its own security's sake to separate China and Pakistan, however onerous and difficult the task may appear to be. It is my view that our first priority today ought to be to recover Indian territory in J&K, known in popular parlance as Pakistan-Occupied Kashmir (PoK).

Second, China is geostrategically located to cause India enormous problems in Kashmir, the UP border, Sikkim and Assam, and also with our neighbours, such as Nepal and Bhutan. Furthermore, in combination with Pakistan's terror menace such problems will have a multiplier effect.

In 1978, the new leadership led by Chairman Deng reached out to PM Morarji Desai. As a Member of Parliament (MP) of the Janata Party headed by Morarji, I made a demi-official trip to China, the first since 1962, and was received by Ji Pengfei in Beijing. Ji headed the international department of the CPC after a stint as foreign minister of China. Thus began the 'beginning of the beginning' of a thaw. Both Morarji and I were widely known as diehard anti-Soviet, so the welcome in China was very warm.

In January 1980, the Congress party ousted the Janata Party government and came to power at the Centre. Mrs Gandhi returned to power as PM for the second term. She, however, seemed disillusioned by the Soviet Union by their earlier distancing from her to pacify Morarji as PM (1977–79).

A little later, in 1980, I was specifically requested by Mrs Gandhi and External Affairs Minister P.V. Narasimha Rao to discover any Chinese intentions on the then ongoing Assam students' agitation, by raising the issue—which I did—with Chairman Deng Xiaoping.

Following my meeting with Chairman Deng on 8 April 1981, I obtained a Chinese commitment not to permit such an eventuality of interfering in the Assam agitation. Chairman Deng had relented and his word was honoured by China's PLA till he lived. It is an established fact that since that year, China has consistently discouraged any attempt by the extremist Assamese student agitators to illegally cross the borders to China to internationalize the Assam separatists' issue. Deng accepted Mrs Gandhi's request, which I had carried at her suggestion, asking China to help India by not providing arms to the Assamese student agitators. Deng not only agreed (after grimacing), but joked about her opponent (that is me) carrying her message to China. I said in reply that I was carrying India's message for the sake of better relations with China. India thus gained tremendously from this cooperative non-interference by China from then on.[23]

Another successful initiative that I spearheaded during this landmark visit was the reopening of the holiest Kailash Mansarovar route for Hindu pilgrims after decades of closure, a request that Deng had accepted. In late August 1981, I became the first Hindu from India to trek from Delhi to Uttarakhand by bus. I then walked for 110 km over several days to cross the Lipulekh Pass at an altitude of 17,000 ft. and across to Taklakot in Tibet, where I rested for the night. The following morning, I visited Ravana Hranga ('Hranga' in Tibetan means 'lake'), which is where Ravana had bathed. The water was poisonous. From there, an hour later we drove by Jeep to Mansarovar for a visual darshan of Kailash. It was by then September first week and snowing heavily, so I could not trek further to Kailash. But I vowed to return, which I did in June 2016 as a guest of the Chinese government and saw the abode of Lord Shiva and Goddess Parvati in full splendour, and under the brilliant sun and spotless blue sky.

Following my meeting with Deng, China and India started regular dialogue at the level of vice foreign minister. However, the Chinese side explained in the meetings, held regularly thereafter with Indian officials, that the boundary issue was 'too complicated'

---

[23] See Appendix III, wherein is set out the details of my discussion with Chairman Deng Xiaoping on 8 April 1981.

for quick resolution, and that for the time being, India and China should first develop friendly and cooperative relations in other fields to create a better atmosphere for a final settlement of the boundary question. In retrospect, the Chinese were perhaps right. Our Northeast's insurgency problem, for example, became easier to manage because of the bilateral initiatives taken to improve relations between India and China from 1977 to 1997. The India–China border is incapable of settlement by prolonged picayune discussions of bureaucrats. Hence, other initiatives, such as confidence-building, are imperatives required to be given top priority. However, the Indian side insisted that until the settlement of the boundary dispute, there could not be a breakthrough in other fields.

Thus an impasse slowly developed till 1988. Other hangovers from 1962 remained, too. In 1986, for example, India's then minister of state for personnel told parliament in Answer to a Question, that the ban on Chinese publications and its import into India would *not* be withdrawn since these publications supported 'class struggle and other seditious Marxist ideas'. In 1986, Indian and Chinese armed forces clashed in the Sumdorong Chu Valley on the Sikkim border to the grief of the Chinese PLA, since they were pushed out after heavy casualties of Chinese PLA troops.

After the defeat of the Chinese PLA in the Sumdorong Chu stand-off, PM Rajiv Gandhi was invited to Beijing in 1988. During this visit from 19 to 23 December that year, Rajiv met Chairman Deng Xiaoping. It was this visit that broke through the impasse when India acknowledged that the border *is indeed disputed by both sides* and should be delineated and demarcated by negotiations. This reality dawned late, a reality that Rajiv as PM had dared to recognize. (See Table 2.) I had fully briefed Rajiv before his visit. In fact, Rajiv asked me to accompany him, but M.J. Akbar, then Congress MP, persuaded Rajiv to cancel that proposal.

TABLE 2: PM Rajiv Gandhi's and Premier Li Peng's Views on Sino-Indian Relations

	Prime Minister Rajiv Gandhi's view	Prime Minister Li Peng's view
Assessment of the visit	'Very good and positive...has rebuilt friendship between the two countries.' (Xinhua, 19/12/88)	'For reasons known to all, unfortunately bilateral relations took a turn for the worse and the deterioration even amounted to confrontation. We hope such things will never happen again.' (Xinhua, 19/12/88)
Tibet	'Tibet is a region of China. The Indian govt. does not allow any political activities harmful to China's international affairs.' (Xinhua, 19/12/88)	'The Chinese express concern over anti-China activities by some Tibetan elements in India.' (Xinhua, 23/12/88)
Border	'An atmosphere of calm and tranquillity along the border should be maintained.' (Xinhua, 19/12/88)	'The Boundary problem is hindering the improvement of bilateral relations.' (Xinhua, 19/12/88)

Source: Author's original research

Note: It is, thus, clear from the above that Rajiv Gandhi's perception of his visit was entirely optimistic, while the Chinese view in content and tone was patronizing and cold.

Thereafter, the two sides agreed to negotiate a border settlement, and pending that, they pledged to maintain peace and tranquillity on the border. For about a decade thereafter, bilateral relations developed steadily and smoothly. The ban on Chinese publications was also lifted in early 1989.

In February 1991, as Cabinet Minister of Commerce and Law & Justice in the new Chandra Shekhar-led government, I travelled to Beijing and signed a long overdue—pending since 1983—Trade Protocol agreement, thus laying the foundation for bilateral trade. The turnover of bilateral trade, which was a mere $265 million in 1991, increased to more than $2 billion by 1998 and now stands at several billions. Of course, since May 2020, the situation has completely changed as a consequence of the PLA's incursion in Ladakh. India has yet to evict the PLA.

In 1993, PM Narasimha Rao visited China and in return President Jiang Zemin visited India in 1996. These visits laid the institutional foundation for the relations to progress through two important agreements: An *Agreement on the Maintenance of Peace and Tranquillity* along the delineated Line of Actual Control (LAC) in the India–China Border Areas (but not demarcated) and an *Agreement on Confidence-building Measures* in the Military Field along the Line of Actual Control in the India–China Border Areas. The institutionalized bilateral interaction based on the India–China Agreement of 1993 enabled the two sides to hold several rounds of talks covering a wide range of issues, including clearer delineation of the LAC, no new troop deployments along the LAC and a range of military-technical Confidence-building Measures (CBMs) detailed at the command levels. None of this China has observed since May 2020.

Relations Still in a Tinderbox

However, after a decade of confidence-building by previous Indian governments, these measures were undone by a series of events after India conducted underground nuclear tests in the deserts of Pokhran, Rajasthan, on 11 and 13 May 1998. The sharp Chinese reactions, however, came only after 15 May 1998, when it called the tests an 'outrageous contempt of the common will of the international community' and that these 'not only threatened China but other neighbours as well'. Thereafter, China progressively hardened its stand, and practically froze any politically significant interaction with the Indian government till 2003.

So what happened between 12 May and 15–18 May 1998 that had so thoroughly shaken the Chinese and embittered them? After the tests, PM Vajpayee wrote a secret letter to US President Bill Clinton on 12 May (which was leaked by the US administration to the *New York Times* on 13 May), implicitly accusing China of posing a nuclear threat to India.

By sheer diplomatic insensitivity, the letter cited China as the major reason for its nuclear explosions. Vajpayee wrote in the letter that:

> We have an overt nuclear weapons state on our borders, a state which committed armed aggression against India in 1962. Although our relationship with that country has improved in the last decade or so, an atmosphere of distrust persists mainly due to the unresolved border problem. To add to the distrust, that country has materially helped another neighbor of ours to become a covert nuclear weapon state.

In Vajpayee's letter, there are clear references to the 'threats' from China and Pakistan. If what happened in 1962, 1965 and 1971 with China and Pakistan constitute a continuing threat in 1998, as Vajpayee pointed out, then is it also not true that the US despatched into the Bay of Bengal the 1971 warships of its Seventh Fleet task force led by aircraft carrier USS Enterprise, with enough nuclear weapons on board to wipe out India's civilization? Did not this constitute by the same logic a continuing threat from the US in 1998?

This omission of the 1971 US role from Vajpayee's letter could not be treated as an oversight. It was obviously to placate the US. The Clinton administration nevertheless chose to leak Vajpayee's letter to the *New York Times*, which is closely read by Chinese strategists.

At one level, there was nothing startlingly new or revealing in Vajpayee's letter as regards the Indian position on China. These views had appeared in the Annual Defence Reports brought out by India's Ministry of Defence. For instance, the Annual Report for 1996–97, at the height of the new bonhomie with China, clearly spelt out that 'India's concerns regarding China's defence cooperation with Pakistan's clandestine nuclear-programme and the sale of missiles and sophisticated weapons systems by it to Pakistan,' were 'conveyed to the Chinese side'. The report also mentioned the '...progress that China has made in the recent years in upgrading her nuclear arsenal and missile capabilities (which) will continue to have relevance for India's security concerns. Upgradation of China's logistic capabilities all along the India–China border for strengthened air operations has to be noted.'

The Chinese at first, did not express any negative reactions when India exploded its hydrogen bomb as a test in May 1998, which was the unfinished task of PM Narasimha Rao. And obviously so, since the Vajpayee government took oath of office on 19 March 1998, just two months earlier to the H-bomb's successful test. The entire planning was done by Rao's government. Vajpayee showed courage in executing the unfinished work of Rao.

The problem arose instead because these were articulated by Vajpayee not to the Indian parliament, which was in session then, but to the US President in a secret letter, almost in a supplicant fashion. Vajpayee's letter hence confirmed, and placed in a disastrously negative perspective, the anti-China allegations frequently made by his defence minister. George Fernandes had publicly referred to China as 'the number one potential threat to India'. At that moment of time, this was not the prevalent view of the country.

Thus, the crystalizing effect of Vajpayee's letter and the Chinese shift in tone from mild to harsh, in just four days after the 11 May test, had shredded Sino-Indian normalization, which had been progressing steadily since 1981, when I had a 100-minute meeting with Chairman Deng Xiaoping accompanied by the Indian ambassador to Beijing (see Appendix III). It was never made clear by the PMO as to why such a letter to President Clinton was written in the first place. As a consequence, the glory of the Indian test exploding a hydrogen bomb within two months of the National Democratic Alliance (NDA) coming to power, was vitiated.

In his subsequent clarificatory statement to parliament in September 1998, Vajpayee stressed 'the fundamental Indian desire to have friendly relations with China' and a satisfactory solution to the border dispute through negotiation. He also emphasized that by working together, India and China would serve not only bilateral interests, but regional and global ones as well. In October, the principal secretary to Vajpayee, Brajesh Chandra Mishra, also stressed that India did not regard China as an enemy! However, none of these proposals pacified the Chinese till Vajpayee's surrender on Tibet autonomy within Chinese sovereignty during his visit to Beijing in 2003.

A year later after the H-bomb test, in June 1999, External Affairs Minister Jaswant Singh requested Beijing for talks with his Chinese counterpart. Chinese Foreign Minister Tang Jiaxuan pointed out that the prerequisites for the development of bilateral relations should be that neither side should view the other as a threat and that the Five Principles of Peaceful Coexistence should be taken as the basis. It was only after Jaswant formally and humbly announced the withdrawal of the earlier statement of 'China is a threat to India', that China relented to a scheduling of a meeting of the Joint Working Group (JWG) on the Boundary Question in April 2000. However, examining the outcome of the India–China dialogue and interaction after the twelfth JWG meet, it is apparent that there has been no forward movement at all in Sino-Indian relations.

Disconcerting indications of tense relations became increasingly apparent when noted writer on strategic affairs, Brahma Chellaney, wrote in the *Hindustan Times* on 31 January 2000, that the Chinese president Jiang Zemin had made some highly derogatory references to India in a meeting with the head of state 'of one of the world's major powers'.

Jiang reportedly told the foreign head of state that he had decided to test India's defence preparedness by sending Chinese military patrols across the LAC. This happened first in Ladakh, while Pakistan was waging a war in the Kargil and Dras sectors during May–July 1999, and later along the Arunachal Pradesh frontier as well. Later, when the BJP-led NDA government returned to power in 1999 after fresh elections, with Vajpayee again as the PM, the Chinese built up tensions at the other end of the border with India, in Arunachal (Tawang sector), through aggressive military moves in October 1999.

For this caricature of an intervention, Jiang had summoned chief executives of the two Chinese provinces that adjoined India to Beijing and discussed 'India's military alertness and response capability'. Quoting Jiang, Chellaney reported that Jiang had said mockingly: 'Each time we tested them [Indians] by sending patrols across, the Indian soldiers reacted by putting their hands up.'

Most insulting indeed! Did we respond? It is never too late for a nation to do so. We have an opportunity on the ground today in Ladakh.

The scorn Jiang poured on India and the warning he delivered were extraordinary. Chellaney opined that for India, Jiang's comments were a reminder that 'without a clear-headed, long-term China policy, it risks further trouble'. The then Indian government suppressed and censored this news from official briefings. No newspaper or agency had reported this foray then, but this report has not been denied either.

Since then, the latent mistrust deepened on both sides. In September 2000, in a major shift of gears, China blamed India for the scant progress in Sino-Indian border talks. In an interview to a group of visiting Indian journalists in Beijing, Chinese Assistant Foreign Minister Wang Yi (now a Cabinet minister), said: 'What is important is that the two sides should have the sincerity and show mutual accommodation instead of one-way accommodation.'[24]

By India's reckoning, China is in illegal possession of 43,180 sq. km of Kashmir, which includes 5,180 sq. km ceded to China by Pakistan under the Sino-Pakistan Agreement of 1963 (also known as the Sino-Pakistan Frontier Agreement and Sino-Pak Boundary Agreement). China, on the other hand, holds that Indian maps show an estimated 90,000 sq. km of Chinese territory as being in India's possession, nearly all of which constitutes Arunachal Pradesh.

Furthermore, expounding China's stand on the Kashmir issue, Wang noted that it has long become stalemated. 'So I think,' he said, 'the only way out is peaceful settlement with help from the international community.' This indicated yet another change from

---

[24] 'China blames India for slow progress in border talks: PTI,' rediff.com. Available at https://www.rediff.com/news/2000/sep/10china.htm, last accessed on 28 September 2020.

the position of neutrality that had been in evidence since 1991 and that had been given shape during Jiang Zemin's 1996 visit to India. Thereafter, Beijing began referring to the UN Resolution on Kashmir in the context of solving that problem. In a series of articles, China's official media articulated this view holding that the Kashmir issue involved three parties: India, the Kashmiri people and Pakistan. All these facts demonstrate that Sino-Indian relations were still in a tinderbox. The 2003 Agreement on Tibet, signed by Vajpayee in Beijing, which permitted the Chinese government to partition Tibet into four parts, dealt yet another disastrous blow to India's self-esteem.

A chill thus descended in the bilateral relations between the two countries; later, post-2004, this changed to a lacklustre and routine relationship during the tenure of the United Progressive Alliance (UPA) government (2004–14) under Dr Manmohan Singh.

The period since 1998 had seen a new phase of incremental hostility between India and China. Though, prior to 2014, both the countries had maintained normal relations, the bare fact today is that India–China relations have not been warm and cooperative since 2015, which assessment I regularly communicated to the PM in writing, and orally to the then defence minister Manohar Parrikar and the then home minister Rajnath Singh. In 2016, I had informed PM Modi, on the sidelines of the BJP National Executive Meeting at Prayagraj, that the signals from my well-placed friends in China and Chinese scholars in the US point to *a souring mood at the highest level in China*. I had earlier informed BJP President Amit Shah when we spoke in late 2015, about my accepting the PM's offer to take up the post of president of the BRICS Development Bank (now New Development Bank [NDB]), headquartered in Shanghai, China. I declined the offer since having left the teaching job at Harvard to face the rough and tumble of India, and having survived it admirably and to my satisfaction, I was not inclined to accept any foreign assignment. In reply to Shah's question, I told him that relations with China were deteriorating and may end up in a major conflict in three to four years. Shah was dismissive of this and sang the usual tune of Modi being highly popular everywhere. However, subsequent events indicate the accuracy of my assessment of the situation.

The question today is: why this deterioration? Especially since Modi has had 18 one-to-one meetings with China's president Xi Jinping during a six-year period? The net result of these meetings has been that China is back in an unusually aggressive mode, having forcibly occupied about 1,000 sq. km of land on the Indian side of the LAC (*The Hindu* quotes it as 1,000 sq. km)[25], that separates Aksai Chin and Ladakh. The assault by the PLA on our soldiers and the wooing away of our closest ally, such as Nepal, was a concomitant effect. On 15 June 2020, violent clashes between Chinese and Indian troops, arising from the Chinese PLA units crossing the LAC, caused significant casualties on both sides, but significantly more in numbers on the Chinese side. We are thus in a very hostile situation in Ladakh, which appears to lead towards a major assault across the Himalayas, perhaps by a coalition of China, Nepal and Pakistan. India needs contingency planning for this possibility.

The negative developments leading to the killing of soldiers on both sides denote a steep paradigm deterioration in India's relations with China. Not only is this a brazen and outrageous violation of the five agreements signed by the two governments in 1993, 1996, 2005, 2012 and 2013, but it is also a challenge directed at the personal stature of PM Modi. This is almost similar

---

[25]Vijaita Singh, 'China Controls 1,000 sq. km of Area in Ladakh,' *The Hindu*, 31 August 2020. Available at: https://www.thehindu.com/news/national/china-controls-1000-sq-km-of-area-in-ladakh-say-intelligence-inputs/article32490453.ece, last accessed on 9 October 2020.

to the actions of Chinese PM Zhou Enlai and PM Nehru before 1962, and with the same result thus far.

First, there must be a determination as to whether Modi failed to understand the nuances of what Xi said to him in the 18 meetings the two had. Or did Xi mislead Modi of his real intention? Second, is this rivalry leading to one-upmanship, or a mere border dispute or something else more sinister which China was planning? It is important hence that India's leadership study China's strategy more seriously than hitherto. China cannot be taken for granted, because starting from Mao's declaration that 'China has stood up', China is well on its way to becoming a global economic and military power, second only to the US.

Of course, India needs to understand that it is important, strategically, to be prepared for a war to resolve the border dispute with China, but it is always better, if possible, to remove the deeper causes that fuel the China–India tensions, and to lay a secure foundation for future normal relations. If India does so, we would have learnt the real lessons of the past.

LAC Explained

The first lesson, therefore, is to understand the contours and extent of the LAC. India and China have a territorial dispute over the Aksai Chin region, which is a high-altitude, barren plateau that is almost unpopulated and has vast natural resources. Situated between China's Xinjiang and Tibet provinces, the region is 'administered' by China as part of Hotan County in the Hotan Prefecture of Xinjiang Autonomous Region. Though part of the Ladakh Union Territory, this region in the Ladakh province of the princely state of J&K was not part of British India, although it was a part of the British empire. Thus, the eastern boundary was defined in 1914, but in the west in Ladakh, it was not.

The line that divides Ladakh from Chinese-occupied Aksai Chin is known as the LAC. It is, therefore, the delineated line that separates Indian territory from China-controlled Indian territory. India's claim line is the line seen in the official boundary on the maps as released by the Survey of India, including both Aksai Chin and Baltistan, also known as Baltiyul or Little Tibet. In China's case, it corresponds mostly to its claim line, but in the Eastern Sector, it claims entire Arunachal Pradesh as 'South Tibet', although the entire Arunachal is within India's secure control.

Lawyer and constitutional expert A.G. Noorani wrote that the Sardar Patel-led Ministry of States had published two White Papers on India. The first, in July 1948, had two maps: one had no boundary shown in the Western Sector, only a partial colour wash; the second one extended the colour yellow to the entire state of J&K, but mentioned 'boundary undefined'. The White Paper was republished in February 1950, after India became a Republic. In it, the map again had boundaries which were undefined.

India maintains that the LAC divides its territory into three sectors: (i) the Eastern Sector, which spans Arunachal Pradesh and Sikkim, (ii) the Middle Sector, bordering Uttarakhand and Himachal Pradesh and (iii) the Western Sector in Ladakh. The alignment of the LAC in the Eastern Sector is along the controversial 1914 McMahon Line. There are minor disputes about the positions on the ground in this sector. The line in the Middle Sector is the least controversial, but for the precise alignment to be marked on the Barahoti plains in Uttarakhand.

The major disagreements are in the Western Sector, where the LAC emerged after two letters written by Zhou Enlai to Nehru in 1959, after he had first mentioned such a 'line' in 1956. In his letter dated 7 November 1959, Zhou said the LAC consisted of 'the so-called McMahon Line in the east and the line up to which each side exercises actual control in the West'.[26]

After the 1962 War, the Chinese claimed they had withdrawn to 20 km behind the LAC of November 1959. Zhou clarified on the LAC in another letter to Nehru thus: 'To put it concretely, in the Eastern Sector, it coincides in the main with the so-called McMahon Line, and in the western and middle sectors, it coincides in the main with the traditional customary line which has consistently been pointed out by China.'

India rejected the concept of LAC in both 1959 and 1962, with Nehru stating: 'There is no sense or meaning in the Chinese offer to withdraw twenty kilometres from what they call "line of actual control". What is this "line of control"? Is this the line they have created by aggression since the beginning of September?'

India insisted that 'the Chinese LAC was a disconnected series of dots on a map that could be joined up in many ways. The acceptable line should omit gains from the aggression in 1962, and hence should be the actual position on 8 September 1962, before the Chinese attack; and the vagueness of the Chinese definition left it open for China to continue its attempt to change facts on the ground by military force'.

It was during Chinese Premier Li Peng's 1991 visit to India that the current LAC was discussed. Narasimha Rao and Li reached an understanding to maintain peace and tranquillity at the LAC. Later in 1993, India formally accepted the concept of the LAC when Rao paid a return visit to Beijing. This was when the two sides signed the Agreement on the Maintenance of Peace and Tranquillity along the Line of Actual Control in the India–China Border Areas.

The 1993 Agreement was the first of the five border agreements between India and China that clearly mentions that both sides

---

[26]Bhasin (op. cit., p.2807).

will 'strictly' observe the LAC. It is the first agreement post-1962, and also the most weighty of the agreements.

Article 1 of the Agreement clearly states that the two sides will work to ensure peace and tranquillity at the border and will not indulge in activities that undercut that peace. Therefore, the amassing of troops by China breached Article 1 of that Agreement, which states that:

> ...Neither side shall use or threaten to use force against the other by any means. Pending an ultimate solution to the boundary question between the two countries, the two sides shall strictly respect and observe the line of actual control between the two sides. No activities of either side shall overstep the line of actual control. In case personnel of one side cross the line of actual control, upon being cautioned by the other side, they shall immediately pull back to their own side of the line of actual control. When necessary, the two sides shall jointly check and determine the segments of the line of actual control where they have different views as to its alignment.

Further, the reference to the LAC was unqualified. Thus, it was made clear that it was not the LAC of 1959 or to the LAC of 1962. To reconcile the differences about some areas, the two countries agreed that the JWG on border issues would take up the task of clarifying the exact alignment of the LAC.

The process of clarifying the LAC has been going on since 2002. So far however, only the LAC maps pertaining to the Middle Sector of both sides have been 'shared'. There are no publicly available official maps depicting the demarcated LAC, since there never has been any demarcation.

During PM Modi's visit to China in May 2015, the proposal to finalize the LAC was rejected by the Chinese. This was an ominous signal, which the NDA government should not have ignored.

Huang Xilian, deputy director general with the Asian Affairs department in the Chinese foreign ministry, later told Indian journalists about the rejection as follows:

> We tried to clarify some years ago but it encountered some difficulties, which led to even complex situation. That is why whatever we do we should make it more conducive to peace and tranquillity for making things easier and not to make them complicated.

The two countries had agreed to maintain the LAC as the *de facto* boundary pending its negotiated settlement. However, despite the Agreement on the LAC frontier and the many rounds of dialogue and engagement, there has been little let-up in tensions between the two sides. Serious issues of dispute have again emerged in the relations that could embitter the bilateral relations in the rest of the twenty-first century.

Indian army planners today contemplate the possibility of further Chinese intrusions along the contested 3,488-km border. For that, the army would have to post soldiers for a 'hardened LAC' round the year, like the Line of Control (LoC) with Pakistan.

India has to retaliate with force *locally* with China to recover the land up to the 1996 LAC, which was mutually agreed upon by delineation on the map, *but not demarcated on the ground as yet*. That is a tactical action to persuade China that India is no more the country of 1962, and therefore India of 2020 can geographically send China back to where it belonged in 1993.

The government spokesperson, for some inexplicable reason, have been sending out confusing signals about the ongoing India–China stand-off on the LAC since April 2020. Four questions arise: (i) Did the Chinese soldiers indeed cross the LAC and capture Indian territory? If not, then where did the 20 jawans and officers of the Indian army die in hand-to-hand combat with the Chinese PLA? (ii) Is the PLA currently squatting on Indian territory? (iii) What exactly is the agenda of the two sides and the scope of their discussions on 'disengagement', which is different from withdrawal from Indian territory? (iv) How does New Delhi plan to retake lost territory if China does not vacate and return to the ex-ante position?

While the PM had claimed on 20 June 2020 that 'neither has anyone intruded into Indian territory nor has anyone captured Indian posts', the GoI Press Note of 17 June had said that 'the Chinese side sought to erect a structure in Galwan Valley on our side of the LAC'. Which is correct?

What is also becoming clear is that the government is seeking soft measures in stitching together a response to China. The government's approach, as External Affairs Minister S. Jaishankar stated the other day, is that 'a solution has to be found in the domain of diplomacy'. Really?

The government's inability to take an unambiguous position on the LAC is disturbing and fraught with national security consequences. Acknowledging Chinese possession of Indian territory cannot be treated as bad optics for the nation. Only good optics is the truth and the nation's determination to act according to the truth.

Lessons of History

The Chinese may have been offensive to Indian sentiments by stating that they 'taught India a lesson in 1962', a refrain repeated by Deng Xiaoping in 1979, when China invaded Vietnam. However, in defeat there were lessons to be learnt by India's leadership which, regrettably, even today, have not been learnt.

Those who do not learn by history are condemned to relive it—as we saw in the summer of 2020.

Nevertheless, the core truth on the Sino-Indian border dispute remains even today: neither the Indians nor the Chinese have an uncontestable case on the border. China has taken full advantage of that since the 1950s. It took the GoI 38 years, from 1950 to 1988, to acknowledge that the Sino-Indian border was indeed disputed and undemarcated, and needed to be settled by negotiations. However, the national cost paid in strategic terms for that late realization has been high. Besides the human lives lost, it is the formation of a Sino-Pakistan axis, which did not exist explicitly before 1962 but came into existence because of events leading up to the 1962 border war, which was the real cost of the India–China conflict that poses the most formidable challenge to India's national security.

What is required today is for India to first shed all remnants of the old British imperialist-inspired policy and the implied concepts on Tibet, and then press for the most advantageous settlement of the Sino-Indian border (which could include Chinese recognition of the McMahon Line with a different nomenclature, as with Burma). As Zhou Enlai candidly admitted in 1959 in a letter to Nehru that China could acknowledge the McMahon Line as the border in the East, as with Burma, provided we are ready to negotiate the border in the West (Ladakh/Aksai Chin).

It would then be pragmatic for geographers and military experts of both countries to engage in talks, and once for all demarcate on the ground a mutually convenient and maintainable border. From the points put across by the Indian government, it would seem that the 'ideal' border line would approximate the LAC on 7 September 1962 or a mutually accepted date prior to the outbreak of the Sino-Indian border war of October 1962.

Before exploring whether there can exist a negotiated solution to the Sino-Indian border dispute, a question which must be faced is the 1962 and 1994 Indian Parliament Resolutions pledging the recovery of 'lost territories'. Legally, it cannot be argued that a resolution does not survive beyond a session of the Lok Sabha that had passed it. However, the really appropriate question is what parliament and the people would consider today as 'lost territories'. There is reason to believe that a settlement based broadly on the lines we suggest here would be received with satisfaction by an overwhelming majority of Indian people, as fulfilling the Parliament Resolution.

This would depend, of course, on the trade-offs that India works out with China. A settlement as a fresh determination of the border made jointly on agreed principles would be much better than one seen to result from 'concessions' and 'adjustments' by one side or the other. Thereby, the groundwork would be laid to explore a future amity and perhaps strategic partnership with China.

However, India's long-term relationship with China is subject to several imponderables. If China seeks superpower status, with a veto in Asian affairs, then India will face fresh problems. Alternatively, India can become a partner with China in international initiatives, as well as in IT and cultural propagation. It is incumbent on the Indian leadership to make a determined effort to investigate these possibilities. However, a settled border and relations normalized in the meantime would allow India to face that eventuality with greater preparedness. The real goal for India is to be entitled and qualified by economic power and clear strategic advantages to be considered an equal superpower, thus globally being a part of the triumvirate of the US, India and China.

6
STRATEGIC CHOICES: CONTAINMENT OR ENGAGEMENT?

Foreign policy of a nation, it must always be remembered, is not based on interpersonal etiquette or attractive photo ops between leaders of nations. Instead, it has to be structured on a substantive basis—that is, with a clear statement of a nation's objectives, its priorities, strategy and resource mobilization consistent with its economic power and past history—to enable it to maximize its geostrategic advantage by both transparent as well as covert initiatives. In addition, nations need to continually search for fresh options to foster national security. A nation's defence capability is based on adequate hardware of weapons and economic sustainability. Its foreign policy is based on other nations' intentions, which in turn, are based on the software of international alliances and common ideology on peacekeeping.

By 'national security', I mean peace on our borders, control of internal insurgency and a mutually beneficial understanding with key countries of the neighbourhood with common borders, for joint action. *These three components are interconnected.*

Foreign policy, thus, is the outcome of the synchronization of the structured substantive basis of a nation's objectives, priorities, strategy and resource mobilization with the three components of national security mentioned above.

The fulcrum of redesigning our global foreign policy is balanced on mature India–China relations. However, a fundamental problem in policymaking towards China is that there is no clear or apparent consensus in India on the objectives of engagement with China. The domestic strategic discourse so far has also failed to come up with a clear criterion for evaluating the 'means to be adopted' in this regard. Even if India had defined objectives, there must also be a set of priorities, a strategy in place to achieve those objectives, as well as a financial and institutional architecture to sustain that achievement.

China is an ancient and cultured country with a long-standing peaceful interaction with India in the long history of more than 2,500 years. However, today it is a Communist Party-ruled nation. Indian democracy stands for transparency and access to information—something Indians have been used to for ages. China under Communism can never be as transparent in its political and security matters. Therefore, Indians have to decode the nuances of the Chinese expressions and reactions, and not be deluded by atmospherics, as we have seen. This is the lesson of 2020 from the 18 one-to-one meetings between PM Modi and President Xi Jinping. This basic strategic understanding and a sense of history have eluded the comprehension of China-baiters in India, most of whom, unfortunately, exercise influence in policymaking. Much of this baiting is encouraged by those nations that are apprehensive of the influence of an India–China understanding, if ever, on global politics.

It is now time to cut through the barriers and begin by seeing the importance of China for India, and understand the reality of the present unequal economic and military endowment; and see this with clarity, and in a perspective based on cold analysis.

Our mutual interactive history shows that nothing innate or intrinsic stands in the way of India and China having friendly relations, with equal respect. In my view, China would not regard the border dispute as an obstacle worthy of prior removal if there was a strategic partnership with India based on matching defence hardware and cogent foreign policy. Nor is rivalry the reason, since there are hardly any international issues in which India and China have irresolvable fundamental conflicts of interest. Issues of conflict have been the outcome of compulsions of unstructured thinking, such as China's view that the '1962 debacle' can be repeated and India's conviction that China is expansionist. Therefore, we must concern ourselves with the national security imperatives that necessitate developing stable India–China relations.

Good bilateral relations in the twenty-first century depend on the cost-benefit calculus of India and China coming together. I have, therefore, focussed on what India must do to motivate China so that it responds appropriately to Indian interests and the cost we are willing to incur for it. All said and done, the bottom line is that it takes two to make a durable friendship. China, too, has to do the same type of cost-benefit analysis to earn India's friendship, and not bond with the US against it.

The question before the nation, therefore, is not whether India can be dismissive of China at one end or placate China at any cost. The crucial query instead is: what should our preferred policy towards China be: cordial or hostile, and the costs and benefits to India of that choice. In the larger interest of global peace, this requires elucidation and formulation of a policy to normalize the situation.

During the next two decades, India will, therefore, need to

make a crucial choice: whether to come into an understanding of global significance with China and befriend it in a fundamental and strategic sense of demonstrating India's self-reliant capability (Option A) or make only proactive efforts with the US to keep China 'contained' (Option B). What is to be determined is the choice to be made and how that choice is to be made.

Nuclear Powers at a Crossroads

To make that choice, India needs to be clear on its nuclear posture vis-à-vis China as well as China's military might and economic prowess. The first point requiring clarification is the content of India's nuclear doctrine. The GoI has stated that the doctrine envisages 'no first use (NFU)' of nuclear weapons and only seeks to establish a 'survivable second-strike capability'. Once India is able to launch missiles from aboard ships or from submarines, these delivery capabilities will significantly lend content to the otherwise vague concept of 'second-strike capability', a concept incidentally in disuse in the West.

Beijing has also committed to NFU and 'non-use against non-nuclear powers'. This, on the face of it, cannot end nuclear confrontation between China and India, since the latter is not a non-nuclear power. However, does China's NFU declaration prevent its use on its 'own territory', or in the Sino-Indian context, in any of the 'disputed' territories claimed by China, e.g., Arunachal or Aksai Chin? Thus, it is possible for China to launch a pre-emptive first strike, using tactical nuclear weapons, against Indian counterforce targets in a disputed region without violating the letter of NFU declaration.

There is, of course, also the possibility that China could launch a massive nuclear first strike against strategic targets in India; for example, if India launches a pre-emptive strike against Pakistan, or even in second strike use of nuclear weapons against Pakistan. This, China could hold, is not 'first use'.

The Indian doctrine must aim for a second-strike capability that would survive a Chinese first strike and retaliate by inflicting unacceptable damage upon the adversary. Theoretically, the well-known strategy theories envisage second-strike capacity on counterforce targets (such as missile silos) and major countervalue targets (population centres) in the Chinese heartland.

In the tactical domain, it envisages capacity to launch strikes against select counterforce targets near the border. According to present defence plans, India would be in a position to deploy the naval version of the Prithvi missile and the Sagarika submarine-launched ballistic missile (SLBM). Both of these missiles, capable of sea-skimming and radar-evading flight trajectories, would complement its land-based deterrent options against China.

However, as the Indian government elaborates its nuclear doctrine, the paradigm of 'minimum deterrence' has to be visualized prudently, in qualitative and quantitative terms. For example, if India were to include reactor-grade fuel to fabricate nuclear weapons, the total nuclear stockpile required would be between 390 and 470 weapons, as compared to China's 450 weapons. Is India inclined to tread this expensive path? A credible Sino-Indian understanding on disarmament is therefore inevitable for India's national security.

Since the 1950s, the vital question that still awaits a conclusive answer is whether China would like the emergence of another Asian giant and non-communist neighbour. In any case, thanks to Nehru's gross stupidity in turning down the UNSC veto holding seat, China is the only UNSC permanent member from Asia. Thus, unless this vital question is answered, India–China relations will always be on a roller-coaster ride, as we have seen since 1950. Especially since India, too, threw away the suffocating Soviet-style Five-year Plan rigmarole and embarked on economic reforms in 1991. Post 1996, India has been closing the economic gap with China, albeit in a jerky sequence. The moment of truth arrived in 2020. China decided to settle this question. They chose India's weakest moment: the coronavirus pandemic, effects on an already tailspinning economy during the period 2015–20, and unpreparedness in Ladakh.

A series of actions and words of the Vajpayee government since it came to office, in 1998, culminating in the letter marked 'secret' that was written by the PM to US President Clinton in May 1998 had, according to my understanding, convinced the Chinese leaders that the Indian government was laying the foundation for emerging as a 'counterweight' to China with US help, and pursuing policies that would seek to undermine China's security and integrity. The tone and content of Vajpayee's letter to Clinton, which was to be kept confidential but revealed by Clinton, indicated that the Indian PM wanted the US patronage to emerge as the counterweight. That is, China perceived that India had chosen Option B.

The inclusion of China and Pakistan in Vajpayee's letter to Clinton, and the omission in that letter of the reference to the 1971 US nuclear threat, which according to a biography of the then US Secretary of State Henry Kissinger was real and ominous, was seen by the Chinese, justifiably, as an attempt to make India curry favour with the US, and India's response of inviting the same Kissinger in 1974 to visit India as an oblique suggestion that India was ready to be considered as a counterweight to China. Of course, if India ultimately emerged as a counterweight to China by pulling herself up by her own bootstraps through economic reforms and military R&D, the world would respect that and adjust to it. However, to expect that the sole superpower of today—the US—would invest in a large country such as India to develop it as a counterweight to another large nuclear weapons country, and a neighbour to boot, is not only unrealistic, but reflects a failure to understand history. It is unbelievable that any Indian PM would expect the US to appreciate India's need for nuclear weapons, and in fact hope to enhance India's capability to match China's in this area. Thus, there is considerable area of ambiguity that would need to be cleared up with the US before we can partner with the Americans against the Chinese. At the present state of relations, however, it seems China would prefer that the ambiguity remains, and will hope that a new dispensation following the US Presidential Election in November 2020 is of the same thought.

Flexing Military Might

Next, an in-depth understanding of the India–China military distance is essential to appreciate India's capability to meet China's potential threat.

According to the 2018 report of the International Institute for Strategic Studies (IISS), at approximately $225 billion, China's defence budget is four times that of India, which is approximately $55 billion. According to the Stockholm International Peace Research Institute (SIPRI), China's expenditure on its military has trended from 2.5 times that of India's in 2010 to 3.7 times that of India's in 2019. This difference is partly explained by the fact that while India's defence expenditure as per cent of GDP has drastically declined from 2010 to 2019 as per Budget FY20 figures, China's expenditure on its military has stayed largely consistent since 2010, at around 1.9 per cent of its GDP (not including the paramilitary expenditure of the PLA). Mostly, however, the primary reason for the gap is the sheer size of China's GDP, which is estimated by the World Bank to have reached $13.61 trillion in 2018 as compared to India's $2.72 trillion. China's GDP growth rate per annum has also increased rapidly since 2010 (see Table 3).

TABLE 3: SIPRI Estimates of Military Expenditure
(In current US$)

Year (FY)	China	India	Ratio of China–India military expenditure (A:B)
	(A) Military expenditure	(B) Military expenditure	
2010	$115.772	$46.09	2.5 : 1
2011	$137.967	$49.63	2.8 : 1
2012	$157.390	$47.22	3.3 : 1
2013	$179.881	$47.40	3.8 : 1
2014	$200.772	$50.91	3.9 : 1
2015	$214.472	$51.30	4.2 : 1
2016	$216.404	$56.64	3.8 : 1
2017	$228.466	$64.56	3.5 : 1
2018	$253.492	$66.26	3.8 : 1
2019	$261.082	$71.13	3.7 : 1

Source: https://www.sipri.org/databases/milex

A major fault line for India is the sluggish weapons procurement procedure, which is weighed down by bureaucratic red tape and risks, thus widening the technological gap with China and reducing with Pakistan.

According to Harsh V. Pant and Anant Singh Mann:

> On land, the PLA is estimated to have approximately 3,500 tanks, 33,000 armoured vehicles, 3,800 self-propelled artillery, 3,600 towed artillery, and 2,650 rocket projectors. The Indian Army, on the other hand, is estimated to have 4,292 tanks, 8,686 armoured vehicles, 235 self-propelled artillery, 4,060 towed artillery, and 266 rocket projectors.[27]

---

[27]Harsh V. Pant and Anant Singh Mann, *The India–China military matrix and their modernisation trajectories,* Observer Research Foundation (ORF). Available at: https://www.orfonline.org/expert-speak/the-india-china-military-matrix-and-their-modernisation-trajectories-68631/, last accessed on 29 September 2020.

Apart from this, a peculiarity of the demographic profile of the armed forces is a significant increase in the expenditure on military pensions, with alarming projections of further increase in the near future. At this rate, the Indian military will expend more funds on pensions than salaries. Hence, for security, India *must* raise its defence expenditure to 5 per cent of GDP by the 2021–22 Budget, from the present 1.8 per cent, and then onwards at a steady 6 per cent of GDP till 2030.

In terms of military manpower, China and India possess the second and third largest in the world, respectively. In terms of GDP, *evaluated at purchasing power parity rates*, the ranking is the same: China and India after the US, in that order.

According to the London-based IISS, the Chinese PLA is nearly double the size of the Indian army. China has over 2 million troops deployed in active military service compared to 1.3 million on the Indian side. However, it may be noted that the Indian paramilitary forces, which have presently been deployed for border and internal security, could be, if required, deployed for other military purposes. China possesses an additional 1,00,000 manpower force for its strategic forces, which India does not have. However, the fact that India has 'gone nuclear' would mean that in the near future it needs to have a nuclear weapons strategic force as well, if the avowed goal of 'minimum deterrence' of the Indian government is to have content.

China has deployed about 60 per cent of its forces between the North and the East, which indicates Northeast Asia as being the major concern of China, where the interests of three nuclear-armed nations (the US, Russia and China) intersect. Russia, as I will argue below, is rapidly becoming a junior partner to China. China has deployed only about 16 per cent of its armed personnel in the areas bordering India, while India has more than half of its total armed forces in the Northern and Eastern periphery. The major deployment of the Indian forces is in the areas bordering China and Pakistan. India's paramilitary forces are also mostly deployed in these two areas. The balance, in terms of personnel deployed, indicates a tilt in favour of India in case hostilities break out between the two. But of course, it is strategy, tactics and morale that will ultimately decide the outcome in a war, and not the arithmetic size of armed forces.

PLA's Experience in the Crucible of Combat

The hangover of 1962 is yet to be erased from the Indian consciousness. Therefore, Indian strategists are often weighed down by the general impression that the PLA is an invincible and formidable force. This impression about the PLA is not based on a realistic assessment. Obviously, China appears to have successfully taught the 'lesson' it had wanted. However, in the recent (2020) clashes with the Chinese PLA troops, it is the Indian army that has come out with flying colours. Hence, India is on the verge of teaching China a bigger lesson in 2020. However, this will depend on the tough and risky decisions of the civil masters of the army. At present, the political authority is busy exhausting its energy in fruitless negotiations on disengagement when it should be issuing 'vacate, withdraw' warnings. But the Chinese lesson is still in the mindset of our political authority.

The main question is whether a close scrutiny of the PLA's performance during the past 50 years validates the Indian hangover. During Chairman Mao's reign, the PLA had seen action five times: three times to fight a war with its neighbours, once to fight US 'imperialism' and once to occupy the Paracel Islands in the South China Sea. Based on a large number of studies in books and papers of various think tanks, the following facts emerge.

The first cross-border Chinese military action was in 1950–51, when the PLA met US forces head-on in the Korean War. Whatever may be the counterclaims, the PLA was perceived to have suffered heavy casualties, and the advance of North Koreans with the PLA south of the 38th parallel was stopped. Some argue that the technological superiority of the US-led UN forces played the decisive role in this defeat of the PLA, but the casualty suffered by US troops were found unacceptable by a then war-weary American public. This had diverted public attention from the real poor performance of the PLA.

A decade later, China decided to commit to the use of force on the Sino-Indian border in October 1962. The PLA moved in swiftly, defeated the Indian army and declared a unilateral ceasefire after taking possession of approximately 90,000 sq. km of Indian territory. Analysis, however, indicates that the Chinese succeeded largely on the northeastern border of India due to the failure of the Indian politico-military leadership in correctly assessing the PLA's capabilities, the failure to budget sufficiently for defence hardware and the collapse of the morale of senior generals who were handpicked by Nehru and Menon, such as Lt Gen B.M. Kaul.

Between 11–15 September 1967, the PLA confronted the Indian armed forces at Nathu La, on the Sikkim-Tibet border. The six-day 'border skirmish' included exchange of heavy artillery fire when the PLA soldiers tried to cross that border in large numbers. The attack was repulsed at all points. The PLA had received a severe mauling in the artillery duels across the barbed wire fence boundary. Indian gunners scored several direct hits on Chinese bunkers, including a command post from where the Chinese operations were being directed. The Chinese army suffered at least twice as many casualties as the Indians in this encounter. Many recent books by (now) retired officials on this episode are available in bookstores. Here is a gist of these.

From the Nathu La and Cho La ('La' means 'pass') episode on the Sikkim-Tibet border, the Indian armed forces demonstrated beyond doubt that the PLA had met its match. In both the areas, a series of military clashes took place between India and China on the Sikkim border. These clashes started on 11 September 1967, when the PLA launched an attack on Indian posts at Nathu La. This lasted till 15 September 1967. On 5 October 1967, another military duel took place at Cho La and ended on the same day.

The decision to control the disputed borderland in the Chumbi Valley was the major cause of these incidents. India achieved decisive advantage and held its own against Chinese forces. Many PLA fortifications at Nathu La were destroyed, where Indian troops drove back the attacking Chinese forces. These clashes indicated a decline of 'claim of strength' of China's decision to initiate the use of PLA force. Justifiably, our military was pleased with the combat performance of its forces in the Nathu La clashes, seeing it as a sign of improvement since its defeat in the 1962 Sino-Indian War.

In the morning of 11 September 1967, the engineers and jawans (soldiers) of the Indian army started laying the stretch of fencing from Nathu La to Sebu La along the perceived border. According to an Indian account, immediately a Chinese Political Commissar asked the Indian Colonel to stop laying the wire. The Indian soldiers refused to halt, saying that they were given orders. An argument started which soon turned into a scuffle. After that, the Chinese went back to their bunkers and the Indians resumed laying the wire.

Within a few minutes of this, a whistle was blown from the Chinese side, followed by medium machine gun firing against Indian troops from the north shoulder. Shortly thereafter, the Chinese also opened artillery fire. A little later, Indian troops opened artillery fire from their side. The clashes lasted through the day and the night, for the next three days, with the use of artillery, mortars and machine guns, during which the Indian troops beat back the Chinese forces. Five days after the clashes started, an uneasy ceasefire was arranged. Due to the advantageous position the Indian troops got because of their occupation of high grounds at the pass in Sebu La and Camel's Back, they were able to destroy many Chinese bunkers at Nathu La. The corpses of fallen soldiers were exchanged on 15 and 16 September. Independent Western sources attributed the initiation of these clashes to the Chinese. The Chinese, however, blamed the Indian troops for provoking the clashes, alleging that the firing had started from the Indian side. However, the bottom line was that the 1962 lesson fell flat.

On 1 October 1967, another clash took place between India and China at Cho La, a few kilometres north of Nathu La. The duel was initiated by the Chinese troops after a scuffle, when the Chinese troops infiltrated into the Sikkim side of the border, claimed the pass and questioned the Indian occupation of it.

The military duel lasted for a day, and boosted the Indian army's morale. According to Maj. Gen. Sheru Thapliyal, the Chinese were forced to withdraw nearly 3 km into Cho La during this clash.

The defence ministry reported casualties as 88 killed and 163 wounded on the Indian side, while 340 were killed and 450 injured on the Chinese side during the two incidents at Nathu La and Cho La.

Thereafter, the Sino-Indian border remained peaceful till the 2020 China-India skirmishes, starting on 5 May 2020. The incidents of 15 June were the worst, but despite heavy casualties, the Indian army did us proud yet again.

Interestingly, in 2005, the Chinese PM Wen Jiabao stated that 'Sikkim is no longer the problem between China and India'.

Although Xi Jinping had agreed to PM Modi's request to open the Sikkim route to Kailash Mansarovar in 2015, it was closed down in April 2020 in the wake of the COVID-19 pandemic. The route through Lipu Lekh that I got opened in 1981 through my discussions with Chairman Den Xiaoping is still open.

On 2–3 March 1969, there were 'border skirmishes' in the area of the Nizhnemikhallovka border post on the Ussuri River. The intruding PLA men were confronted by the Soviet Red Army and a stalemate ensued. Again, on 15 March, the PLA launched a fresh attack with an infantry regiment strength (estimated to be 2,000 men) with support units at Zhenbao/Damansky Island on the Ussuri River. At first, the Chinese succeeded in penetrating the island under the cover of artillery and mortar fire from their side of the river, but a massive retaliation by the Red Army restored the status quo ex ante.

In 1977, the Soviet Union decided to retaliate by sending troops to Tibet via India. PM Morarji Desai was contacted by Premier Kosygin to invoke the 1971 Indo-Soviet Friendship Treaty. Morarji bhai contacted me as a China expert (although I was a Janata Party Lok Sabha MP). I reminded him that in 1962 the USSR had told India that the Soviet Union was China's 'brother' but Indians were 'just friends'. So, I advised Morarji bhai to just say that to Kosygin. We decided not to comply, thereby reducing the Indo-Soviet Treaty to waste paper. Thus began a new thaw.

In 1974, in a swift move, the PLA captured the disputed Paracel Islands in the South China Sea. With the ongoing conflict in Indo-China at that time, the Association of Southeast Asian Nations (ASEAN) and Vietnam, who also claim part of these islands, did not offer any resistance to the PLA's occupation of the islands. Virtually without firing a shot, this time, the PLA achieved total success.

In the now-famous 17 February 1979 war with Vietnam, Chairman Deng Xiaoping announced that he wanted 'to teach a lesson' to the Vietnamese. However, in the ensuing Sino-Vietnam War, the PLA was severely mauled and forced to retreat. With better strategy and motivation, the battle-hardened Vietnamese were able to take on the 'out-of-practice' PLA and inflict heavy casualties. Chairman Deng, a pragmatist, then realized that there was a need to improve the technological superiority of the PLA.

Consequently, the military modernization segment of the Four Modernizations programme (the other three being agriculture, industry, and science and technology) was initiated. Accordingly, greater allocations for defence were made in the Chinese budget, but were well-disguised. The PLA's decision-making apparatus was also restructured in the 1990s.

In mid-1986, it came to the notice of India that the PLA had built a helipad at Wandung in the Sumdorong Chu Valley in Arunachal Pradesh. India reacted swiftly and the PLA had an eyeball-to-eyeball confrontation with the Indian army in the Sumdorong Chu Valley in August 1986. After a week of tense moments, both sides mutually agreed to withdraw their forces inside their respective territories and create a no-man's land. The Chinese posture at that time clearly indicated that Beijing quickly realized that 1962 could not be repeated. Afterwards, the PLA's official organ, *People's Liberation Army Daily*, wrote about the 'new' professionalism in the Indian armed forces. This paved the way for Rajiv Gandhi's 1988 visit, and the Chinese willingness to talk seriously.

The Spratly Islands—situated at 350 km from Vietnam's coast and 1,000 km from China's—consist of about 150 reefs, sandbanks and islands in the South China Sea. They straddle busy shipping lanes and are, therefore, strategically important.

Both China and Vietnam claimed the Spratlys for centuries, but up to 1987, they had been content with a war of words. On 14 March 1988, the PLA Navy (PLAN) clashed with the Vietnamese Navy for the first time. Though it was a very short confrontation, both sides suffered a considerable number of casualties. Though a war-weary Vietnam proposed bilateral talks with China to resolve the issue, the Chinese rejected the offer.

However, fresh tensions erupted in May 1992, when the Chinese authorities leased an oil concession to an American firm, Creston Energy, for oil exploration in and around the Spratlys. Vietnam took strong objection to it. Soon enough, China chose to agree to bilateral talks with Vietnam. From 1993 onwards, both China and Vietnam started negotiations. It would suffice to say that the PLA was not able to enforce its authority to the extent it wanted to in the Spratlys to overrun the Vietnamese.

The PLA's success story is usually due to the timing of the campaign, like in the Paracel Islands. An assessment of these PLA actions indicates that *whenever it confronted an adversary without any element of surprise, its performance was poor.* This is clear from the Korean War, and the Nathu La and Ussuri incidents. In fact, in the Nathu La and Ussuri incidents, the PLA did not offer even stiff resistance. From all accounts, it made a retreat the instant the adversary offered stiff resistance or acted decisively.

Naval and Air Superiority

China has a massive lead in naval aviation units compared to India.

> China's PLA Navy (PLAN) has a total of 777 naval assets which include two aircraft carriers, 36 destroyers, 52 frigates, 50 corvettes, 74 submarines, 220 patrol vessels, and 29 mine warfare crafts. The Indian Navy, meanwhile, has a total of 285 naval assets which include one aircraft carrier, 10 destroyers,

13 frigates, 19 corvettes, 16 submarines, 139 patrol vehicles, and three mine warfare crafts.[28]

However, Chinese naval aviation is completely land-based. This creates a disadvantage for China because it reduces the range of combat aircraft in maritime operations. Indian naval capabilities have increased significantly both in numbers and quality. The proposed induction of a second aircraft carrier from Russia will enhance India's 'blue navy' attack capability, provided the repair work on the decommissioned carrier is properly carried out. It may be noted here that China does not have 'blue water' fighting capability; therefore despite its huge lead over India in this category of naval weaponry, China does not pose a serious threat to India as yet from the Ocean.

However, the induction of nuclear-armed submarines off the waters of Thailand would alter that position. India will also need to rethink its naval strategic doctrine and shift focus from surface forces to subsurface forces. This arm of the navy is cost-effective since India presently does not seem to face any major sea-borne threat, except in exceptional circumstances from the US Seventh Fleet.

According to most Western writers, China has been working on a 'String of Pearls' strategy in the Indian Ocean to surround the Indian peninsula and contain it to within the South Asian sphere, making it a dominant power in Asia. Once China starts to surround India with the String of Pearls, will it be game over for India as far as regional influence is concerned?

The BJP government has been quietly constructing its own port and basing arrangements, a 'Network of Diamonds',

---

[28]Harsh V. Pant and Anant Singh Mann, *The India–China military matrix and their modernisation trajectories*, Observer Research Foundation (ORF). Available at: https://www.orfonline.org/expert-speak/the-india-china-military-matrix-and-their-modernisation-trajectories-68631/, last accessed on 26 October 2020.

outflanking China's attempts to box India into the subcontinent. As of 2020, India has agreements for port and basing rights with the Maldives, Madagascar, Singapore and Oman, and is close to finalizing a deal with the Seychelles for the use of Assumption Island. Additionally, India now has reciprocal deals with Australia and France to use each other's Indian Ocean facilities for military purposes, as well as disaster relief and other non-war missions. Finally, India has greatly strengthened its forces with an eye for monitoring the critical Strait of Malacca area in the future. It has created a tri-service command, Andaman and Nicobar Command (ANC), for the strategic Andaman and Nicobar island chains, and now has advanced, long-range weapons based there, such as the P-8I Poseidon MPA. This advantageous position near a critical choke point in maritime trade for China gives India immense leverage in strategic confrontation.

In terms of quantity, China's air force capabilities have a massive lead over the Indian Air Force. Since the 1990s, China has modernized its air force at a rapid rate. In that decade, it had 5,000 aircrafts, but most of them were obsolete, such as the Soviet MiG 19s and MiG 21s.

China has now upgraded its fleet into new-generation aircrafts.

> China's PLA Air Force (PLAAF) is considered to have a total strength of around 3,210 which include 1,232 fighters, 371 dedicated attack aircrafts, 224 transport aircrafts, 314 trainers, 281 attack helicopters, 911 helicopters, and 111 maintained for special missions. For its part, the Indian Air Force has a strength of 2,123 which include 538 fighters, 172 dedicated attack aircrafts, 250 transport aircrafts, 359 trainers, 23 attack helicopters, 722 helicopters, and 77 reserved for special missions.[29]

---

[29]ibid.

However, qualitatively, China is not so far ahead of India because of the long logistics as compared to India's access to the Sino-Indian LAC.

So, will China deploy its entire air force on the India–China front? The answer is 'no', according to a study by Group Captain Ravinder Chhatwal (retd), the author of *The Chinese Air Threat: Understanding the Reality*.

He suggests:

> To launch any air campaign, fighter aircraft have to be deployed close to the border, roughly about 200 km to 300 km from the border of your enemy. Against India, China will have to deploy its fighter aircraft in Tibet and adjacent airfields in Xinjiang. China has 2,100 combat aircraft but most of them are deployed on its eastern seaboard. They cannot deploy all of them against India because of limited number of airfields in Tibet.
>
> Tibet, unfortunately for them and fortunately for us, is a high-altitude plateau with mountainous terrain. They have just about five main airfields in Tibet (Kongka Dzong, Hoping, Pangta, Linzhi and Gargunsa) and another two in Xinjiang (Hotan and Kashgar). They are developing three more airfields in Tibet which are likely to be ready by 2022.
>
> The second point is that to carry out sustained fighter aircraft operations, airfields have to be mutually supporting. By mutually supporting, I mean, that if you take off from an airfield, there should be another airfield nearby within 100 or 200 km, so that in case of requirement for diversion etc., you have an alternative airfield. In the northern Xinjiang sector's two airfields Hotan and Kashgar, the distance between them is 450 km, while the distance between Hotan and Gargunsa is 550 km. Hotan to Korla (in central Xinjiang), the distance is 750 km, so they are not mutually supportive. In western

Tibet, there is only one airfield, Gargunsa. If Gargunsa is bombed by the Indian Air Force, there will be a gap of 1,500 km between Hotan and the nearest airfield Hoping.

Moreover, as Group Captain (retd) Chhatwal states:

> There is another limitation which they have. In the airfield, when you park aircraft for fighter operations, there has to be blast proof or protected shelters, e.g., concrete shelters. China doesn't have any blast proof protected shelters at any of the airfields. After Doklam, they have realized their mistake and have now started building these in Kongka Dzong (Lhasa) airfield.

China's nuclear capabilities, operated by the PLA Rocket Force (PLARF), are estimated to have a total of 104 missiles, which include the Dongfeng (DF)—31A, DF31 and DF21— missiles. India, on the other hand, is estimated to have around 10 Agni-III launchers and eight Agni-II launchers. Furthermore, it is estimated that India has around 51 aircrafts (Jaguar IS and Mirage 2000H fighters), which are capable of launching nuclear warheads.[30]

In the next few years, the planned acquisition by China of multirole combat aircraft, interceptors and submarines, and other air force and navy weapon systems from countries such as France, Britain and South Africa, will significantly enhance its capability vis-à-vis India, both in terms of quantity and quality. India, presently, does not have any major plans to match these, but it will need a phased modernization plan of its air force with a special focus on induction of more multirole capable aircrafts.

India's security posture against China should seek qualitative sufficiency and not be a search for parity recognition. Despite

---

[30]ibid.

Chinese missile deployments in Tibet and upgrading of surveillance capability in the Coco Islands (some 25 miles off the Andaman and Nicobar Islands), the strategist in India has to formulate a plan on the basis of present as well as emergent threats. The political leadership has to harmonize that strategy with other dimensions of policy, and developments that would and could take place subsequently in the future.

In hardware terms, the Chinese possess a massive lead over the Indians in all three arms of the military. Hence, in actual war-fighting machines, China seems to have acquired a distinct edge over India. However, in case of a future armed conflict between the two, India's qualitatively more sophisticated navy and air force, provide, inter alia, a clear-cut edge. If this is backed by a clear strategic military doctrine, India can compensate for the imbalance in quantitative terms.

Sino-Pak All-Weather Friendship

The fundamental strategic proposition in this present situation is that it is the axis with Pakistan which provides the necessary force multiplier to make China (or Pakistan) formidable.

In the years 2000 onwards, the Sino-Soviet rivalry has ceased to be a factor, because of the dismantling of the Soviet empire from 1991 onwards. Today all that remains is the rump Russia, which Vladimir Putin as Supremo of Russia is fiercely working to restore as a superpower. Although Putin has restored to Russia the social stability that was lost during President Boris Yeltsin's tenure, it is yet to be an economic power to reckon with. Owing to its poor financial conditions and being dependent on the sale of crude oil and gas to Europe, which President Donald Trump has shut by sanctions, and Europe has complied, Russia has become dependent on bail outs from China.

But ever since India purchased the S-400 air defence missile systems from Russia in 2018, it has been increasingly relying on Russia as a *de facto* mediator in its conflict with China since 18 April 2020 in Ladakh.

However, this is most inadvisable since Xi Jinping described Russian President Putin as 'my best friend and colleague' in a meet in Moscow in June 2019. This was not a casual compliment usually paid at banquets during bilateral summits, and for the media.

The Associated Press quoted that *The Moscow Times* and TASS (Russia's press agency) had on 23 October 2020 reported Putin as stating to a meeting of experts that 'a future military alliance with China cannot be ruled out'. Putin added that 'already Russia is sharing sensitive military technology with China'.[31] As former foreign secretary Vijay Gokhale maintains in his perceptive op-ed piece in *The Hindu*, 'Moscow is in real danger of permanently becoming the "junior partner" of Beijing.'[32]

The S-400 missile system built by Russia and sold to India has Chinese electronics. This has alienated the US, which was about to sell advanced military hardware to India, but had put it

---

[31] *The Moscow Times*, 23 October 2020, on Putin's admission. Available at: https://www.themoscowtimes.com/2020/10/23/russia-china-military-alliance-quite-possible-putin-says-a71834, last accessed on 29 October 2020.

Eugene Rumer, Richard Sokolsky and Aleksandar Vladicic, 'Russia in the Asia-Pacific: Less Than Meets the Eye,' Paper, Carnegie Endowment for International Peace, 3 September 2020. Available at:https://carnegieendowment.org/2020/09/03/russia-in-asia-pacific-less-than-meets-eye-pub-82614, last accessed on 29 October 2020.

[32] Vijay Gokhale, 'China-Russia Ties as a Major Determinant,' *The Hindu*, 20 August 2020. Available at: https://www.thehindu.com/opinion/lead/china-russia-ties-as-a-major-determinant/article32397585.ece, last accessed on 6 October 2020.

Russia – China's Junior Partner, Warsaw Institute, 2 November 2019. Available at: https://warsawinstitute.org/russia-chinas-junior-partner/, last accessed on 29 October 2020.

on hold because it could not risk Chinese or Russian espionage in India on advanced US weapons systems.

The Soviet Union, of which Russia was a component, had become a bitter enemy of China after 1958, when Chairman Mao launched the Great Leap Forward project. To collapse this project, the Soviets, led by Nikita Khrushchev, cancelled all the industrial projects that were being implemented to modernize China, and also withdrew all the experts along with the blueprints sent to China. Not only was the Great Leap Forward a disaster and industrial growth stunted, an ensuing famine in 1960–61 led to 16–32 million deaths.

For the US, this opened up the road to Beijing. Within the decade of the 1960s, US and Chinese negotiators met in Warsaw, Poland, to work out a thaw in relations. In 1971, the US changed its two-decade-old stand and voted to admit China into the UN and invited it to take the seat of a permanent member with a veto at the UNSC. China greatly benefitted by the US granting the most favoured trade clause, thus opening US markets to China, as well as for joint ventures to enable China to produce with its cheap and captive labour. This helped accelerate the Chinese GDP at more than 10–12 per cent growth rate for a decade. China soon rose from the ninth position in GDP rankings to the second position (after the US) by the year 2000.

For three decades, the US had occupied the favoured position in terms of its relations with Russia and China. China seems to have assumed that position now. Second, as Gokhale states, the disintegration of the Soviet Union essentially negated the Russian threat in Chinese eyes. Both these trends will likely continue despite the recent tensions in Sino-US relations.

The Sino-Russian partnership currently rests on peace at the frontier, trade and Chinese funds for Russia to escape the effects of US sanctions, and a shared distrust of American democracy and intensions.

Currently, Sino-Russian trade has more than doubled and Russia's central bank has increased its Chinese currency reserves from less than 1 per cent to over 13 per cent. Germany is no more the principal supplier of industrial plant and technology to Russia, China is.

Action in multilateral forums such as BRICS, increasingly sophisticated joint military exercises and pooling of influence with countries such as Iran are other reliable indicators of a growing alliance between Russia and China.

Hence, today, a proper appraisal of the Sino-Russian relationship will be critical to our foreign policy calculus. Clearly, India has to make a choice: either we partner the US strategically, or Russia and China. If we have a conflict with China, Russia cannot be trusted, nor if we do, the US will not trust us. Hence, this dream of isolating China is short-sighted.

It is dangerous, therefore, for India to consider Russian help against China. Russia under Putin will have no hesitation in misinforming us about PLA mobilization and intention. For example, in the recent Ladakh incursions, the Russian highest authority had assured India that China was only amassing troops along the LAC for routine annual exercises. It was wrong information and India was caught unawares. Today, compared to the economic progress made by China, the rump Russia seems like a poor cousin coming in from the cold. Instead, for India, the Sino-Pakistan axis is the main security concern through which prism India's future China perspective must be viewed, and the policy towards China structured.

In military strategy and tactics, the Sino-Pakistan axis or nexus has a significant bearing on India's security environment. This nexus has remained remarkably stable over the last four decades, and ideologically neutral and immune to tumultuous changes in international relations, even after the dismemberment of Pakistan in 1971.

When Pakistan joined the Southeast Asia Treaty Organization (SEATO) in 1954 and the Central Treaty Organization (CENTO) in 1955 (military alliances which were established to contain communist influence), surprisingly, China did not object to it. In fact, PM Zhou Enlai took the extraordinary step of explaining to the Afro-Asian Conference in Bandung (in April 1955) that 'the Prime Minister of Pakistan told me that although Pakistan was party to a military treaty, Pakistan was not against China. Pakistan had no fear that China would commit aggression against her. As a result of that, we achieve a mutual understanding, although we are still against military treaties'.

The PM of Pakistan even reiterated that in the event of a global war launched by the US against China, Pakistan would not be a party to it.

Zhou told the Associated Press of Pakistan that because of 'certain Pakistan assurances since 1954 onwards, China "approved" of Pakistan's objectives of acquiring political and military superiority over India in joining SEATO and CENTO, since otherwise Pakistan had no other motivation in joining the pacts'. Pakistan had joined these pacts, according to Premier Zhou, for 'defensive' reasons, and therefore, it would not adversely affect the overall Sino-Pak relations.

In 1956, China had made its first pronouncement, in an India-related dispute (despite the Panchsheel Declaration of 1954), when in talks with a Pakistani press delegation in Beijing, Zhou said: 'China accepted the existence of the Kashmir dispute and hoped that it would be settled peacefully.'

In January 1961, China entered into negotiations with Pakistan for the demarcation of the border (in PoK). In May 1962, the two governments recognized the need to 'locate and align their common border' and expressed their wish to demarcate the boundary between China's Sinkiang Province (or Xinjiang

Province) and the contiguous areas, 'the defence of which is under the actual control of Pakistan'.

The statement said that the agreement would be of a 'provisional nature', and that China would renegotiate with the 'sovereign authority' after the settlement of the dispute over Kashmir between India and Pakistan. India's strong protest, of course, fell on deaf ears.

On 27 December 1962, a month after the Sino-Indian border war, a joint Sino-Pak communique clearly expressed that 'an agreement in principle has been reached on the location and alignment of the boundary actually existing between the two countries'.

The Sino-Pak boundary agreement was effective from 2 March 1963, under which Pakistan ceded to China 3,200 sq. km of Kashmir territory to China. In July that year, Foreign Minister Zulfikar (Zulfiqar) Ali Bhutto told Pakistan's National Assembly that Pakistan could now rely on Chinese support in the event of an Indo-Pak war. Obviously, China had decided to make Pakistan a strategic ally, for which the latter was willing to pay a price.

From 1966 to 1968, Pakistan acquired a hundred T-9 (Soviet variant) tanks, 80 MiG-19s (F-6) and 10 Ilyushin-28 bombers. This substantially made up for the losses during its 1965 war with India over Kashmir. Since then, China has been one of Pakistan's main suppliers of military equipment. From 1966 to 2018, arms transfer from China to Pakistan has amounted to more than an estimated $200 billion. Military supplies were given free of cost till 1978, and since then at cost price.

There has also been considerable nuclear collaboration between China and Pakistan since 1965. The credit for procuring Chinese nuclear technology for Pakistan goes to Zulfikar Bhutto. During his visit to Beijing in May 1976, two crucial agreements were signed: one for scientific cooperation in nuclear energy, and the other for military cooperation.

Pakistan obtained most of its equipment and fissile uranium from North Korea with a benevolent nod from China. Beijing has been a constant supplier, direct and indirect, of a variety of nuclear products and services to Pakistan, ranging from uranium-enrichment technology and heavy water to research and power reactors. For the first time, a joint China-Pakistan Military Committee was also established. There was to be cooperation between the two countries in plutonium reprocessing and collaboration on uranium enrichment through the centrifuge method. The degree of indirect Chinese participation in Pakistan's nuclear programme remains an indication of the degree of its commitment to Pakistan's security.

In 1978, when the French government informed the Zia-ul-Haq government that it would be unable to proceed with the Chashma reactor deal unless Pakistan agreed to revise the original agreement of 1978, providing for co-processing of spent fuel, the Chinese came to Pakistan's rescue.

A study published by the Centre for Nonproliferation Studies at the Monterey Institute of International Studies in the US (in September 2000) reveal details about how China helped Pakistan become a significant nuclear and missile power in South Asia. The study had concluded as early as 1983 that Beijing had by then transferred a complete nuclear weapon design to Islamabad, along with enough weapons-grade uranium for two nuclear weapons.

On 15 September 1986, a formal agreement was signed between Pakistan and China on cooperation in the nuclear field during the visit of Pakistan's PM to Beijing. The agreement was for cooperation in the 'peaceful' uses of nuclear technology and had safeguard provisions against the proliferation of nuclear weapons in accordance with the ones laid down by the International Atomic Energy Agency (IAEA).

After concluding this comprehensive nuclear cooperation agreement with Pakistan, China began assisting Islamabad with the enrichment of weapons-grade uranium. China also reportedly transferred enough tritium gas to Pakistan for 10 nuclear weapons. The study claimed that in 1989, China involved Pakistani scientists in a nuclear test at its Lop Nor test site in the northwest. In 1994–95, China sold 5,000 ring magnets to the Abdul Qadeer (A.Q.) Khan Research Laboratory at Kahuta, Pakistan, which were used in gas centrifuges to make weapons-grade-enriched uranium. The destination of these magnets—to the research lab which is not subject to IAEA safeguards—is believed to be for use in Pakistan's nuclear weapons programme.

Today, China's nuclear weapon programme has reached a stage where its SLBM, the CSS-N-3, can be deployed aboard the nuclear-powered Xia-class submarines in large numbers. These missiles have a range of 2,800 km and can pose a threat to the Indian landmass; when these submarines start entering the waters of the Indian Ocean, India will face a serious threat. The Chinese nuclear submarines entering the Indian Ocean would need R&R (military abbreviation for rest and recuperation) and the Karachi one has excellent port facilities for that purpose.

Sino-Pak nuclear understanding against India is not an improbability in the future. Therefore, if India does not restructure its foreign policy suitably, it would become highly vulnerable to a possible nuclear blackmail by Pakistan.

The Sino-Pak axis has also been strategically strengthened by the reopening of the old silk route—the Karakoram Highway—which linked Chinese Xinjiang with Pak-occupied Hunza Valley in PoK in 1967. This meant the opening of a direct route for supply of arms that would remain undisturbed in any future contingency.

However, this supply route potentially poses a more serious threat to India's security than any quantum of armaments that Pakistan may receive. The safety of this particular Sino-Pak highway against possible attack has been guaranteed by the construction of a number of military bases all along the route. The Karakoram Highway linking Gilgit with Beijing was formally inaugurated in June 1978. These roads are demonstrations of China's firm commitment to consolidate and perpetuate its close ties with Pakistan.

Pakistan by itself, however, can never be a major threat to India's security. If China shares with Pakistan a common hostility towards India, only then India's security is seriously threatened by Pakistan. Also, terrorism in Kashmir could again flare up if Pakistan is able to coordinate with a China hostile to India. Hostility with neighbouring countries makes it possible for the insurgents to have safe supply routes, and to find easy places for R&R. However, India presently seems to be losing neighbours, not gaining any. India's deteriorating relations with China have serious implications for neighbourliness with the South Asian Association for Regional Cooperation (SAARC) countries too, as demonstrated by the about-turn of Nepal recently when, for the first time, it demanded a part of Uttarakhand as belonging to it. As of mid-2020, India has managed only to drive Pakistan and China strategically closer, and China getting more allies or neutrality in SAARC nations.

In the last five decades, India has seen military action with Pakistan on three occasions: in 1947, 1965 and 1971. A direct Chinese intervention on behalf of Pakistan in 1965 and 1971, however, did not occur for fortuitous but unforeseen reasons.

In 1965, this was because China was on the verge of a domestic turmoil that led to the Cultural Revolution, in which the PLA became embroiled. China did nevertheless engage in some verbal brinkmanship. At that time, on 16 September 1965, an official note was sent by China to India which accused India of 'setting up 56 posts on the Tibetan side of the Sikkim sector, kidnapping Tibetan civilians, and committing 300 infiltrations since 1962'. China demanded dismantling of the so-called posts within 72 hours, and began amassing troops along the Sino-Indian border. China also demanded that India return 1,000 yaks that it allegedly stole! However, because of the internal constraint, the Chinese did not act on their ultimatum; and on the day the UN-mediated ceasefire came into effect on 22 September 1965, China announced that India 'had met the conditions'. Nevertheless, the 1965 Pakistani aggression against India was encouraged by the increasingly strong vocal support that Beijing had given to Pakistan's position on Kashmir, which made the Pakistani leaders believe that if it made a move against India, it would have strong Chinese military backing as well for its actions.

China nevertheless vehemently opposed the 1966 Tashkent Declaration as a Soviet conspiracy. Soon thereafter, China began its military supplies to Pakistan to prevent a possible further improvement in Soviet relations with Pakistan.

The Chinese also did not intervene in the 1971 Liberation War of Bangladesh on behalf of Pakistan because around that time, it, too, was engulfed in the September 1971 aborted coup attempt by Defence Minister Lin Biao. As a consequence of the failed attempt, Chairman Mao ordered all air force planes to be grounded and the PLA demobilized.

Hence, twice India was luckily assisted by unrelated internal developments in China, which had prevented a joint China-Pakistan operation against India. However, no nation can structure its strategic perceptions and options on the presumption of such luck obtaining every time. India has to start restructuring its military strategy on the assumption that there could be a

Sino-Pak joint attack, which could be widened with Nepal and Myanmar joining it. Defence strategy has to be based on capacity of the opponents, while foreign policy is based on the intentions expressed.

In the future too, the Sino-Pakistan nexus will test the Indian political leadership's practical sense and street smartness in international affairs. India's most important diplomatic and strategic goal is thus to unhinge and undo the Sino-Pak axis. The Indian leadership must be astute and alert to any possibility of a rupture in relations, and then to seize it when it happens.

Chasing the Dragon

The next requirement for India is to close the gap in economic development with China, which developed from zero in 1980 to four times by 2010. From 1980 onwards till the end of the remainder of the twentieth century, China had outperformed India in economic growth, accelerating to twice as fast in GDP growth rate. Thereafter and till 2015, the gap remained unchanged. Since 2015, the gap-ratio widened again to 4.6 in 2020 (see Table 4).

TABLE 4: Author's Estimates of GDP Growth in India and China, 2010–20

Year	2010	2011	2012	2013	2014	2015	2016	2017	2018	2019	2020
China	10.6%	9.5%	7.9%	7.8%	7.3%	6.9%	6.8%	6.9%	6.7%	6.1%	1.2% (est)
India	10.3%	6.6%	5.5%	6.4%	7.4%	8%	8.3%	7%	6.1%	4.2%	1.9% (est)

Since 2016, the lack of a deep understanding of how economies can be made to grow has resulted in a steady decline in India's growth rate. In the financial year 2019–20, that is before the onset of the coronavirus pandemic, India's GDP growth rate had declined to 4 per cent. For a projected estimate for 2020–21, it is estimated to be less than *minus* 5 per cent. Is it credible anymore that India can catch up with China, leave alone overtake that country?

The China–India gap can be measured in four dimensions of economic progress:

   i. Growth factors;
  ii. Globalization;
 iii. Financial structure;
  iv. Human Development Index.

Growth Factors

Between 1980 and 2004, the GDP growth rate of China was maintained at a much faster pace, which made for a widening gap with India's. During this period, typically the Chinese average growth rate was 75 per cent higher than the Indian rate of growth. The per capita income, which was almost the same in 1980 for both countries, diverged sharply in the two decades that followed, to China's advantage.

Evaluated in purchasing power parity (PPP) terms, the gap was 86 per cent in favour of China, not only because of a higher growth rate of GDP but also because of a lower growth rate of population. In 1952, China's population was 57 per cent higher than India's. In the 1990s, it was just 28 per cent higher. At present, China's population is growing at less than 1.0 per cent per year while India's is expanding at 1.7 per cent per year.

At this rate, India will overtake China's population by 2025. Earlier, China had an ambitious plan to reach zero population growth by 2020 to level at 1.5 billion people. If that were so, India would have overtaken China in population size by 2016. However, since 2005, China has realized that its drastic one child per family policy was ageing its population, judging by the average age of the population. Thus, the one child per family target has been abandoned. At present, the average age of the Indian population is 27 years, while for China it is 35 years.

China has had a higher GDP growth rate than India since 1980. However, it should be noted that the gap has narrowed partly due to China's growth rate slowing down since 2005, and partly because India's growth rate rose during Narasimha Rao's tenure as PM, from less than 4 per cent average during the 1980s to 8 per cent in 1995–96. China's higher growth rate was made possible by a much higher rate of gross domestic investment (GDI; as a ratio of GDP), which is about 70 per cent more than that of India. The rate of growth of GDI in China during this period is double the rate in India.

One can, therefore, conclude that the wide gap between India and China in per capita incomes (the gap was about zero in 1980) was partly due to a lower population growth, but primarily due to a much greater investment effort in China. India cannot close this per capita income gap by 2025 without a much faster GDP growth rate (e.g., 10 per cent per year), for which an even greater effort to raise the level of investment will have to be made. This is, of course, easier said than done. Table 5 highlights the current gap sectorally for industrial products between China and India.

Since 1997, GDI as a ratio of GDP has been declining, albeit erratically, due to consumerism and low interest rates on fixed deposits and savings. Hence, a dynamic policy design for such an accelerated effort will have to be resolutely implemented to raise the level of saving.

TABLE 5: Sectoral Gap in Industrial Products between China and India

Steel Production (10:1)	Global Trade (3:1)
China ~1000 Mn Tonnes India ~110 Mn Tonnes	China ~$4.5 Trillion India ~$1.2 Trillion
Cement Production (7:1)	**Cellphone Export (40:1)**
China ~2000 Mn Tonnes India ~350 Mn Tonnes	China ~$125 Bn India ~$3 Bn
Services Export (2:1)	**Telecom Export (40:1)**
China ~$200 Bn India ~$120 Bn	China ~$200 Mn India ~$5 Mn
Foreign Trips (5:1)	**Textile Export (6:1)**
China ~150 Mn People India ~30 Mn People	China ~$120 Bn India ~$20 BN
APIs Export (10:1)	**Automobile Export (4:1)**
China ~10 Mn Tonnes India ~1 Mn Tonnes	China ~$120 Bn India ~ $30 BN
Box Office Collection (6:1)	**Ecommerce Sales (40:1)**
China ~$9000 Mn India ~$1500 Mn	China ~$2000 Bn India ~ $50 BN

Source: GoI estimates

However, judging by indicators of productivity in agriculture, China is not that far ahead of India. In 2018, the proportion of irrigated land in agriculture was only 16 per cent higher in China. Gross cropped area under good crops was, however, 30 per cent lower, although yield was 2.87 times higher. Agriculture value added per agricultural worker is just 17 per cent more in China. Surprisingly, while commercial energy use per capita (in kgs) of oil equivalent is almost double in China, the efficiency in its use measured by its ratio to GDP is higher in India. This despite China having 2.35 times more scientists and engineers in R&D (research and development) activities than India. It is clear that if productivity in agriculture is systematically raised in India, then India can overtake China. At the level of Chinese yield per hectare, India can produce 579 million tonnes of foodgrains as compared to less than half that amount in India at today's technology and ground reality.

Globalization

In the field of IT, China has completely outstripped India in hardware items of technology, even if it is behind India in software. High-technology exports as a percentage of manufacturing exports are almost double than that of India's. The per 1,000 people availability of computers in China is four times that of India. Even in number of internet hosts, despite China being a controlled society, the per 10,000 people ratio is only slightly higher than that of India. China has 10 times more mobile phones per capita than India, almost three times more telephone main lines and four times more TV sets per capita.

In 2015, China had 6.2 times more patent applications filed by foreigners. Chinese residents filed 7.1 times more such applications than Indians in their own country. Indians need not, therefore, be too smug in the thought that India is ahead of China in software because Indian computer engineers are already beginning to get priced out by huge salaries being paid by Fortune 500 companies in outsourcing. Thus, sometime in the future, Chinese, Russian and Irish engineers can be lower-cost alternatives to Indians; and Fortune 500 companies would not hesitate to give up sourcing from India then. Therefore, India has to move from being servers, to design and domain specialists in IT.

Thus, at present, there is without doubt an unambiguous and wide gap in favour of China over India in overall globalization. Surprisingly, therefore, an open democratic market economy—India—has to make special efforts to catch up with a controlled communist 'social market' economy—China—and that too ironically in the area of globalization!

Financial Structure

In growth terms then, the China–India gap can be sealed if India designs its fiscal architecture in such a way that the rate of investment rises to above 36 per cent of GDP from the present 29 per cent, while it reduces the incremental capital-output ratio, which measures the efficiency or productivity (larger the ratio, higher the inefficiency), from 4.0 to 3.0.

China has not only managed a high rate of investment, but has kept the Prime Lending Rate (PLR) at a relatively low 8 per cent; the interest rate spread between lending and deposit rates was confined to 2.6 per cent. In India, the PLR is 12 per cent, while the interest rate spread is at 3.4 per cent.

Clearly, China's configurations are more conducive to high domestic investment. Even though Indian stock markets were established much before China's, as regards market capitalization, China is ahead of India by 2.20 times. Chinese banks extend credit, measured as a ratio of GDP, at a rate two and a half times India's. Marginal tax rates on corporate incomes are at a maximum of 30 per cent, while in India it is 40 per cent. Even in fiscal decentralization, the Chinese central government transfers 51.4 per cent of the tax revenue to the provinces, while in India it is 36.1 per cent.

However, despite China being ahead of India in various financial factors, these gaps are not unbridgeable. A sincere and determined effort at financial restructuring by India can close the China–India financial gap within a decade.

Human Development Factors

According to the 2016 Human Development Report of the UN, China had a higher ranking in human development index than India. The index for China was 1.29 times that of India.

Public expenditure on health in China as ratio of GDP was three times more. Surprisingly, the Gini index of income inequality was also higher in China than in India, because the urban average income as ratio of rural per capita income was much higher in India. No surprises because China's modernization and foreign investment were urban-focused. Economic reforms in China had caused a sharp increase in urban incomes in the eastern seaboard areas, and this caused the ratio to rise, since the rural and western provinces lagged behind.

To put it simply, India can overtake China if the Indian households and corporate sector are encouraged by abolition of income tax, reduction of corporate taxes and increase in fixed deposit rate of return to encourage savings—to save more for national investment. If the interest rate for loans is lowered, the nation will have a boom in savings, which can be converted to investment.

If production can become more efficient through efficient processes, e.g., by introducing new innovation or computerizing routine procedures to lower the capital output ratio, the growth rate will rise without more investment. For example, if the rate of investment as a ratio of GDP is 36 per cent, and if by reducing waste and cost, the incremental capital ratio (which at present is 4.0 in India) is reduced to 3.6, then 36 divided by 3.6 is equal to 10 per cent growth rate. So, to overtake China, India has to grow annually at 10 per cent for 12 years continuously.

India, once having been a most developed nation, should not despair today even though faced with the huge crisis caused by a conjunction of the past decade of mismanaged economy

(2010–20), a coronavirus pandemic that has paralysed us for eight months running so far as the book goes to print and a looming cross-border war with China. In the end, India has always prevailed, no matter what crisis or holocaust is imposed on us.

China's India Policy Dilemma

It is equally important to understand reactions of China's India watchers. At one end are those who believe that the current conflict is an 'inevitable development' of the covert strategy of India for an infrastructure race at the LAC. Hence, the upset PLA wants 'to teach India a lesson', as in 1962. Of course, subsequent events ended up with China learning a lesson instead. The Indian government, ruled since 2014 by the BJP, is made of sterner stuff. At this juncture in time, India, burdened with the COVID-19 pandemic, has yet not been able to reverse what the PLA had taken by nibbling away since 2002 and encroaching on the mutually agreed 1993 LAC.

On the other side of the debate there are those influential political scientists, who in their analysis of the Galwan Valley incident, have been concerned about China's policies towards India, which they say remain mostly tactical, of a 'reactive nature', and are characterized by a 'tit-for-tat' approach, but devoid of any clear strategic intent. This, according to them, stokes aggressive nationalism in India, which not only harms China's interests, but might eventually draw China into an untimely global military conflict.

China, they argue, has failed to fathom that India, as a rising power, is very important to enable China–India relations to evolve for global positioning as the most important pair of relations after China–U.S. If China–India ties are damaged beyond repair, they warn, India alone or in association with other countries will cause 'endless trouble for China'. For instance, an openly hostile India will use every possible means to prevent China from reaching the Indian Ocean.

Moreover, the ending of China–India relations will strengthen the encirclement of China by the US, India, Japan, Australia, Vietnam, Indonesia and other nations, who will actively take the initiative of reshaping global industrial chains and the Indo-Pacific Strategy to checkmate China's military and economic power, and to expand international organizations such as the G7 to reduce China's influence in international affairs.

Strategically too, the alternate view is that it is 'unwise' for China to get into a military conflict with India, which is a large country with commensurate and thus comparable military strength at this point in time. A few Chinese military analysts even hold that if China has an advantage in terms of psychological preparation, equipment and careful logistics mobilization, India too has strategic and tactical advantage on other dimensions, such as ease of deployment, shorter supply lines, modern war experience since World War I, less challenging topography and battle-compliant climate. China's biggest hurdle is its long supply lines, which pass through the difficult terrain of Tibet and Xinjiang. Therefore, only if the military conflict ends in a short period of time, will it benefit China. However, if it is prolonged, China will be at a disadvantage. And there lies imbedded the military zero-sum game. That is, India must not agree to a unilateral declaration of ceasefire by China.

If a war starts, India should make all efforts to prolong it as far as possible, a prospect that worries Chinese military strategists. And if the US and Israel decide to help India to attain this objective, especially with air-to-surface missiles fitted with F-18s and laser-based explosives, then China's defeat seems probable. Even if war between the two sides ends in a stalemate,

India will be counted as the victor, and the national morale of Indians will rise sharply. On the contrary, in China, the morale will decline if it cannot beat India as decisively as it did in 1962. Therefore, in their internal discussions, Chinese experts are worried that in its effort to 'teach India a lesson', China may land in a Catch-22 fix. They fear that whatever the outcome, China would in any case lose more than it would gain. In India too, we have yet to stop swinging from one end of euphoria to the other end of remorse.

Meanwhile, China will simultaneously carry out its strategy of weakening India internally by leveraging its social and political differences, completing its strategic encirclement, improving troop deployment in the Tibet region to secure the China-Pakistan Economic Corridor (CPEC), pushing India out of Chabahar Port in Iran, prodding Nepal to make outrageous demands on India and stationing Chinese troops in the Gwadar Port (Arabian Sea) and in Doklam, so as to destabilize the Indian people's support to the Modi government and also secure China's Indian Ocean sea routes, among other interests. China has to try to obtain a comprehensive presence in geopolitics vis-à-vis India—which, I feel, China knows that it cannot alter by a full-scale war with India.

Thus, despite all the propaganda through its official media, China is clearly in a serious dilemma today over its outdated India policy. We should, therefore, pay attention to the ongoing Chinese debate on India, and factor in its inadequacies and vulnerabilities vis-à-vis India. As a matching military power, India has arrived, and its policymakers have leveraged this matrix of advantages and disadvantages to assert themselves as a global power, in the same league as the US and China. World peace will depend on this developed triumvirate.

The Power of Two

However, the events of April–October 2020 show that the Indian political class is still obsessed with the 1962 War, when Indian leadership moved from bravado and spin to abject fear of China. India, thus, needs a mental renaissance in the perception of the Chinese threat, which is bound to come with educated political class in future. In this final analysis, it would be appropriate to quote Deng Xiaoping's statement made at his meeting with PM Rajiv Gandhi in Beijing on 21 December 1988:

> In recent years there has been comment about the next century being the Asia-Pacific century, as though its arrival is imminent. I do not agree with this viewpoint. When we talk of the Asia-Pacific region, if the United States is excluded then we find that only Japan, the 'four small dragons', Australia, and New Zealand are comparatively developed, and yet, they have 200 million people at most. Even if the far eastern region of the Soviet Union and the western part of the United States and Canada are included, the population comes to only about 300 million, whereas the combined population of our countries is 1.8 billion. If India and China fail to develop, it cannot be called an Asia century.[33]

Given the strategic realignment of forces in Asia, India should reconfigure and recast its relationship with China. An induced Sino-Indian proper understanding would dramatically change the strategic and economic map of Asia. India, thus, has to define its perspective on China with clarity and transparency: does India want a compact with China in the twenty-first century (Option A), or does India want to participate in the growing prospect to

---

[33] Selected Works of Deng Xiaoping Vol. III, excerpts from *Beijing Review* (Beijing), 17–23 January 1994.

contain China with the US or Russia (Option B)? The choice can be made once we Indians demonstrate on the ground that we can defend and impose heavy costs against China on our own strengths and military preparedness.

My conclusion, thus, is that from cultural, historical and strategic perspectives, the maximum and stable strategic gains to India in the twenty-first century obtain in Option A. However, clearly a trade-off between China's relations with Pakistan and India's transparency in Tibet are the cornerstones of that structuring of policy. What Indian security needs today is moderated, normal (but not intimate) Sino–Pakistan relations, for which India has to offer a transparent commitment to respect China's interest in its own autonomous province of Tibet as a trade-off.

Rather than paint it as a clear and present danger, or a new-found ally, India needs to take the middle path in its interaction with China. This new policy should be grounded in pragmatism, not out of fear or overreaction. It should be derived from Indian and not Western assessments of China's strategic calculus, priorities and propensities, and India's position in that calculation. Accordingly, once India's national interests are defined vis-à-vis China, the tasks for the foreign policy establishment become clear. They can contribute both to formulating the Indian response as well as to implementing the resultant strategy.

However, for such a compact to come within the realm of possibilities requires a change in the mindset of the Chinese and Indian leadership, and a washing off of the 1962 hangover. In particular, the new mindset would make future Indian leaders recognize that Pakistan, despite its nuclear capability, is not in India's league, and for China to recognize that India is very much in China's league and that it is no more possible for China to 'teach any lesson' to India, without itself coming to grief.

This Indian commitment has value for China's strategic

calculations, especially in the context of its recent growing vulnerability to Islamic fundamentalism in the Xinjiang province. It is, however, not as simple as that, since China values Pakistan as a reliable conduit to West Asia and even to the US. However, even there, the evolving relations between Israel and China may reduce Pakistan's importance as a gateway to the US. Nevertheless, a modern non-Talibanized Pakistani state would still be an invaluable asset to Beijing in the Arab world, unless Pakistan crumbles to the Talibanization onslaught, which is not a remote possibility.

It must be stressed that just as India wishes to be liberated from ignominious comparisons with Pakistan, it needs to better calibrate its relations with China, freeing it from odious and sterile comparisons of arithmetic parity. Only then will India be able to play a larger role in Asian affairs, in a compact with China.

Such a compact would thus have multidimensional possibilities, including a joint supervision of the Malacca Straits, which would control nearly 75 per cent of the world's commercial sea traffic. However, it is not easy to affect it. Although, it is not impossible either. It depends on the astuteness of leadership on both sides of the Himalayan mountain range. However, if China wishes to continue to be obstinate, the same Malacca Straits with an India-Indonesia alliance can strangulate Chinese foreign trade. The onus today is on China, but it also requires a little diplomatic finesse from India, backed by a modernized armed force.

For the moment, leaving aside the other possible positive gains from an India–China friendship, such as in the UN, in bilateral trade, etc., immutable strategic facts make it imperative that any Indian government ought, in the national interest, to strive for India–China rapprochement without being carried away by peripheral issues and wallow in spin dished out by the media.

In brief, after having demonstrated to China that 1962 was

a mirage for their hardliners, India is ready to demonstrate the same any time again. Global peace will be greatly facilitated if China and India cease hostilities, since it will end in a stalemate for China. Working together has a more fruitful and productive endgame.

BIBLIOGRAPHY

BOOKS:

Bhasin, Avtar Singh: *India–China Relations 1947–2000: A Documentary Study*. Published in cooperation with the Ministry of External Affairs, Volumes I to V. New Delhi: Geetika Publishers, 2018.

Bowie, Robert R. and John F. Fairbank: *Communist China, 1955–1959: Policy Documents with Analysis*. Cambridge, Massachusetts: Harvard University Press, 1965.

Dalai Lama: *Freedom in Exile: An Autobiography*. London: Abacus, 1998.

Gopal, S. (ed.): Sardar Patel's Correspondence: 1945–50, Vol. 8 (Ahmedabad, 1973), p.8. See also, Bhasin *op.cit*. Vol. I, pp. 441–47.

Galbraith, John Kenneth: *Ambassador's Journal*. Boston: Houghton and Mifflin Company, 1969.

Government of India (GoI), Report of the Officials of the Governments of India and the People's Republic of China on the Boundary Question, New Delhi: The Government of India Press, 1962.

_____, White Papers: Notes, Momoranda, Letters Exchanges Between the Governments of India and China, 1954–64, Faridabad: The Government of India Press, Nos. I-IX.

Kaul, B.M.: *The Untold Story*. Bombay: Allied Publishers, 1967.

Krishnan, Ananth: *India's China Challenge*. HarperCollins, 2020.

MacFarquhar, Roderick: *The Politics of China*, Second Edition. Cambridge University Press, 1997.

_____, *Origins of the Cultural Revolution*. Oxford University Press, 1997.

Mankekar, D.R.: *The Guilty Men of 1962*. Bombay: The Tulsi Shah Enterprises, 1968, Penguin Edition, 1998.

Maxwell, Neville: *India's China War*. New York: Pantheon Books, 1970.

Panikkar, K.M: *India and China: A Study of Cultural Relations*. Bombay: Asia Publishing House, 1957.

_____, *Two Chinas: Memoirs of a Diplomat*. London: George Allen and Urwin, 1955.

People's Republic of China: *Concerning the Question of Tibet*. Peking: Foreign Language Press, 1959.

_____, *The Sino-Indian Border Question*. Peking: Foreign Language Press, 1962.

Ranganathan, C.V. and Vinod Khanna: *India and China: The Way Ahead*. New Delhi: Haranand Publications, 2000.

Swamy, Subramanian: *India's China Strategic Perspectives*. New Delhi: Haranand Publications, 2019.

Wang, Jia Nei and Nyima Gyain Cain: *The Historical Status of China's Tibet*. Beijing: China Intercontinental Press, 1997.

PAPERS:

Acharya, Alka: 'Prelude to the Sino-Indian War: Aspects of Decision-Making Processes during 1959–62,' China Report, Vol. 32, No. 4, October–December 1996, pp. 363–93.

Bakshi, Z.C.: 'Sino-Indian Relations in the 1992s,' USI Journal, Vol. 122, No. 510, October–December 1992, pp. 450–55.

China Pictorial Magazine, No. 95, July, 1958, pp. 20–21.

Fischer, Margaret W. and Leo E. Rose, 'Ladakh and the Sino-Indian Border Crisis,' *Asian Survey*, Vol. 2, February 1962, pp. 27–37.

Foot, Rosemary, 'Chinese-Indian Relations and the Process of Building Confidence: Implications for the Asia-Pacific,' *Pacific Review*, Vol. 9, No. 1, 1996, pp. 58–76.

_____, 'Sino-Indian Rapprochement and the Sino-Pakistan Entente,' *Political Science Quarterly*, Vol. 111, No. 2, 1996, pp. 322–47.

Horn, Robert C: 'Soviet Union and Sino-Indian Relations,' *Orbis*, Vol. 26, No. 4, Winter 1983, pp. 47–59.

MacFarquhar, Roderick: 'The Last Red Bastion,' in Pande, Ira (ed.): *India China*, HarperCollins & India International Centre, New Delhi, 2010.

Maxwell, Neville: 'India's Forward Policy,' *The China Quarterly*, No. 45, January–March, 1971, pp. 157–58.

_____, 'The Sino-India Border Dispute Reconsidered,' *Economic and Political Weekly*, April 10, 1999 p. 905.

_____, 'China and India: The Unnegotiated Dispute,' *The China Quarterly*, No. 43, July-September, 1970, pp. 47–80.

Shih, Hu: *The Indianization of China: A Case Study in Cultural Borrowing, Independence, Convergence and Borrowing*, Harvard University Tercentenary Publications, Cambridge, Mass., 1937, p. 247.

Swamy, Subramanian: 'Predictions and Meditations,' in Pande, Ira (ed.): *India China*, HarperCollins & India International Centre, New Delhi, 2010.

_____, 'Economic Distance Between China and India, 1955-73,' *The China Quarterly*, Vol. 70, June 1977, pp. 371–83.

Wang, Shaoguang, 'Estimating China's Defence Expenditure,' *The China Quarterly*, 1996.

Appendix I

HOME MINISTER VALLABHBHAI PATEL'S NOTE TO THE PRIME MINISTER

7 November 1950
New Delhi

My dear Jawaharlal,

1. Ever since my return from Ahmedabad and after the Cabinet meeting the same day which I had to attend at practically 15 minutes' notice and for which I regret I was not able to read all the papers, I have been anxiously thinking over the problem of Tibet and I thought I should share with you what is passing through my mind.
2. I have carefully gone through the correspondence between the External Affairs Ministry and our ambassador in Peking and through him the Chinese Government. I have tried to peruse this correspondence as favorably to our Ambassador and the Chinese Government as possible, but I regret to say that neither of them comes out well as a result of this study. The Chinese Government have tried to delude us by professions of peaceful intentions. My own feeling is that at

crucial period they managed to instill into our Ambassador a false sense of confidence in their so-called desire to settle the Tibetan problem by peaceful means. There can be no doubt that during the period covered by this correspondence the Chinese must have been concentrating for an onslaught on Tibet. The final action of the Chinese, in my judgment, is little short of perfidy. The tragedy of it is that the Tibetans put faith in us; they chose to be guided by us and we have been unable to get them out of the meshes of Chinese diplomacy or malevolence. From the latest position, it appears that we shall not be able to rescue the Dalai Lama. Our Ambassador had been at great pains to find an explanation or justification for Chinese policy and actions. As the External Affairs Ministry remarked in one of their telegrams, there was a lack of firmness and unnecessary apology in one or two representations that he made to the Chinese Government on our behalf. It is impossible to imagine any sensible person believing in the so-called threat to China from Anglo-American mechanization in Tibet. Therefore, if the Chinese put faith in this, they must have distrusted us so completely as to have taken us as tools or stooges of Anglo-American diplomacy or strategy. This feeling, if genuinely entertained by the Chinese in spite of your direct approach to them, indicates that even though we regard ourselves as friends of China the Chinese do not regard us their friends. With the Communist mentality of "whoever is not with them being against them", this is a significant pointer, of which we have to take due note. During the last several months, outside the Russian camp, we have practically been alone in championing the cause of Chinese entry into the UNO and in securing from the American assurances on the Formosa (now Taiwan) question. We have done everything we could to assuage Chinese feelings, to allay its apprehensions and to defend its legitimate claims in our discussions and correspondence with America and Britain and in the UNO. In spite of this, China is not concerned about our disinterestedness; it continued to regard us with suspicion and the whole psychology is one, at least outwardly, of skepticism, perhaps mixed with a little hostility. I doubt if we can go any further than we have done already to convince China of our good intentions, friendliness and goodwill. In Beijing we have an Ambassador who is eminently suitable for putting across the friendly point of view. Even he seems to have failed to convert the Chinese. Their last telegram to us is an act of gross discourtesy not only in the summary way it disposes of our protest against the entry of Chinese forces into Tibet but also in the wild insinuation that our attitude is determined by foreign influences. It looks as though it is not a friend speaking in that language but a potential enemy.

3. In the background of this, we have to consider what new situation now faces us as a result of the disappearance of Tibet, as we know it, and the expansion of China almost up to our gates. Throughout history we have seldom been worried about our north-east frontier. The Himalayas have been regarded as an impenetrable barrier against any threat from the north. We had a friendly Tibet which gave us no trouble. The Chinese were divided. They had their own domestic problems and never bothered us about our frontiers. In 1914, we entered into a convention with Tibet which was not endorsed by the Chinese. We seem to have regarded Tibetan autonomy as extending to independent treaty relationship. Presumably, all that we required was Chinese counter-signature. The Chinese interpretation of suzerainty seems to be different. We can,

therefore, safely assume that very soon they will disown all the stipulations which Tibet has entered into with us in the past. That throws into the melting pot all frontier and commercial settlements with Tibet on which we have been functioning and acting during the last half a century. China is no longer divided. It is united and strong. All along the Himalayas in the north and north-east, we have on our side of the frontier a population ethnologically and culturally no different from Tibetans or Mongoloids. The undefined state of the frontier and the existence on our side of a population with its affinities to Tibetans or Chinese have all the elements of potential trouble between China and ourselves. Recent and bitter history also tell us that Communism is no shield against imperialism and that the Communists are as good or as bad imperialists as any other.

Chinese ambitions in this respect not only cover the Himalayan slopes on our side but also include important parts of Assam. They have their ambitions in Burma also. Burma has the added difficulty that it has no McMahon Line round which to build up even the semblance of an agreement. Chinese irredentism and Communist imperialism are different from the expansionism or imperialism of the Western Powers. The former has a cloak of ideology which makes it ten times more dangerous. In the guise of ideological expansion lie concealed racial, national or historical claims. The danger from the north and north-east, therefore, becomes both communist and imperialists. While our western and north-western threat to security is still as prominent as before, a new threat has developed from the north and north-east. Thus, for the first time, after centuries, India's defense has to concentrate itself on two fronts simultaneously. Our defence measures have so far been based on the calculations of a superiority over Pakistan. In our calculations we shall now have to reckon with Communist China in the north and in the north-east, a Communist China which has definite ambitions and aims and which does not, in any way, seer friendly disposed towards us.

4. Let us also consider the political conditions on those potentially troublesome frontier. Our northern or north-eastern approaches consist of Nepal, Bhutan, Sikkim, the Darjeeling (area) and tribal areas in Assam. From the point of view of communications, they are weak spots. Continuous defensive lines do not exist. There is almost an unlimited scope for infiltration. Police protection is limited to a very small number of passes. There, too, our outposts do not seem to be fully manned. The contact of these areas with us is by no means close and intimate. The people inhabiting these portions have no established loyalty or devotion to India. Even the Darjeeling and Kalimpong areas are not free from pro-Mongoloid prejudices. During the last three years we have not been able to make any appreciable approaches to the Nagas and other hill tribes in Assam. European missionaries and other visitors had been in touch with them. But their influence was in no way friendly to India or Indians. In Sikkim, there was political ferment some time ago. It is quite possible that discontent is smoldering there. Bhutan is comparatively quiet, but its affinity with Tibetans would be a handicap. Nepal has a weak oligarchic regime based almost entirely on force; it is in conflict with a turbulent element of the population as well as with enlightened ideas of the modern age. In these circumstances, to make people alive to the new danger or to make them defensively strong is a very difficult task indeed and that difficulty can be got over only by enlightened firmness, strength and a clear line of policy. I

am sure the Chinese and their sources of inspiration, Soviet Russia, would not miss any opportunity of exploiting these weak spots, partly in support of their ideology and partly in support of their ambitions. In my judgment, therefore, the situation is one in which we cannot afford either to be complacent or to be vacillating. We must have a clear idea of what we wish to achieve and also of the methods by which we should achieve it. Any faltering or lack of decisiveness in formulating our objectives or in pursuing our policy to attain those objectives is bound to weaken us and increase the threats which are so evident.

5. Side by side with these external dangers, we shall now have to face serious internal problems as well. I have already asked (H.V.R.) Iyengar to send to the E.A. Ministry a copy of the Intelligence Bureau's appreciation of these matters. Hitherto, the Communist Party of India had found some difficulty in contacting Communists abroad, or in getting supplies of arms, literature, etc. from them. They had to contend with the difficult Burmese and Pakistan frontiers on the east or with the long seaboard. They shall now have a comparatively easy means of access to Chinese Communists and through them to other foreign Communists. Infiltration of spies, fifth columnists and Communists would now be easier. Instead of having to deal with isolated Communist pockets in Telengana and Warangal we may have to deal with Communist arsenals in China. The whole situation thus raises a number of problems on which we must come to an early decision so that we can, as I said earlier, formulate the objectives of our policy and decide the methods by which those objectives are to be attained. It is also clear that action will have to be fairly comprehensive, involving not only our defense strategy and

state of preparations but also problems of internal security to deal with administrative and political problems in the weak spots along the frontier to which I have already referred.

6. It is, of course, impossible for me to be exhaustive in setting out all these problems. I am, however, giving below some of the problems which, in my opinion, require early solution and round which we have to build our administrative or military policies and measures to implement them:

(a) A military and intelligence appreciation of the Chinese threat to India both on the frontier and to internal security.

(b) An examination of our military position and such predisposition of our forces as might be necessary, particularly with the idea of guarding important routes or areas which are likely to be the subject of dispute.

(c) An appraisement of the strength of our forces and, if necessary, reconsideration of our retrenchment plans for the Army in the light of these new threats.

(d) A long-term consideration of our defence needs. My own feeling is that, unless we assure our supplies of arms, ammunition and amours, we should be making our defence position perpetually weak and we would not be able to stand up to the double threat of difficulties both from the west and north-west and north and north-east.

(e) The question of Chinese entry into UNO. In view of the rebuff which China has given us and the method which it has followed in dealing with Tibet, I am doubtful whether we can advocate its claims any longer. There would probably be a threat in the UNO virtually to outlaw China in view of its active participation in the Korean War. We must determine our attitude on this question also.

(f) The political and administrative steps which we should take to strengthen our northern and north eastern frontiers. This would include the whole of the border, i.e. Nepal, Bhutan, Sikkim, Darjeeling and the tribal territory in Assam.

(g) Measures of internal security in the border areas as well as the states flanking those areas, such as UP, Bihar, Bengal and Assam.

(h) Improvement of our communications, road, rail, air and wireless, in these areas and with the frontier outposts.

(i) Policing and intelligence of frontier posts.

(j) The future of our mission at Lhasa and the trade posts at Gyantse and Yatung and the forces which we have in operation in Tibet to guard the trade routes.

(k) The policy in regard to the McMahon Line.

7. These are some of the questions which occur to my mind. It is possible that a consideration of these matters may lead us into wider questions of our relationship with China, Russia, America, Britain and Burma, This, however, would be of a general nature, though some might be basically very important, e.g., we might have to consider whether we should not enter into closer association with Burma in order to strengthen the latter in its dealings with China. I do not rule out the possibility that, before applying pressure on us, China might apply pressure on Burma. With Burma, the frontier is entirely undefined and the Chinese territorial claims are more substantial. In its present position, Burma might offer an easier problem for China and, therefore, right claim its attention.

8. I suggest that we meet early to have a general discussion on these problems and decide on such steps as we might think to be immediately necessary and direct quick examination of

other problems with a view to taking early measures to deal with them.

Yours,
Vallabhbhai Patel

The Hon'ble Shri Jawaharlal Nehru
New Delhi

(*Source:* Dr S. Gopal [ed.], Sardar Patel's Correspondence, pp. 335–41)

Appendix II

PRIME MINISTER JAWAHARLAL NEHRU'S NOTE ON CHINA AND TIBET

18 November 1950

(The Note was obviously forwarded to Sardar Patel as it answered indirectly some of the matters raised in Patel's letter of 7 November 1950)

1. The Chinese Government having replied to our last note, we have to consider what further steps we should take in this matter. There [is] no immediate hurry about sending a reply to the Chinese Government. But we have to send immediate instructions to Shri B.N. Rau as to what he should do in the event of Tibet's appeal brought up before the Security Council or the Central Assembly.
2. The content of the Chinese reply is much the same as their previous notes, but there does not appear to be a toning down and an attempt at some kind of a friendly approach.
3. It is interesting to note that they have not referred specifically to our mission [at] Lhasa or to our trade agents or military

escort at Gyantse etc. We had mentioned these especially in our last note. There is an indirect reference, however, in China's note. At the end, this note says that "As long as our two sides adhere strictly to the principle of mutual respect for territory, sovereignty, equality and mutual benefit, we are convinced that the friendship between China and India should be developed in a normal way and that problems relating to Sino-Indian diplomatic, commercial and cultural relations with respect to Tibet and to our trade agent and others in Tibet may be resolved. We had expected a demand from them for the withdrawal of these agents etc. The fact that they have not done so has some significance.

4. Stress is laid in China's note on Chinese sovereignty over Tibet, which we are reminded, we have acknowledged, on Tibet being an integral part of China's territory and therefore a domestic problem. It is however, again repeated that outside influences have been at play obstructing China's mission in Tibet. In fact, it is stated that liberation of Changtu proves that foreign force and influences were inciting Tibetan troops to resist. It is again repeated that no foreign intervention will be permitted and that the Chinese army will proceed.

5. All this is much the same as has been said before, but it is said in a somewhat different way and there are repeated references in the note to China desiring the friendship of India.

6. It is true that in one of our messages to the Chinese government we used "sovereignty" of China in relation to Tibet. In our last message we used the word "suzerainty". After receipt of the China's last note, we have pointed out to our Ambassador that "suzerainty" was the right word and that "sovereignty" had been used by error.

7. It is easy to draft a reply to the Chinese note, pressing our

viewpoints and countering some of the arguments raised in the Chinese note. But before we do so we should be clear in our own minds as to what we are aiming at, not only in the immediate future but from a long-term view. It is important that we keep both these viewpoints before us. In all probability China, that is present-day China, is going to be our close neighbour for a long time to come. We are going to have a tremendously long common frontier. It is unlikely, and it would be unwise to expect, that the present Chinese government will collapse giving place to another. Therefore, it is important to pursue a policy which will be in keeping with this long-term view.

8. I think it may be taken for granted that China will take possession, in a political sense at least, of the whole of Tibet. There is no likelihood whatever of Tibet being able to resist this or stop it. It is equally unlikely that any foreign power can prevent it. We cannot do so. If so, what can we do to help in the maintenance of Tibetan autonomy and at the same time avoiding continuous tension and apprehension on our frontiers?

9. The Chinese note has repeated that they with the Tibetan people have what they call "regional autonomy and religious freedom". This autonomy can obviously not be anything like the autonomy verging on independence which Tibet has enjoyed during the last forty years or so. But it is reasonable to assume from the very nature of Tibetan geography, terrain and climate, that a large measure of autonomy is almost inevitable. It may of course be that this autonomous Tibet is controlled by communist elements in Tibet. I imagine however that it is, on the whole, more likely that what will be attempted will be a pre-communist China administration rather than a communist one.

10. If world war comes, then all kinds of difficult and intricate problems arise and each one of these problems will be inter-related with others. Even the question of defence of India assumes a different shape and cannot be isolated from other world factors. I think that is exceedingly unlikely that we may have to face any real military invasion from the Chinese side, whether in peace or in war, in the foreseeable future. I base this conclusion on a consideration of various world factors. In peace, such an invasion would undoubtedly lead to world war. China, though internally big, is in a way amorphous and easily capable of being attacked on its sea [coasts] and by air. In such a war, China would have its main front in South and East and it will be fighting for its very existence against powerful enemies. It is inconceivable that it should divert its forces and its strength across the inhospitable terrain of Tibet and undertake a wild adventure across the Himalayas. Any such attempt will greatly weaken its capacity to meet its real enemies on other fronts. Thus I rule out any major attack on India by China. I think these considerations should be borne in mind, because there is far too much loose talk about China attacking and overriding India. If we lose our sense of perspective and world strategy and give way to unreasoning fears then any policy that we might have is likely to fail.
11. While there is, in any opinion, practically no chance of a major attack on India by China, there are certainly chances of gradual infiltration across our border and possibly of entering and taking possession of disputed territory, if there is no obstruction to this happening. We must therefore take all necessary precautions to prevent this. But again, we must differentiate between these precautions and those that might be necessary to meet a real attack.
12. If we really feared an attack and had to make full provision for

it, this would cast an intolerable burden on us, financial and otherwise, and it would weaken our general defence position. There are limits beyond which we cannot go, at least for some years, and a spreading out of our army on distant frontiers would be bad from every military or strategic point of view.

13. In spite of our desire to settle the points at issue between us and Pakistan, and developing peaceful relations with it, the fact remains that our major possible enemy is Pakistan. This has compelled us to think of our defence mainly in terms of Pakistan's aggression. If we begin to think of, and prepare for China's aggression in the same way, we would weaken considerably on the Pakistan side. We might well be got in a pincer movement. It is interesting to note that Pakistan is taking a great deal of interest, from this point of view, in developments in Tibet. Indeed it has been discussed in the Pakistan Press that the new danger from Tibet to India might help them to settle the Kashmir problem according to their wishes. Pakistan has absolutely nothing in common with China or Tibet. But if we fall out completely with China, Pakistan will undoubtedly try to take advantage of this, politically or otherwise. The position of India thus will be bad from a defence point of view. We cannot have all the time two possible enemies on either side of India. This danger will not be over, even if we increase our defence forces or even if other foreign countries help us in arming. The measures of safety that one gets by increasing the defence apparatus is limited by many factors. But whatever that measures of safety might be, strategically we would be in an unsound position and the burden of this will be very great on us. As it is, we are facing enormous difficulties, financial, economic etc.

14. The idea that communism inevitably means expansion and war, or to put it more precisely, that Chinese communism

means inevitably an expansion towards India, is rather naive. It may mean that in certain circumstances. Those circumstances would depend upon many factors, which I need not go into here. The danger really is not from military invasion but from infiltration of men and ideas. The ideas are there already and can only be countered by other ideas. Communism is an important element in the situation. But, by our attaching [too] great importance to it in this context, we are likely to misjudge the situation from other and more important angles.

15. In a long-term view, India and China are two of the biggest countries of Asia bordering on each other and both with certain expansive tendencies, because of their vitality. If their relations are bad, this will have a serious effect not only on both of them but on Asia as a whole. It would affect our future for a long time. If a position arises in which China and India are inveterately hostile to each other, like France and Germany, then there will be repeated wars bringing destruction to both. The advantage will go to other countries. It is interesting to note that both the UK and the USA appear to be anxious to add to the unfriendliness of India and China towards each other. It is also interesting to find that USSR does not view with favour any friendly relations between India and China. These are long-term reactions which one can fully understand, because India and China, [at] peace with each other, would make a vast difference to the whole set-up and balance of the world. Much, of course, depends upon the development of either country and how far communism in China will mould the Chinese people. Even so, these processes are long-range ones and in the long run it is fairly safe to assume that hundreds of millions of people will not change their essential characteristics.

16. These arguments lead to the conclusion that while we should

be prepared, to the best of our ability, for all contingencies, the real protection that we should seek is some kind of understanding of China. If we have not got that, then both our present and our future are imperilled and no distant power can save us. I think on the whole that China desires this too for obvious reasons. If this is so then we should fashion our present policy accordingly.

17. We cannot save Tibet, as we should have liked to do and our very attempts to save it might well bring greater trouble to it. It would be unfair to Tibet for us to bring this trouble upon her without having the capacity to help her effectively. It may be possible however that we might be able to help Tibet to retain a large measure of her autonomy. That would be good for Tibet and good for India. As far as I can see, this can only be done on the diplomatic level and by avoidance of making the present tension between India and China worse.

18. When then should be our instructions to B.N. Rau? From the messages he has sent us, it appears that no member of the Security Council shows any inclination to sponsor Tibet's appeal and that there is a little likelihood of the matter being considered by the Council. We have said that (we) are not going to sponsor this appeal, but if it comes up we shall state our viewpoint. This viewpoint cannot be one of full support [to] the Tibetan appeal, because that goes far and claims full independence. We may say that whatever might have been acknowledged in the past about China's sovereignty or suzerainty, recent events have deprived China of the right to claim that. There may be some moral basis for this argument. But it will not take us or Tibet very far. It will only hasten the downfall of Tibet. No outsiders will be able to help her and China, suspicious and apprehensive of these tactics, will make sure of much speedier and fuller possession of Tibet

than she might otherwise have done. We shall thus not only fail in our endeavour but at the same time have really hostile China on our doorstep.

19. I think that in no event should we sponsor Tibet's appeal. I would personally think that it would be a good thing if that appeal is not heard in the Security Council of the General Assembly. If it is considered there, there is bound to be a great deal of bitter speaking and accusation, which will worsen the situation as regards Tibet as well as the possibility of widespread war, without helping it in the least. It must be remembered that neither the UK nor the USA, nor indeed any other power is particularly interested in Tibet or the future of that country. What they are interested in is embarrassing China. Our interest, on the other hand, is Tibet, and if we cannot serve that interest, we fail.

20. Therefore, it will be better not to discuss Tibet's appeal in the UN. Suppose, however, that it comes up for discussion, in spite of our not wishing this, what then? I would suggest that our representative should state our case as moderately as possible and ask the Security Council or the Assembly to give expression to their desire that the Sino-Tibetan question should be settled peacefully and that Tibet's autonomy should be respected and maintained. Any particular reference to an article of the charter of the UN might tie us up in the difficulties and lead to certain consequences later, which may prove highly embarrassing for us. Or a resolution of the UN might just be a dead letter, which also will be bad.

21. If my general argument is approved, then we can frame our reply to China's note accordingly.

J. Nehru
18 November 1950

(*Source*: Dr S. Gopal, Sardar Patel's Correspondence, pp. 342–47)

Appendix III

'WE FACE COMMON PROBLEMS': DENG XIAOPING IN A MEETING WITH DR SUBRAMANIAN SWAMY IN BEIJING ON 8 APRIL 1981 (AS PUBLISHED IN *INDIA TODAY*)

Dr Subramanian Swamy, 41, the Janata Party MP, was back in the head-line-grabbing business following his historic 100-minute interview with Chinese strongman Deng Xiaoping in Beijing's Great Hall of the People. Deng is vice-chairman of the Communist Party of China and currently the most powerful man in Beijing. His remarks on improving Sino-Indian relations are the first such high-level statements since the diplomatic freeze between the two countries following India's recognition of the Heng Samrin regime in Kampuchea last year.

China, for Swamy, has been familiar ground. This was his third visit to China since 1978 and though he was not an official emissary of the Government, the presence of the India ambassador in Beijing, S.K. Bajpai, at the interview, elevated the meeting to an inter-governmental communication.

Swamy agreed to give *India Today* exclusive rights to the full transcript of his meeting with Deng, which is reproduced below.

Swamy: It is great honour for me to meet a great leader of China. I have been your admirer for 15 years.

Deng: Well, this year you are 41. You are in the prime of life. Me, I am already very old.

Swamy: You look very young. It is like my party's former prime minister Morarji Desai. He is 85 but acts younger than I.

Deng: I have never met Mr Morarji Desai but I would like you to give him my regards.

Swamy: Thank you. Excellency, in the last few years there has been a good development of our relations but we are countries with such a long history, and with so much that need our cooperation, it pains me if we do not have the greatest of friendship. I hope that we can develop this much more.

Deng: Yes, we are two big countries. We have had over 2,000 years of good relations and we should have more friendship and cooperation. We have both had great civilisations. We have also had common misfortunes. India was a colonial country and we were semi-colonial. Now we are the two biggest countries in the world. If our two populations were put together it could come to more than one-third of the world but when we talk of ourselves as big countries what do we mean?

Really just that we have these big populations. We are also poor countries. We face common problems. India is a Third World country, so is China. It is necessary for us to work together. In the early '50s we had very close friendship. Premier Chou En-lai visited India and had a very good visit. Later on Prime Minister Mr Nehru came to China. Then in the late '50s problems developed between us. We had this long period of strain. After that we started to normalise relations.

Actually, what do we mean by this word normalisation? We already have ambassadors in both countries so in that sense relations are normal. However, if we mean that we should have more friendship then certainly that is correct. There is no reason why we should not improve our relations and no reason why we should not have more exchanges between us. This has always been my view. Even when I went to Nepal I said so and in fact there was some positive response from your side to my statement. Even earlier the late Chairman Mao Zedong was of the same view. I recall that he spoke to your charge d' affaires and then we started trying to improve our relations. Your foreign Minister paid us a visit. There have been all these twists and turns in our relations. We even had to postpone the visit of our Foreign Minister Huang Hua. However, it is necessary to work for better relations and we have decided that Huang Hua will visit India soon.

Swamy: I am very glad to hear that Foreign Minister Huang Hua will be visiting us soon. You may be sure he will be given a warm welcome. Actually, the people of India have very warm feelings for China and visitors from China are made welcome. Even the groups we just had [had] some acrobats who were very well received and you will find that your foreign minister will have nothing but affection from the people of India. They will give him good reception as I am sure the Government of India also will.

Deng: Your Prime Minister Mrs Gandhi was good enough to receive our acrobats. Please thank her for this.

Swamy: Certainly. But you know, Excellency, this has been said before the Xinhua commentary of last June made the point that the only real outstanding problem between us is the border question. Once that is solved then all questions between us can go and we can really develop our relations into the best of friendship. What is your view on this border issue, how can we solve it?

Deng: Our position on this is very clear. Not only our newspapers but that is the position of the Government that if we both approach the problem with understanding there will be no difficulty in reaching a solution through repeated discussions. There is my own proposal for a package deal. Until that can be settled let us develop contacts in other fields. Then there is this question of threat. Some people talk of threat in India, that there is a threat from China and in China that there is a threat from India. How can there be any threat? There is the whole Tibetan Plateau between us. There is very little oxygen and it is not even possible to deploy a large number of troops. From the beginning of the People's Republic of China (PRC) we have hardly any troops near you. We can never be a threat to you nor do we think you are a threat to us. Actually, we are told that you have many [more] troops on your side of the border than we have on ours but that does not make you a threat.

Even if you were to take part of Tibet, that would not be a threat to China. It is not India by itself that could be a threat. What we consider a danger is that some other force may take a land there. The real threat is from the North. There are a million troops deployed there. Moreover, the Soviet Union is instigating Vietnam to make it a threat from the South.

Swamy: I entirely agree with you but you know there is one problem—people in India wonder you know in all the years after our crisis, [inspite] of our differences India never changed its position: whether on your admission to the United Nations, whether on Taiwan question, whether on Tibet, the Indian position was to support you completely but on your side, statements used to be made—all sorts of things are said and our public wonders about your wanting to be friends, so some sort of gesture would be useful. On Sikkim for instance why can't you accept that it is part of India? As to the way it happened, our former prime minister, Mr Morarji Desai has said he did like the way it was done but he also made it clear these things are irreversible.

India is a merger of states and once merged nothing can be done. I ask because your maps show it separate and so questions are asked by people in India that you do not want our relations to improve. The Soviet lobby is very active every day. The Soviet Union has it in papers that we should not trust you, that you are [too] clever and will fool us. There are so many planted stories, So if you do not recognise the position on Sikkim, there are many people who take advantage of this whereas if you were to recognise it, it would [be] a [good] gesture of your intentions and it would help people like me who want to advocate friendship with China.

Deng: On Sikkim our position is very clear. We made [an] official statement at the time of annexation that we could not accept annexation. We disapprove because it is contrary both to international norms and to morality. We will not change our position on this. Indeed, there is no reason why we should change our position. We can never approve of the annexation. However, we have also said that we will not mention or make use of the subject when discussing Sino-Indian relation. Actually, I told this both to a journalist [from] India and to your Foreign Secretary, Mr Gonsalves, when he came here. I repeat again, we will not mention or make use of this subject in discussing the improvement of Sino-Indian relations.

It is important that we improve our bilateral relations. We have to take note of the situation in the world and act in the larger context.

Swamy: I believe that when President Zia-ul-Haq of Pakistan was here last year, [he] had said to you that he would like to improve relations with India. Actually, there was some progress. Our ambassador here used to be ambassador in Pakistan and I know he did a very good job, it is very necessary for us to have good relations with Pakistan. Lately there have been some hold ups. I mention our Sino-Indian bilateral relations because of the importance I attach to friendship but I agree with you that it is not only our bilateral relations, [it] is our relations with neighbours and the position of China and India in the subcontinent and in Asia as a whole that are important. I wonder if you could comment on how we could bring about better relations in the subcontinent and what China could do in the context.

Deng: It is certainly very important that you improve your relations with your neighbours. They worry about you. It is not only Pakistan, there is Nepal, there is Bangladesh, even Sri Lanka. We know these countries. We have contact with them and we hear their views about you and their relations with you. There is Bhutan also. We do not know very much about Bhutan but generally, where your neighbours are concerned you are so big and they are so small. Actually in the subcontinent you are the big brother. The big brother has to show more understanding of the smaller.

Swamy: I agree with you entirely that you know these neighbours. When you have a smaller neighbour there are problems. You have neighbour Vietnam which is very afraid of you. Would you tell me how you think you could improve relations with Vietnam?

Deng: As regards Vietnam I do not think you are well informed. We could not understand their attitude towards us. Look at it from the very beginning, China had excellent relations. We helped them all along, first in their struggle against the colonial masters

France, then during their war with America. We were a poor country—we are a poor country—but we tighten[ed] our belts and gave them everything we could, even if we had to help. We could not understand why they turned against us. Soviet Union has instigated them. They are an ungrateful nation.

When Cambodia was having to fight its war against imperialists we also have had to help Cambodia. We have no common border with Cambodia. Everything we sent had to go through Vietnam, then we found they were taking it themselves. Nothing that we sent reached Cambodia. The greedy Vietnamese were keeping it all even though that meant denying help to our friends in Cambodia. The Russians have been at work and the leadership in Vietnam has been instigated by Russians to be a threat to us. We were very patient but everyday there were provocations. Finally, we decided we had to teach them a lesson. I said this when I was in America. Mr Carter did not like it. He did not approve but we said it had to be done. We have no enmity against Vietnam but when they behaved like that, it was necessary to teach them a lesson, so we sent our forces and after we have taught them a lesson that they could not behave like that, then we withdrew our forces.

Actually on this there was a lot of questioning because it happened when your foreign minister was here and you all said why you not told us in advance. The fact is we forgot about it. We had been saying it for so many months, we thought everybody knew. There was no secret. We had said so many times. I can assure you there was no intention on our part to do it while your foreign minister was here. It just happened but we had no aggressive intentions towards Vietnam. We would like friendship but they did not allow it.

Swamy: In regard to the international situation, would you say that the danger of war has increased? The situation in Poland is very worrying. The Soviet Union has already moved into Afghanistan and there is this danger now in Poland. You used to say that another world is inevitable but do you think the danger had increased?

Deng: Certainly there is great danger but we do not think it necessary to say that it is immediate and that it does not have to happen now. However, if it is to be delayed we have to be vigilant. The first two world wars started over small things. Whether it is Afghanistan, whether it is Poland we have to be vigilant, whether these are beginnings of other thing.

Swamy: Thank you. You are a very busy man. You have very important responsibilities but I would like to just ask three more questions. First, your relations with the United States. How do you view them?

Deng: With the United States there is no reason, from the beginning, why we should not be friends except Taiwan and their two China theory. If they do this, it will not only put an end to progress in Sino-US relations, it would be retrogression. We have made this clear to the Americans. We have spoken to them many times and said that we would like to be friends but this is one matter which we cannot stand. They have assured us that they have no such intention. They too have talked to us. We have said what about Reagan's campaign speeches? They have said his campaign speeches were only for the campaign and that is now over. However, we must remember the Reagan Administration is less than three months in office and we should wait and see whether its foreign policy stabilises.

Swamy: What about Sino-USSR relations? You said that the danger is from the North and I agree with you but do you see any possibility of your improving relations with the Russians?

Deng: As for improving relations with the USSR, there is nothing in the way if the USSR gives up hegemonies. That is what has caused the problem with us and with other countries. We could be friends easily if they were to give up their hegemonies but is it possible to imagine that? Their policy is that of the Czars. Actually, that was the problem. We wanted to improve relations and we started having talks with them but then they moved into Afghanistan and we had to break off the talks. They behave as expansionists. They have been instigating Vietnam as I have already told you. Then there is their action in Afghanistan. You know this is an attempt to get to the Indian Ocean. Actually, this is a matter for you to worry about, the Russians always tried to use others, even the war between China and India. Khrushchev visited India in 1959 and what developed from that. It is Soviet hegemonies that is the danger and it is for your country to consider it also.

Swamy: I again agree entirely with you, but to change to another subject. You have lately been laying stress, you have moved away from [the] earlier emphasis on heavy industry and have been stressing the need to develop light industry and provide more consumer good for your people. There is this readjustment going on. Is this a permanent shift in your economic strategy or is this emphasis on light industry only for a short period?

Deng: This is while we complete our readjustment. The fact is that we have made mistakes from the beginning and we find we have gone wrong because we started the wrong way. We now have to start again and we find we have made other mistakes. So it is necessary for us to look carefully and [make] the necessary readjustments but our present approach is [for] this period of readjustment.

Swamy: One last question. Excellency, you are good enough to note that I am still young. I would like to develop my political career and serve my people in the years to come. You have done so much, as I said. I have been your admirer [for] the last 15 years. Is there any advice you would give me?

Deng: The only thing that I can say is that I have always been an optimist. Even when things were going wrong I have remained an optimist and have always been right. When I look back I think one should be calm and never give up. I remain an optimist also about [our] relations.

Swamy: Thank you, I must remember that.

Deng: (starting to get up) Thank you for your visit.

Bajpai: Excuse me. I do not wish to delay you, Mr Vice-Chairman, [but] I would like to say a few words.

Deng: Please.

Bajpai: I did not wish to intervene before because this is Dr Swamy's day. It is his call on you and [I] am here by courtesy. Actually, I have just returned from Delhi and I have already spoken to your Foreign Office that I had an opportunity to talk with my leaders and in the light of my discussions I hope to call on the leaders here in due course. I hope that someday soon I can call on your Excellency and perhaps I can then discuss some of these matters more fully. At the moment I would not go into details but I am bound to say that on a number of formulations the Government of India would agree with either of you—your Excellency or Dr Swamy—whether it is what you said about Sikkim or when you referred to an unfortunate period of our relations with you and to our being egged on by Mr Khruschev.

I have been most encouraged by many of your remarks and by your basic approach that you would like to see further improvement of relations with India. That is also the policy of the Government of India and we would like to see further improvement of relations with China but if you are going to have misconceptions about us—if for example you assume that India [can] be instigated in a particular policy by another country then I am afraid the task of improving relations becomes very much more difficult. I think we have both to realise that we are each sovereign independent countries and just as you take your decisions on the basis of your own judgement and analysts, India also decides for itself. If misconceptions to the contrary persist then as I say it becomes much more difficult to improve relations. If however, we respect each other's independence of judgement and action then I am sure the Government of India would share the optimism you have expressed just as we share the desire for improvement of relations.

Deng: That is all right, does not matter if we do not agree on some points.

India Today
1–15 May 1981

Appendix IV

INDIA'S VOTING RECORD ON ISSUES RELATING TO CHINA IN THE UNITED NATIONS

	'50	'51	'52	'53	'54	'55	'56	'57	'58	'59	'60	'61	'62	'63	'64	'65	'66	'67	'68	'69	'70	'71
1. Resolution regarding the seat of China in United Nations	F																					
2. China as an aggressor in Korea (1951)		A																				
3. 'Moratorium' Resolution		A	A	A	A	A	A	A	A	A	A	A										
4. Request for including China's question for discussion in agenda							F	F	F	F	AB	AB	AB	AB	AB	AB	AB	AB	AB	AB	AB	AB
5. Resolutions regarding 'genocide' in Tibet (1959–66)											AB		AB				F					
6. China's membership an important question or not (1961–70)													A	A	A	A	A	A	A	A	A	A
7. Resolution regarding China's replacement of Taiwan (1961–70)													F	F	F	F	F	F	F	F	F	F

F—Favour, A—Against, AB—Abstained

Appendix V

DECLASSIFIED CIA PAPERS:
THE SINO-INDIAN BORDER DISPUTE*

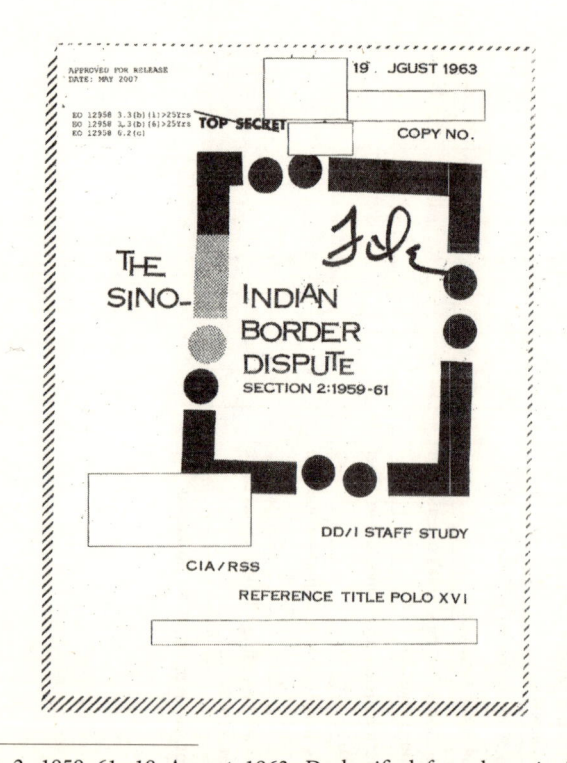

*Section 2, 1959–61, 19 August 1963. Declassified for release in May 2007 (an extract).

~~This document contains classified information affecting the national security of the United States within the meaning of the espionage laws, US Code Title 18, Sections 793, 794 and 798. The law prohibits its transmission or the revelation of its contents in any manner to an unauthorized person, as well as its use in any manner prejudicial to the safety or interest of the United States or for the benefit of any foreign government to the detriment of the United States.~~

It is to be seen only by US personnel especially indoctrinated and authorized to receive [   ] information; its security must be maintained in accordance with [   ] REGULATIONS.

No action is to be taken on any [   ] which may be contained herein, regardless of the advantages to be gained, unless such action is first approved by the Director of Central Intelligence.

~~TOP SECRET~~

Off. Ser. No. 2

THE SINO-INDIAN BORDER DISPUTE
SECTION II. (1959-1961)

This is the second in a series of three working papers on the Sino-Indian border dispute. This Section II deals with the period from late 1959 to early 1961. Section III will cover the remainder of 1961 and most of 1962, through the Chinese attack of 20 October.

Useful comments by P. D. Davis and H. G. Hagerty of OCI have been incorporated. The DDI/RS would welcome comment, addressed either to the Chief or to the writer, Arthur Cohen,

TOP SECRET

SECTION II. (1959-1961)

Summary

By fall 1959 the Chinese leaders were convinced of the need for negotiations with Nehru, in order to prevent their international prestige--including their position in the world Communist movement--from deteriorating. Shortly after the August 1959 clashes they also recognized, or were made aware by Indian party boss Ghosh, that Nehru's advisers might use these skirmishes to push him and the entire government further to the "right"--i.e. towards a militant anti-China policy and a willingness to accept some degree of American support in this policy. The practical strategic danger such a development posed was that the arc of U.S. bases "encircling" China would be extended through India. They continued to see Nehru as still having a "good side" (anti-Western) as well as a "bad side" (anti-Chinese) and therefore as possibly still amenable to persuasion through personal diplomacy on the matter of a border settlement. This meshed well with their new-found concern with preventing the establishment of a military government in New Delhi.

As they moved toward negotiations, however, they took an irrational action which temporarily clouded the atmosphere for talks in New Delhi. The Chinese physically and mentally coerced the leader of a small Indian police party they had captured during a clash in October 1959, in order to secure a "confession" that the Indians had sparked the incident. When it became public knowledge that the Indian prisoner had been manipulated by Maoist methods used in forced confession, popular and official Indian resentment caused a reaction which hurt Peiping more than the charge that Chinese troops had fired first. Having learned the lesson, the Chinese have since made a special point of their "brotherly" concern for Indian prisoners.

By late fall, Chou began to press Nehru hard to begin talks with him. During an exchange of ministerial letters, Nehru raised certain pre-conditions for talks, stipulating on 16 November the requirement that the Chinese withdraw from Longju and that both sides withdraw from the disputed

TOP SECRET

area in Ladakh. In the latter area, Indian troops would withdraw south and west to the line which Peiping claimed on its 1956 maps, and Chinese troops would withdraw north and east of the line claimed by India on its maps. In effect, Nehru's stipulation would be tantamount to a Chinese withdrawal from the Aksai Plain and the Sinkiang-Tibet road, and the Chinese said as much. Chou En-lai's reply of 17 December went right to the point of realpolitik, arguing from actual Chinese possession, complaining that Nehru's concession would be only "theoretical" as India had no personnel there to withdraw, and insisting on the area's importance for "it has been a traffic artery linking up the vast regions of Sinkiang and Tibet." The Indian leaders indicated some sensitivity on Chou's additional point that New Delhi was "utterly unaware" of Chinese roadbuilding in the area until September 1958--"proving" continuous Chinese jurisdiction--and informed their embassies to take the line that intrusions cannot give a neighboring country any legal right to an area "merely because such intrusions were not resisted by us or had not come to our notice earlier." Turning a conciliatory side, Chou in this 17 December letter stated that following the 21 October 1959 clash Peiping had stopped sending out patrols, and he requested a personal meeting with Nehru to establish "principles" for negotiating the dispute. Chou then hinted that Peiping would be willing to exchange its claim to the area south of the McMahon line for New Delhi's claim to the Aksai Plain. Nehru was reluctant to meet personally with Chou, and persisted in this attitude until January 1960, when, on the advice of his ambassadors and certain cabinet members, he agreed to drop his pre-conditions.

In this period, Khrushchev made several public statements in which he deplored the border dispute, clearly implying that Chinese military actions were jeopardizing Moscow's relations with New Delhi. In November, he described the dispute as a "sad and stupid story"--a remark which angered the Chinese leaders--and hinted that he favored a compromise. Soviet officials tried to create the impression among Indian diplomats that Khrushchev had intervened directly with Peiping on New Delhi's behalf, but, when pressed for explicit proof, scaled down their remarks to suggest that the Russians had merely urged talks on Peiping as soon as possible. The Russians, in fact, had no influence with the Chinese leaders. Foreign Secretary Dutt later told an American official that Khrushchev had been no help with the Chinese "at all," remaining just as neutral in private as in public and hoping that these two "friends" of the Soviet Union would settle their dispute. Although the Chinese leaders clearly viewed Khrushchev's public remarks as hostile to them, and Peiping subsequently claimed that Sino-Soviet polemics logically followed the September 1959 TASS statement of neutrality between China and India, the Soviet position on the Sino-Indian dispute in fact remained a peripheral issue in the Sino-Soviet dispute.

In January 1960, the Chinese moved quickly to bring the Burmese to Peiping for a Sino-Burmese border agreement, in order to provide an "example" of how a friendly country should settle its border problems with China. Prior to that time, the Chinese for several years had been parrying Burmese requests for a settlement, but, once the decision to bring Nehru to negotiations had been made (October-November 1959), the Chinese leaders apparently calculated that a speedy border agreement with Prime Minister Ne Win would make it more difficult for Nehru to reject similar talks. The Chinese also used the Sino-Burmese agreement against their critics in the Soviet bloc, and Ne Win speculated on 30 January that the Chinese leaders had been "quite anxious" to settle the border dispute with Burma prior to Khrushchev's stopover in New Delhi, trying thus to undercut Nehru's argument to the Soviet leader on the intransigence of the Chinese on the border issue.

Constantly under pressure from Parliament and the press not to take a soft line with Peiping, Nehru was compelled to make even an agreement "to meet" with Chou appear as part of a hard, anti-China policy. Nehru's 5 February 1960 letter to Chou agreed to a meeting but not to substantive negotiations, as the Chinese claim that the entire border had never been delimited was "incorrect...and on that basis there can be no negotiations." Nevertheless, he invited Chou to meet with him in New Delhi to explore every avenue for a settlement, and he defended this formal invitation in Parliament by calmly insisting that no policy change was involved: he had always said he was prepared "to meet" anybody, anywhere. It was Nehru's intention merely to determine what Chou "really wants"--as Foreign Secretary Dutt put it--and to probe Peiping's long-term intentions on the border. The firmness of Nehru's letter of invitation was intended partly to scotch rumors that he and his advisers were willing to exchange the Aksai Plain for formal Chinese recognition of the McMahon line--rumors fed by Krishna Menon's slip in a speech to the effect that India would not yield "...any part of our administered territory along the border," i.e. would remain silent on areas occupied by the Chinese. In February and early March, there were other indications that Nehru was looking for some way to accept Chinese use of the Sinkiang-Tibet road while retaining nominal Indian sovereignty over the Aksai Plain.

The Chinese leaders apparently read these early signs as tantamount to an invitation to further probe the apparent soft spot--relating to the Aksai Plain--in the Indian position, and prepared for substantive negotiations rather than meaningless "exploratory" talks. They attempted to make credible their expressed willingness to negotiate a settlement, not only by agreeing to send Chou to India in the face of two Nehru refusals to go to China but also by acting quickly to sign a border agreement with Nepal in March, just two months after Chou's success with the Burmese. But when Chou indicated to Nehru his intention to spend six days in New Delhi (despite Nehru's busy schedule) and to come at the head of a high-level delegation, Nehru and his advisers were taken aback. Nehru's advisers noted that whereas New Delhi was approaching the Chou-Nehru meeting merely in terms of improving relations, Chinese notes and Chou's acceptance letter had looked toward a concrete border "settlement." When asked what Chou would be doing in New Delhi for six days, Nehru replied that Chou was quite capable of talking steadily for three or four hours at a stretch. When Nehru in April contemplated and discussed the line to take during the anticipated bargaining Chou would conduct, the advice he received from all sides was to be adamant. Thus Chou, who in late April came with a business-like delegation and a real hope of gaining agreement in principle that the border was not delimited and was therefore subject to negotiation, was confronted by an Indian prime minister who had already rejected bargaining.

In probing the presumed soft spot in the Indian position, Chou departed from diplomatic precedent, working over Nehru and his top advisers, including Krishna Menon, in separate, private, man-to-man sessions. In each session, Chou ran into a stone wall of opposition--even with his "old friend," Menon--and after three days of almost uninterrupted discussions, he had made no dent in the Indian position on Ladakh; in turn, he rejected Nehru's suggestion that Chinese troops be withdrawn from "occupied" areas. The most Chou was able to salvage from his near-total failure was to be able to give an impression that the talks would be continued. The Chinese clearly underestimated Nehru's adamancy in April 1960. They may have read the signs of compromise in New Delhi correctly in February and March, but they carried that estimate into late April, well after Nehru's back had been stiffened decisively by his advisers.

The April 1960 Chou-Nehru talks seem in retrospect to have been Peiping's last chance for a negotiated settlement with Nehru. Nehru rejected Chou's proposal that they meet again, and refused to agree formally either to a "line" of actual control or to stop sending out Indian patrols. Nehru agreed merely to a temporary, informal "understanding" to halt patrolling and to turn the issue over to subordinate officials, who were to meet to examine the historical and legal evidence of each side and draft a joint report, but who were not empowered to recommend a solution.

The border experts talks in middle and late 1960 served as an instrument of the Chinese effort to perpetuate an impression of continuing negotiations, but they eventually proved detrimental to Peiping's historical and legal case. By the end of the third and final session in December 1960, the Indian experts were convinced that the vaunted Chinese case had proved to be in fact a weak one. The Indian case, owing much to the excellent and extensive administrative records the British had maintained in the India Office Library in London, and published in a detailed Report available to the general public, was impressive. It was argued adroitly on many points of fact (i.e. documentary evidence), logic, and international law, demonstrating that New Delhi could produce a respectable legal case

TOP SECRET

when British-educated, first-class legal experts and historians were called on. However, New Delhi's ability to drive home effectively to laymen specially selected points was inferior to Peiping's, and Indian officials later commented that India's position in the dispute had not been understood in Southeast Asia, partly because "All-India Radio is no match for Peiping Radio." That the Chinese themselves were troubled and recognized that the Indian case was at least as strong as their own is suggested by their failing to publish the experts reports, and by their limiting knowledge of the reports' contents to certain CCP members and deputies of the National People's Congress rather than distributing it to the general public and foreigners. (As of mid-1963, Peiping has not made generally available the texts of the separate Indian and Chinese experts reports.)

Following the Chou-Nehru talks, the Chinese leaders apparently followed a two-fold policy of ceasing regular patrol activity along the border while on occasion sending out reconnaissance parties in the immediate vicinity of their border posts. The primary goal was to reduce further the possibility of armed clashes, clashes which had hurt them politically and had spoiled any chance they may have had of negotiating a settlement. The rationale of a policy of only limited reconnaissance was set forth in a captured Tibetan document of November 1960, which warned PLA personnel to remain cool, not to replace political policy with emotions, otherwise

> We would not look to the larger situation and would not ask for orders or wait for directions from above before opening fire and striking back. In that case, we might gain a greater military victory, but politically we would fall into the trap of the other side and would cause only great injury to the party and state--the biggest mistake.

The document also suggested a Chinese estimate as of November 1960 that New Delhi did not intend to re-take large areas of Chinese-held border territory because the Indians did not have the military capability to do so. However, the cessation of regular forward patrolling did not mean an end to the cautious and surreptitious construction of certain new posts at specially selected points, particularly in the more inaccessible valleys in Ladakh. In addition to this stealthy forward movement of individual posts, the Chinese border experts gave the Indian experts in 1960 a new map of the Chinese-claimed "line"--a "line" which in 1960 was at points well to the west of the map-alignment of the same area which Chou had shown Nehru in 1956.

Regarding Indian protests in 1960 that Chinese planes were violating Indian airspace, Chou told Nehru in April that India need only shoot one of the planes down to see that these were not Chinese Communist aircraft. However, the Indian leaders continued to protest, reluctant to believe Peiping's claim that the planes belonged to the U.S., or reluctant to state publicly that they believed the claim.

As of January 1961, the Chinese strategy remained: to work for a rapprochement with New Delhi, to treat India as still nonaligned, and to avoid personal attacks on Nehru. The prospect of a major Sino-Indian war apparently was considered only as an unlikely eventuality, which, if it were to occur, would completely change the nature of the border struggle, then regarded as political. According to a Chinese Communist Foreign Ministry report of January 1961, it was Mao himself who provided the general principle of diplomatic forbearance for the period: "In 1960, Chairman Mao again instructed us repeatedly that in our struggle, some leeway must be provided /to the opponent/." This was conceived as the key part of Mao's dual policy of "unity and struggle" toward India, at times taking a hard line with New Delhi and at other times taking a soft line. The Chinese may have seen this dual policy as flexible, but to New Delhi China was becoming India's most important enemy and the policy of "unity and struggle" toward India meant nothing but "struggle." It may be, therefore, that the Chinese leaders, including Mao, by early 1961 believed that they had some room for future diplomatic maneuvering with New Delhi, when in fact such room no longer existed.

Appendix VI

EXTRACTS FROM A SOVIET DOCUMENT DATED 2 OCTOBER 1959 ACCESSED FROM THE WOODROW WILSON COLD WAR ARCHIVES*

---

*It is a verbatim record of a discussion in Beijing between Khrushchev and Mao Zedong, each accompanied by politburo members.
Source: *India–China Relations 1947-2000: A Documentary Study,* Vol. III introduced and edited by Avtar Singh Bhasin.

(Nehru Papers: Folio 691-I, P.445-48)

❖❖❖❖❖

1502. **Extracts from a Soviet document dated 2 October 1959, accessed from Woodrow Wilson Cold War Archives. It is a verbatim record of a discussion in Beijing between Khrushchev and Mao Zedong, each accompanied by politburo members.**

October 2nd, 1959.

N.S. Khrushchev : You have had good relations with India for many years. Suddenly, here is a bloody incident, as result of which [Prime Minister of India Jawaharlal Nehru] found himself in a very difficult position. We may say that Nehru is a bourgeois statesman. But we know about it. If Nehru leaves, who would be better than him? The Dalai Lama fled from Tibet, he is a bourgeois figure. This issue is also not clear for us. When the events in Hungary took place, then Nehru was against us, and we did not take offence at him, because we did not expect anything from him as a bourgeois statesman. But although he was against it, this did not prevent us from preserving good relations with him. If you let me, I will tell you what a guest should not say the events in Tibet are your fault. You ruled in Tibet, you should have had your intelligence [agencies] there and should have known about the plans and intentions of the Dalai Lama.

Mao Zedong : Nehru also says that the events in Tibet occurred on our fault. Besides, in the Soviet Union they published a TASS declaration on the issue of conflict with India.

N.S. Khrushchev : Do you really want us to approve of your conflict with India? It would be stupid on our part. The TASS declaration was necessary. You still seem to be able to see some difference between Nehru and me. If we had not issued the TASS declaration, there could have been an impression that there was a united front of socialist countries against Nehru. The TASS declaration turned this issue into one between you and India.

Mao Zedong : Our mistake was that we did not disarm the Dalai Lama right away. But at that time we had no contact with the popular masses of Tibet.

N.S. Khrushchev : You have no contact even now with the population of Tibet.

Mao Zedong : We have a different understanding of this issue.

N.S. Khrushchev : Of course, that is why we raised this issue. One could also say the following: both you and we have Koreans who fled from Kim Il Sung. But this does not give us ground to spoil relations with Kim Il Sung, and we remain good friends. As to the escape of the Dalai Lama from Tibet, if we had been in your place, we would not have let him escape. It would be better if he was in a coffin. And now he is in India, and perhaps will go to the USA. Is this to the advantage of the socialist countries?

Mao Zedong : This is impossible; we could not arrest him then. We could not bar him from leaving, since the border with India is very extended, and he could cross it at any point.

N.S. Khrushchev : It's not a matter of arrest; I am just saying that you were wrong to let him go. If you allow him an opportunity to flee to India, then what has Nehru to do with it? We believe that the events in Tibet are the fault of the Communist Party of China, not Nehru's fault.

Mao Zedong : No, this is Nehru's fault.

N.S. Khrushchev : Then the events in Hungary are not our fault, but the fault of the United States of America, if I understand you correctly. Please, look here, we had an army in Hungary, we supported that fool Rakosi - and this is our mistake, not the mistake of the United States.

Mao Zedong : How can you compare Rakosi to the Dalai Lama?

N.S. Khrushchev : If you like, you can to a certain degree.

Mao Zedong : The Hindus acted in Tibet as if it belonged to them.

N.S. Khrushchev : We know. As you know, Nepal wanted to have a Soviet ambassador, but we did not send there for a long time. You did the same. This is because Nehru did not want that Soviet and Chinese ambassadors were there. This should not come as a surprise - nothing else can be expected from Nehru. But this should not be a ground for us for breaking off the relations.

Mao Zedong : We also support Nehru, but in the question of Tibet we should crush him.

N.S. Khrushchev : Why did you have to kill people on the border with India?

Mao Zedong : They attacked us first, crossed the border and continued firing for 12 hours.

Zhou Enlai : What data do you trust more, Indian or ours?

N.S. Khrushchev : Although the Hindus attacked first, nobody was killed among the Chinese, and only among the Hindus.

Zhou Enlai : But what we are supposed to do if they attack us first. We cannot fire in the air. The Hindus even crossed the McMahon line. Besides, in the nearest future [Indian] Vice President [Savrepalli] Radhakrishnan comes to China. This is to say that we are undertaking measures to resolve the issue peacefully, by negotiations. In my letter of 9 September to Nehru we provided detailed explanations of all that had occurred between India and us.

N.S. Khrushchev : Comrade Zhou Enlai. You have been Minister of Foreign Affairs of the PRC for many years and know better than me how one can resolve disputed issues without [spilling] blood. In this particular case I do not touch at all the issue of the border, for if the Chinese and the Hindus do not know where the borderline goes between them, it is not for me, a Russian, to meddle. I am only against the methods that have been used.

Zhou Enlai : We did not know until recently about the border incident, and local authorities undertook all the measures there, without authorization from the center. Besides, we are talking here about three disputed regions between China and India. The Hindus were the first to cross the McMahon line and were the first to open fire. No government of China ever recognized the McMahon line. If, for instance, the Finns attacked the borders of the USSR, wouldn't you retaliate?

M.A. Suslov : We do not have claims against the Finnish government.

N.S. Khrushchev : That the center knew nothing about the incident is news to me. I would tell you, what I was against. On 22 June 1941 Germans began their assault against the Soviet Union. Stalin forbade opening fire in response, and the instruction to open fire was sent only after some time. As Stalin explained, it might have been a provocation. Of course, it was Stalin's mistake. He simply got cold feet [on strusil]. But this case is absolutely different.

Zhu De : Hindus crossed the McMahon line that tears away 90 thousand square kilometers from China.

Chen Yi : After the revolt in Tibet there were several anti-Chinese, anti-communist campaigns in India. There were demonstrations against our Embassy in Dehli and the consulate in Calcutta; their participants reviled the leaders of the PRC and shouted anti-Chinese slogans. We did nothing like that, and the Indian Ambassador in the PRC had not the slightest pretext to claim [that we] were unfriendly.

N.S. Khrushchev : Our Soviet representatives abroad had much more fallen on them than yours. Since the establishment of our state not a few of Soviet ambassadors were killed abroad. And in the Soviet Union only a German ambassador was killed in 1918. True, at some point the windows in the embassies of the United States and Federal Republic of Germany were broken, but we organized it ourselves.

Chen Yi : Speaking of the effectiveness of efforts to pull Nehru to our side, our method will be more efficient, and yours is time-serving [opportunism-prisposoblenchestvo].

N.S. Khrushchev : Chen Yi is Minister of Foreign Affairs and he can weigh his words. He did not say it at random. We have existed for 42 years, and for 30 years we existed alone [as a socialist country] and adjusted to nothing, but carried out our principled communist policy.

Chen Yi : (in great agitation and hastily) The Chinese people evoked pity for a long time and during many decades lived under oppression of British, American, French and other imperialists. The Soviet comrades should understand this. We are now undertaking certain measures to resolve the conflict with India peacefully, and just one fact testifies to this, that perhaps Vice President of India Radhakrishnan will come to us in mid-October. We also have a certain element of time-serving. You should understand our policy correctly. Our line is firmer and more correct.

N.S. Khrushchev : Look at this lefty. Watch it, comrade Chen Yi, if you turn left, you may end up going to the right. The oak is also firm, but it breaks. I believe that we should leave this issue aside, for we have a different understanding of it.

Zhou Enlai : Comrade Khrushchev, even the Hindus themselves do not know what and how it occurred on the Indo-Chinese border.

Lin Biao : During the war between the Soviet Union and Fascist Germany, the Soviet Army routed the fascists and entered Berlin. This does not mean that the Soviet Union began the war.

N.S. Khrushchev : It is not for me, a lieutenant-general, to teach you, comrade Marshal.

M.A. Suslov : Comrade Lin Biao, you are trying to compare incomparable things. During the Patriotic War millions of people were killed, and here is a trivial incident.

Zhou En lai : The Hindus did not withdraw their troops from where they had penetrated. We seek peaceful resolution of the conflict and suggested and do suggest to resolve it piece by piece.

N.S. Khrushchev : We agree with all that you are doing. It is what you have done before that we disagree with.

Zhou En lai : The Hindus conducted large-scale anti-Chinese propaganda for 40 years until this provocation. They were the first to cross the border; they were the first to open fire. Could one still consider under these circumstances that we actually unleashed this incident?

N. S. Khrushchev : We are communists, and they are like Noah's Ark. You, comrade Zhou En lai, understand it as well as I do.

M.A. Suslov : Noah's Ark in a sense that they have a pair of every creature.

Peng Zhen : (in hasty agitation) Nasser has been abusing without reason the Soviet Union that delivers to him unconditional assistance. Here we should keep in mind the reactionary aspects of the national bourgeoisie. If you, Soviet comrades, can lash out at the national bourgeoisie, why we cannot do the same?

N.S. Khrushchev : Nobody says you cannot lash out - but shooting is not the same as criticism.

Peng Zhen : The McMahon line is a dirty line that was not recognized by any government in China.

N.S. Khrushchev : There are three of us here, and nine of you, and you keep repeating the same line. I think this is to no use. I only wanted to express our position. It is your business to accept it or not.

Mao Zedong : The border conflict with India - this is only a marginal border issue, not a clash between the two governments. Nehru himself is not aware what happened there. As we found out, their patrols crossed the McMahon line. We learned about this much later, after the incident took place. All this was known neither to Nehru, nor even to our military district in Tibet. When Nehru learned that their patrols had crossed the McMahon line, he issued the instruction for them to withdraw. We also carried out the work towards peaceful resolution of the issue.

N.S. Khrushchev : If this had been done immediately after the skirmish, the conflict would not have taken place. Besides, you failed to inform us for a rather long time about the border incident.

Liu Shaoqi : On 6 September I informed you through comrade [Soviet charge d'affaires in Beijing Sergei F.] Antonov about the situation on the border. Earlier we could not inform you, since we still had not figured it out ourselves.

Zhou En lai : The TASS announcement was published before you received my letter to Nehru. It was passed to comrade Antonov on the afternoon of 9 September.

M.A. Suslov : It was probably done simultaneously, considering that the time difference between Moscow and Beijing is 5 hours.

A.A. Gromyko : The ambassador of India in the USSR told me that the Chinese letter not only fails to make things calmer, but also actually throws everything back.

M.A. Suslov : At the present moment the temperature has fallen and we can let this issue alone.

Mao Zedong : (peevishly) The temperature has fallen thanks to your announcement?

M.A. Suslov : Not only, but also thanks to the decision of your parliament.

Liu Shaoqi : On 6 September I passed a message to you via comrade Antonov that within a week [we] would deliver retaliation to the Hindus.

M.A. Suslov : The decision of your parliament was considerably softer than your Note.

Peng Zhen : The delegates of the All-Chinese Assembly of People's Deputies asked me how one should understand the TASS announcement, was it that the senior brother, without finding out what was right and who was wrong, gave a beating to the PRC and India.

Wang Jiaxiang : But the first who began to fire were the Hindus, not us.

N.S. Khrushchev : Yes, they began to shoot and they themselves fell dead. Our duty is to share with you our considerations on the incident, for nobody besides us would tell you about it.

Zhou En lai : There could be disputes and unresolved issues between the CCP and the CPSU, but for the outside consumption we always underline unity with the Soviet Union.

Lin Biao : The Hindus began to shoot first and they fired for 12 hours, until they spent all their ammunition. There could be a different approach to this issue, one might admit, but the facts are facts: 1) the Hindus were the first to cross the border; 2) the Hindus were the first to open fire; 3) the Hindus sustained fire during 12 hours. In this situation there might be two approaches to the issue: 1) the Hindus crossed the border and we have to beat retreat; 2) the Hindus cross the border and we offer a rebuff.

Mao Zedong : The rebuff was delivered on the decision of local military organs.

Lin Biao : There was no command from the top.

Mao Zedong : We could not keep the Dalai Lama, for the border with India is very extended and he could cross it at any point.

M.A. Suslov : You should have known in advance about his intentions and plots.

Mao Zedong : We wanted to delay the transformation of Tibet by four years.

N.S. Khrushchev : And that was your mistake.

Mao Zedong : The decision to delay the transformations was taken earlier, after the Dalai Lama visited India [in early 1959]. We could not launch an offensive without a pretext. And this time we had a good excuse and we struck. This is, probably, what you cannot grasp. You will see for yourselves later that the McMahon line with India will be maintained, and the border conflict with India will end.

N.S. Khrushchev : This is good. But the issue is not about the line. We know nothing about this line and we do not even want to know.

Mao Zedong : The border issue with India will be decided through negotiations.

N.S. Khrushchev : We welcome this intention.

Zhou En lai : On 22 January you suggested to Nehru to conduct talks on the border issues. Then he disagreed with this. Today he agrees.

Mao Zedong : You attached to us two labels - the conflict with India was our fault, and that the escape of the Dalai Lama was also our error. We, in turn, attached to you one label time-servers. Please accept it.

N.S. Khrushchev : We do not accept it. We take a principled communist line.

Mao Zedong : The TASS announcement made all imperialists happy.

M.A. Suslov : Precisely on the contrary. This announcement and our recent measures promoted the relaxation of the situation. The imperialists would have been happy, had the relations between India and China been spoiled. We have the information that Americans approached Nehru and offered him their services regarding the conflict between India and China. Our steps cooled the hot expectations of the reactionaries.

Lin Biao : The whole issue is about who was first to shoot, not who was killed.

Zhou En lai : It follows from your reasoning that, if burglars break into your house and you beat them up, then you are guilty.

N.S. Khrushchev : Why may you criticize us, and the senior brother may not censure you. At one meeting with cda. Yudin you, comrade Mao Zedong, very sharply criticized the CPSU, and we accepted this criticism. Moreover, you left the session at the 8th Congress of the CCP during the speech of comrade [Anastas] Mikoyan. This was a demonstrative gesture, and Mikoyan could have left also.

In fact, I can also pack my suitcases and leave, but I am not doing it. When the events in Hungary took place, comrade Zhou Enlai came to us and lectured us. He blamed us both for Bessarabia and for the Baltic countries. We received this lesson. It turns out that you may censure us, and we may not. There are even some members of the CC CPSU Presidium back home who say the following: there is a formula in the socialist camp headed by the Soviet Union, but in reality one lacks even respect for observations of the CPSU. Aren't you talking to us too haughtily?

Mao Zedong : We expressed our observations to you in a confidential manner. And you this time expressed them in the same order. This is good. This will serve the right cause. But when you took a public stand (I have in mind the TASS announcement) this was not good.

A.A. Gromyko : The TASS announcement did nothing to push India away from the People's Republic of China (reads an excerpt).

Peng Zhen : We also must speak out. The Hindus were really the first ones to cross the border, to start shooting, they continued shooting for 12 hours. Comrade Mao Zedong has just said that nobody knew precisely what actually occurred on the Sino-Indian border.

N.S. Khrushchev : You do not tolerate objections, you believe you are orthodox, and this is where our haughtiness reveals itself. Chen Yi attached to us a label, and it is a political label. What ground does he have to do this?

Chen Yi : The TASS announcement was in support of India, in support of the bourgeoisie.

N.S. Khrushchev : You want to subjugate us to yourselves, but nothing will come out of it, we are also a party and we have our own way, and we are not time-servers towards anybody.

Mao Zedong : And what is then our way?

N.S. Khrushchev : We always believed and believe that you and we take one road and we regard you as our best friends.

Mao Zedong : I cannot understand what constitutes our mistake? Kerensky and Trotsky also escaped from you.

N.S. Khrushchev : The Dalai Lama escaped, and you are not guilty? Well, there were also similar mistakes and facts on our side. True, when we allowed Kerensky to escape from the USSR, it was our mistake, but one should keep in mind that this happened literally in the first days of the revolution. Lenin freed on parole generals Krasnov and Kaledin. As for Trotsky, it was Stalin who expelled him. Nehru may go over to the USA. He is among our fellow-travelers who go with us when it is to their advantage. When we delivered assistance to Nasser, we knew that he might turn against us. We gave him credits for construction of the high-altitude Aswan dam. This is tactics. Had we not given him this credit, Nasser would have ended up in America's embrace.

Mao Zedong : You only see our "threatening gestures," and fail to see the other side our struggle to pull Nehru over to our side.

N.S. Khrushchev : We are not confident that Nasser will hold out with us for long. There is only a very fine thread connecting us and it can break off at any moment.

Chen Yi : I am outraged by your declaration that "the aggravation of relationship with India was our fault."

N.S. Khrushchev : I am also outraged by your declaration that we are time-servers. We should support Nehru, to help him stay in power.

Mao Zedong : The events in Tibet and the border conflict - these are temporary developments. Better that we end here the discussion of these issues. Could we assess the relationship between us as follows, that on the whole we are united, and some differences do not stand in the way of our friendship?

N.S. Khrushchev : We took and do take this view.

Mao Zedong : I would like to introduce a clarification - I never attended the session at the 8th Congress when comrade Mikoyan spoke. I would like to speak to Mikoyan personally.

N.S. Khrushchev : You skipped that session precisely because Mikoyan spoke there. Zhou Enlai once delivered to us a fair lecture. He is a good lecturer, but I disagree with the content of his lecture.

Liu Shaoqi : We never told anybody about our disagreements, not to even any fraternal party.

N.S. Khrushchev : This is good, this is correct. You gave us the first lesson, we heard you, and you must now listen to us. Take back your political accusations; otherwise we spoil relations between our parties. We are your friends and speak the truth. We never acted as time-servers with regard to anybody, even our friends.

Chen Yi : But you also lay two political accusations at our door, by saying that both the aggravations of relations with India and the escape of Dalai Lama were our fault. I believe that you are still acting as time-servers.

N.S. Khrushchev : These are completely different matters. I drew your attention only to specific oversights and never hurled at you principled political accusations, and you put forth precisely a political accusation. If you consider us time-servers, comrade Chen Yi, then do not offer me your hand. I will not accept it.

Chen Yi : Neither will I. I must tell you I am not afraid of your fury.

N.S. Khrushchev : You should not spit from the height of your Marshal title. You do not have enough spit. We cannot be intimidated. What a pretty situation we have: on one side, you use the formula headed by the Soviet Union, on the other hand, you do not let me say a word. What kind of equality we can talk about? That is why we raised the question at the 21st Congress of the CPSU about the repeal of the formula the socialist camp headed by the Soviet Union. We do not want any Party to stand at the head. All communist parties are equal and independent. Otherwise one is in a false situation.

Mao Zedong : (in a conciliatory manner) Chen Yi speaks about particulars, and you should not generalize.

Wang Jiaxiang : The whole matter is about wrong translation. Chen Yi did not speak of time-serving as some kind of doctrine.

N.S. Khrushchev : We shot down not only one American plane and always said that they crash by themselves. This you cannot brand as time-serving.

M.A. Suslov : Now you are moving toward negotiations between you and India. This is good.

A.A. Gromyko : Is there a need that the PRC makes a declaration that would promote a relaxation in the situation? I am making a reservation that I am saying this without a preliminary exchange of opinions with cde. Khrushchev.

Zhou Enlai : There is no need to make such a declaration. We informed the Hindus that Vice President Radhakrishnan might come to us at his convenience in the period from 15 October until 1 December.

N.S. Khrushchev : I would also like to express an idea that has materialized just now with regard to the question of the visit of the Vice President. Would there be no bewilderment, if it were the Vice President, and not the President and Prime Minister [i.e., Nehru], to come to the PRC?

Zhou Enlai : The Hindus themselves offered the candidacy of Radhakrishnan. The President and Prime Minister of India sent us best wishes on the 10th anniversary of the PRC. In reply to the address we will remind them again about the invitation of Radhakrishnan to come to the PRC.

Mao Zedong : "Pravda" published only an abridged version of Zhou Enlai's letter to Nehru, and the TASS announcement was published in full. Perhaps we now stop discussing this issue and shift to Laos?

N.S. Khrushchev : Good, let us do this, but I have not a slightest interest in this matter, for this is a very insignificant matter, and there is much noise around it. Today Ho Chi Minh came to see us and had a conversation with us about Laos. I sent him to you, for you should be more concerned with this...

INDEX

Abdul Qadeer (A.Q.) Khan Research Laboratory, 153
Abdullah, Sheikh, 63
Adhocism, 95
Afghanistan, 9, 38–39, 46, 52
Afro-Asian Conference in Bandung, 150
Agreement on Confidence-building Measures, 110
Agreement on the Maintenance of Peace and Tranquillity (1993), 110, 120-21
Agreement on Tibet (2003), 116
Agreement on Trade and Intercourse between Tibet region of China and India, 64, 75
Aitchison Treaties, 53–56
Aitchison, C.U., 53
Akbar, M.J., 72, 87, 92, 108
Aksai Chin, 57–58, 60–66, 71, 74, 76, 79, 97, 117–19, 124, 129
  area as 'boundary undefined, 60
  completion of a motorable road, 73
  status of, 57
  unnotified building of a road by the Chinese government, 82
All India Congress Committee (AICC), 96

Anglo-Chinese Convention, 24
Anglo-Russian Convention, 49
Anglo-Sikh war of 1845–46, 57
Anglo-Tibetan Convention, 24
Anti-China phobia, 38
Armed conflict (1962), 97
Arunachal Pradesh, 40, 66, 77, 83, 114–115, 119, 140
Asceticism, 14
Asian Relations Conference (ARC), 59
Assam separatists issue, 107
Associated Press, 147, 150
Association of Southeast Asian Nations (ASEAN), 139

Bajpai, Girija Shankar, 62, 77
Baltistan, 119
Bamiyan, 8–9
Bangladesh, 39, 47
Bangladesh Liberation War (1971), 104, 155
Bank of China, properties in Calcutta, 104
Beijing Review, 31
Bhagat, P.S., 89
Bharatiya Janata Party (BJP), 39, 114, 116, 142, 163

Bhutto, Zulfikar (Zulfiqar) Ali, 151
Biao, Lin, 155
Bilateral trade, turnover of, 110
Bodhidharma, 2, 14
Bombay Presidency, 62
Border dispute, 29, 68, 74, 76, 81, 98, 113, 118, 128
Brahmin Dance, 19
BRICS, 116, 149
   futile meetings of, 90
BRICS Development Bank. *See* New Development Bank (NDB)
British bureaucracy 'monumental crime' in, 51
British colonialism, 19
Brooks, Henderson, 89–90
Buddha Nature (Ultimate Reality), 14
Buddha's Nirvana, 3–5, 7
Buddhayasas, 12
Buddhism and Buddhist Pilgrims, 5
Buddhism, 2–5, 8–9, 11, 13–16, 18–20, 22–23, 31, 40
   continuance of, 16
   decline in India, 19
   dominance and firm grip, 17
   establishment in China, 2
   Mahayana Buddhism, 3, 5
   monasteries and nunneries of, 20
   progress in the Yangtze Valley, 16
   Tantric Buddhism, 14–15
   three treatise school, 13
Buddhist doctrines, 12, 18
Buddhist missionaries, 2
Bureau of Translators, 13

Camel's Back, occupation of, 138
Caroe, Olaf K., 53, 77
Cartography (visualized exactly on a map), 45
Central Treaty Organization (CENTO), 150
Centre for Nonproliferation Studies, 152

Chabahar Port, Iran, 165
Chandragupta Maurya, 6–7
Chavanne, Émmanuel-Édouard, 16
Chellaney, Brahma, 114–15
Chhatwal, Ravinder, 144-45
China Pictorial, 73
China's India policy, 163-66
   catch-22 fix, 165
   effort to 'teach India a lesson', 165
   Galwan Valley incident, 163
   'inevitable development' of the covert strategy, 163
   initiative of reshaping global industrial chains, 164
   military power matching, 165
   military zero-sum game, 164
   PLA wants 'to teach India a lesson', as in 1962, 163
   strategic and tactical advantage, 164
   'tit-for-tat' approach, 163
China's insistence led to armed conflicts, 46
China's stand on the Kashmir issue, 115
China-Burma border agreement, 73
China-India relations, 42, 118
China-Pakistan Economic Corridor (CPEC), 165
China-Pakistan joint attack, 105
The Chinese Air Threat: Understanding the Reality, 144-45
Chinese civilization, influence on India, 20
Chinese Communist Party (CCP), 30
   Polit Bureau, 92
Chinese de-induction, reasons for, 95
Chinese frontier guards, 87
Chinese historical events, chronology of, 4
Chinese incursions of 1959–60, 68
Chinese Influence on India, 16-21
Chinese Literature, 19
Chinese military patronage, 25

Chinese misunderstanding of India's intentions, 29
Chinese Nationalist Party, 25
Chinese publications, ban lifted on (1989), 110
Chinese recognition of the McMahon Line, 124
Chinese Revolution, 51
Chinese Suzerainty, 24-29
Chuang, Yuan, 2, 11, 20
Clinton, Bill, 37, 111-13, 131
A Collection of Treaties Engagements and Sanads, 53
Communication between India and China, 8
Communism, 69, 98, 127
Communist Chinese intentions on Tibet, 2
Communist Party of China (CPC), 44
Communist Party of the Soviet Union (CPSU), 79
Communist revolution, 3
Confidence-building, 108, 110
Confucianism, 18
'Constitutional fiction', 24
Coronavirus Pandemic, 131, 139, 157, 163
Creston Energy, oil concessions from, 141
Crewe-Milnes, Robert, 49
Cuban Missile Crisis (1962), 88, 100
Cultural and commercial traffic between India and China, 11
Cultural borrowing, 3, 16, 103
Cultural Revolution (1966-76), 30, 154
Curzon, Lord, 24, 40
Czechoslovakia, suppression of democratic movement (1968,), 104

Dalai Lama, 23, 25, 28-34, 41, 43, 67, 82, 98, 102
  escape of, 82
  Gyatso, Ngawang Lobsang, Fifth Dalai Lama, 23
  institution of the, 23, 25
  'Policy towards the Dalai Lama', 31
  ninth Dalai Lama, political head of Tibet, 23
  return of, 31-32
  temporal head of independent Tibet, 32
  veneration of, 32
  safe return to his honoured position, 32
  thirteenth Dalai Lama, 25, 52
Defence capability, 126
Dehuai, Peng, 79
Delineation. *See* Diplomatic negotiations
Demarcation (marked out on the ground), 45
Desai, Morarji, 32-33, 104-6, 139
Dhola-Thagla area, 91
Diplomatic insensitivity, 111
Diplomatic negotiations, 45
Diplomatic relations, 10
Dithering voices, 32-36
Dogra-Tibet Treaty (1842), 57
Doklam, 145, 165
Doordarshan, 105
Dunghuan, 8-9

Economic sustainability, 126
Eisenhower, Dwight D., 100
Encyclopædia Britannica, 52
Enlai, Zhou Premier, 4, 65-66, 72-76, 78-80, 90, 94-95, 97, 101, 118-120, 124, 150
  acceptance of Kashmir dispute, 150
  advocated counter-attack in defence, 101
  cartographic contradictions, 74
  China's claims over the Aksai Chin, 66
  clarification on LAC, 120

extraordinary step of, 150
Indian visit of, 73, 79
letter to Nehru, 78
official meeting with Nehru, 66
press conference 'six points', 80
question of 'wrong maps', 72–73
suggestions for maintaining the status quo on the border, 79
territorial claims to an 40,000 sq. miles of territory in Ladakh and NEFA, 78
three-point proposal for ceasefire and disengagement, 94

Fa-Hsien, 2–7, 11
Far Eastern Economic Review, 31
Fenghi, Wei, 89
Fernandes, George, 32–35, 38, 113
Financial structure, 161
    capital-output ratio, 161
    China–India gap, 161
    fiscal decentralization, 161
    marginal tax rates, 161
    prime lending rate (PLR), 161
Five Principles of Peaceful Coexistence. *See* Panchsheel
Flexing military, 132-35
    China's expenditure on its military, 132
    deployment of Chinese forces, 134
    estimates of military expenditure, 133
    goal of 'minimum deterrence', 134
    India–China military distance, 132
    military manpower, 134
Forceful push in the Dhola-Thagla area in NEFA, 91
Foreign policy, 27, 99, 105, 126–28, 149, 153, 156, 167
    based on other nations' intentions, 126
    components, 126
    cost-benefit calculus, 128

domestic strategic discourse, 127
    fulcrum of redesigning, 127
    national security, 126
    nationalism became a factor, 105
Fortune 500 companies, 160
Forward Policy, 68, 81–83, 86, 92–93
    adventurism, 93
    success of, 84
    India began implementing the provocative offensive, 87
Free Tibet lobby campaign, 33

Galwan Valley, 82, 88, 123, 163
Gandhi, Indira, 34–36, 104, 106–7
    lost the elections in March 1977, 104
    signed Treaty of Peace, Friendship and Cooperation with Soviet Union, 104
Gandhi, Rajiv, 36, 108–9, 140, 166
    invited to Beijing in 1988, 108
    views on Sino-Indian relations, 109
Gayatri Mantra, 15
GDP Growth in India and China, 156
Gelug Sect (Yellow Sect) of Buddhism, 23
Geneva, last-ditch meetings in, 89
George, T.J.S., 86
Globalization, 160-61
    hardware items of technology, 160
    high-technology exports, 160
    patent applications, 160
Gobi Desert, 8
Gokhale, Vijay, 147–48
Good bilateral relations, 128
Gorbachev, Mikhail, 46
Government of India Act (1935), 54
Great Leap Forward, 30, 148
    failure of the, 79, 99
Grey, Edward, 48
Growth factors, 157-60
    APIs export, 159
    automobile export, 159

box office collection, 159
cellphone export, 159
cement production, 159
ecommerce sales, 159
foreign trips, 159
GDP growth rate, 157-58
global trade, 159
gross domestic investment (GDI), 158
population, 157
purchasing power parity (PPP) terms, 157
sectoral gap in industrial products, 159
services export, 159
steel production, 159
telecom export, 159
textile export, 159
The Guilty Men of 1962, 35
Gulab Singh, Maharaja, 57–58
   achievements of 1842, 58
Gupta period, 9. See also Kushan period
Gwadar Port (Arabian Sea), 165
Gyatso, Ngawang Lobsang, Fifth Dalai Lama, 23

Hanfu, Zhang, 89
Hardinge, Charles, 49–51
H-bomb test. See Pokhran nuclear tests
Henderson Brooks Report, 90
Hinayana Buddhism, 3, 13
Hindi Chini Bhai Bhai, 36, 42, 74
The Hindu, 10, 114, 117, 147
Ho, Cheng, 11
Huangdi, Qin Shi, 7
Human Development factors, 162-63
   economic reforms in China, 162
   human development index, 162
   past decade of mismanaged economy, 162
   public expenditure on health in China, 162

Human Development Report of the UN, 162
Hungarian Revolution of 1956, 45

IAEA safeguards, 153
Ideological differences, 45
I-fen, Chen (Ivan Chen), 51
Imperialism, 26, 66, 135
Incidents of Travels in India, 5
India (1888), 47
India's extra-territorial rights in Tibet, 66
India's Tibet Policy, 22-, 22
   Tibet as an integral part of China, 22
India's transparency in Tibet, 167
India–China Agreement in Tibet, 68
India–China Agreement of 1993, 110
India–China bilateral relations, 103
India–China border dispute, 74
India–China delineation of boundary the Treaty (1842), 60
India–China dialogue and interaction, 114
India–China friendship, 78
India–China official meetings between Nehru and Zhou Enlai, 66
India–China relations
   contradiction in, 71
   disaster in, 29
India–China treaty, 66
India-Indonesia alliance, 168
Indian Air Force, 93, 143, 145
   logistic capabilities of, 87
Indian Council of World Affairs (ICWA), 67
Indian expansionism, 97
Indian influence on Chinese, 19
Indian Parliament Resolutions (1962 and 1994), 125
Indian Penal Code (IPC), 55
Indian political class, obsession with 1962 War, 166

The Indianization of China, 16
Indianization of Chinese thought, 20
India-Tibet frontier, 77
Indika, 6
Indo-Soviet Friendship Treaty, 104–5, 139
Industrial system, near collapse of, 79
International anti-Chinese campaign, 100
International Atomic Energy Agency (IAEA), 153
International Institute for Strategic Studies (IISS), 132, 134
Islamic fundamentalism, 168
Islamic invasion, 19

Jaishankar, S., 123
Janata Party, 32–33, 36, 104, 106, 139
The Japan Times, 37
Jiabao, Wen, 138
Jiaxuan, Tang, 113
Jinping, Xi, 90, 117, 127, 139, 147
   mislead Modi of his real intention, 118
   one-to-one meetings between Modi, 127
Jordan, John Newell, 48, 51

Kailash Mansarovar, reopening of route, 107
Kai-shek-led Kuomintang (KMT) government, 25
Kargil and Dras, Pakistan was waging a war, 114
Kaul, B.M., 85, 93, 136
Kennedy, John F., 88
Khalistan movement, 41
Khan, Altan, 23
Khan, Ayub, 90
Khan, Kublai, 15, 23
Khrushchev, Nikita, 79, 100, 148
Khurnak Fort, 74

Kingdon-Ward, Francis, 52
   arrest of, 53
Kissinger, Henry, 131
Korean War, 45, 136, 141
Kosygin, Alexei, 33–34, 105
Ku, Pan, 10
Kumarajiva, 2, 12–13
Kushan period, 9

Ladakh, demilitarized zone in, 97
Lamaism, 15
'Last-ditch' meetings in Geneva, 89
Left-led massive central government employees strike in India (1960), 99
Lhasa Temple, 4
Li, Wan, 30
Line of Actual Control (LAC), 94, 118-23
   1962 War, 120
   India formally accepted the concept (1993,), 120
   agreement on the Maintenance of Peace and Tranquility, 120
   Chinese-occupied Aksai Chin, 119
   contours and extent of LAC, 118
   as the *de facto* boundary pending, 122
   division of territory, 119
   eastern Sector (1914 McMahon Line, minor disputes), 119
   India–China border areas, 110
   India rejected the concept of LAC, 120
   Indian government's inability to take an unambiguous position, 123
   middle Sector (least controversial), 119
   stand-off on, 122-23
   territorial dispute over Aksai Chin, 118
   vagueness of the Chinese definition, 120

western Sector (major disagreements), 119
Lohia, Ram Manohar, 76
Longju incident (1959), 98

Macartney–MacDonald Line, 58
MacDonald, Claude, 58
Madhyamika school, 13
Mahayana Buddhism, 3, 5
Mahayana texts, 13
Mahayana trimmings, 17
Malacca Straits, 168
Mang, Wang, 10
Mankekar, D.R., 35
Mann, Anant Singh, 133
Mantra sect, 14
Mao's Art of War, 81-92
Maritime Province, 46
Matanga, Kashyapa, 12
McMahon Line (called the Red Line because it was marked by McMahon in red pencil), 26–27, 43–45, 48–50, 52–54, 57, 59–62, 65–68, 73–78, 81, 83, 85, 91, 94, 119–20, 124
  as 'undemarcated', 60
  90,000 sq. km of India territory south of the, 97
  as the boundary in the eastern area of the frontier, 78
  cannot be disputed under international law, 45
  Chinese recognition of the, 124
  demarcation of, 83
  fixity of the, 60, 77
  illegal and invalid, 75-76
  India's legal boundary, 57
  in the NEFA Area, 77, 83
  non-starter for 22 years till 1936, 57
  official sanction to the, 53
  a product of the same imperialism, 66
McMahon, Henry, 37, 48–52, 56, 68
  actions at Simla, 52
  dealings with the Tibetans, 51
McMahon-Shatra Agreement on the McMahon Line, 53
Megasthenes, 6–7
Menon, V.K. Krishna, 86–89, 91, 105, 136
Military preparedness, 70, 84, 167
Military-technical Confidence-building Measures (CBMs), 110
Ming dynasty, 23
'Minister-in-waiting' protocol, 33
Minto, Lord, 24
Mishra, Brajesh Chandra, 113
Modi, Narendra, 40, 86, 90, 116–118, 121, 139, 165
  failed to understand the nuances of Xi, 118
  one-to-one meetings with Xi Jinping, 90, 127
  request to open the Sikkim route to Kailash Mansarovar (2015), 139
  visit to China (2015), 121
Monastic Rules, 6
The Moscow Times, 147
Muktapida, Lalitaditya, 66
Müller, Max, 5
My Days as a Military Staff in the Supreme Command, 101
Myopic vision, pathetic commentary on, 103

Nagarahara, 9
Narain, Raj, 32
National Defence Fund, 98
National Democratic Alliance (NDA), 113
National interest and security, 105
National People's Congress, 97
Naval and Air superiority, 141-49
  'blue water' fighting capability, 142
  China's air force capabilities, 143
  China's nuclear capabilities, 145

Chinese acquisition of multirole combat aircraft, 145
Chinese possess a massive lead over the Indians, 146
Indian has agreements for port with Maldives, Madagascar, Singapore and Oman, 143
Indian naval capabilities, 142
induction of nuclear-armed submarines, 142
land-based Chinese naval aviation, 142
naval assets, 141
PLA Rocket Force (PLARF), 145
'String of Pearls' strategy in the Indian Ocean, 142
NEFA, 66, 71, 73, 78, 83, 91, 93
  forceful push in the Dhola-Thagla, 91
  McMahon line, 77, 83
Negative developments leading to the killing of soldiers, 117
Nehru, Jawaharlal, 26–29, 40, 42, 44–45, 59–60, 62–70, 72–92, 95–96, 99–101, 104–5, 118–20, 124, 136
  acquiescence in the 1956, 99
  assertion in parliament about the McMahon Line, 66
  dilly-dallying attitude on Tibet, 59
  exposed as a 'paper tiger', 81
  letter to Zhou, 74–75
  myopic conviction of, 82
  myth as a 'world statesman', 102
  non-alignment policy, 99
  official meetings with Zhou Enlai, 66
  question of 'wrong maps', 72–73
  recognized the Chinese sovereignty over Tibet region, 28
  stupidity in turning down the UNSC veto holding seat, 130
  took control of Tawang, 60

view on Forward Policy', 83
visited China (1954,), 72
Nehru, R.K., 89
Nehru: The Making of India, 87
'Network of Diamonds', 142
New China News Agency (NCNA), 96
New Development Bank (NDB), 116
New York Times, 111–12
'1962 debacle', 128
1914 Convention as a binding agreement, 62
Ninth Dalai Lama, political head of Tibet, 23
Nirvana of Buddha, 5
Noblesse oblige psychology, 95
Non-Aligned Summit, 35
Noorani, A.G., 119
North Atlantic Treaty Organization (NATO), 82
North-east, insurgency problem, 108
North-west frontier of Punjab, 85
Nuclear power, 129-32
  China's military might and economic prowess, 129
  Indian doctrine, 130
  'no first use (NFU)' doctrine, 129
  'non-use against non-nuclear powers', 129
  paradigm of 'minimum deterrence', 130
  'second-strike capability', 129
  'survivable second-strike capability', 129
Nuclear test by India (1998), 37, 112.
  See also Pokhran nuclear tests
Nyingma Sect (Red Sect), 23

One child per family policy, 157

Pacific Ocean, maritime routes to, 9
Pakistan's terror menace, 106
Pakistani aggression against India (1965), 155

Pakistan-Occupied Kashmir (PoK), 106
Panchen Lama, 29–30
Panchsheel, 28, 65, 114, 150
Panikkar, K.M., 2, 10–11, 15, 63–64
Pant, Harsh V., 133
Parliament Resolution, 125
Patel, Sardar, 26–27, 42, 119
 listed 'Ten Points'—problems, 26
Peng, Li, 109, 120
 views on Sino-Indian relations, 109
People's Liberation Army Daily, 140
Peoples Daily, 92, 96
Peoples Republic of China (PRC), 26, 44
 cultural policy of the, 32
Phags-pa script, 15
PLA, defeat of in the Sumdorong Chu stand-off, 108
PLA's combat experience, 135–41
 'border skirmishes' in the area of the Nizhnemikhallovka, 139
 built a helipad at Wandung, 140
 captured the disputed Paracel Islands (1974), 139
 clash between India and China at Cho La (1967), 138
 confronted the Indian armed forces at Nathu La (1967), 136-38
 decision to control the disputed borderland in the Chumbi Valley, 137
 decision-making apparatus, 140
 eyeball-to-eyeball confrontation with Indian army in the Sumdorong Chu Valley, 140
 fight US 'imperialism', 135
 first cross-border Chinese military action, 136
 four modernizations programme, 140
 an invincible and formidable force, 135

Paracel Islands in the South China Sea, 135
PLA Navy (PLAN) clashed with the Vietnamese Navy (1988), 141
 scrutiny of the PLA's performance, 135
 success story, 141
 use of force on the Sino-Indian border (1962), 136
 war with its neighbours, 135
 war with Vietnam (1979), 140
Pokhran nuclear tests, 110-11
Political and military weakness of China, 82
Pragmatic policy (1954), 70
Prithvi missile, 130
Propagators of Indian thought, 11
Putin, Vladimir, 38, 146–47, 149

Qin emperor, 12
Qing Dynasty, 9, 15, 23, 25
Qinghai Province, 23, 37

Raghu Vira, 14–15
Rajagopalachari, C., 93
Rao, P.V. Narasimha, 35, 106, 112, 120, 158
 visited China (1993), 110
Realpolitik approach, 36–43
A Record of Buddhist Countries, 5
Red Guards, 30
Renmin Ribao (*People's Daily*), 96, 99–100
Research and Analysis Wing (RAW), 34
Rinpoche, Guru, 15, 23

S-400 missile system built by Russia, 147
Sagarika submarine launched ballistic missile (SLBM), 130
Sagya Sect (Flower Sect), 23
Samarkand, 9

Sandrocottus, 6–7
Sanskritization movement, 18
Sanskritization of China, 2-8
　Buddha attained nirvana, 4
　Buddha's Nirvana, 3
　cultural borrowing from India, 3
　Hinayana Buddhism, 3
　Mahayana Buddhism, 3
　relation between Asoka and the Chinese kings, 4
Sanskritization, source of, 15
Sarvastivadin, 12
Saunders, Trelawney, 58
Sebu La, 137–38
17-Point Agreement, 28–30, 62
Shah, Amit, 116–17
Shanghai Cooperation Organisation (SCO), 89
Shashtrata, 10
Shatra, Lonchen, 48–49, 76
Shekhar, Chandra, 110
Shih, Hu, 3, 6, 11, 14, 16–20
Simla Convention (1914), 48–54, 57, 59–60, 65, 67–68
Singh, Charan, 33
Singh, Jaswant, 113
Singh, Manmohan, 116
Singh, Rajnath, 89–90, 116
Singh, Zorawar, 57
Sino-Indian Agreement (1954), 71
Sino-Indian border, 2, 45, 47, 65–68, 71, 90–91, 100, 115, 124–25, 136, 138, 151, 155
　capturing of Indian military personnel, 96
　core truth on, 124
　delineated through age-old customs, 45
　focal point of dispute, 45
　settlement of the, 124
　tragic verdicts of research on the, 97
　talks, 115

Sino-Indian history, 2, 6
Sino-Indian military conflict, 101
Sino-Indian normalization, 113
Sino-Indian relations, 2, 10, 20, 22, 109, 114, 116
Sino-Indian War (1962), 29, 93, 120, 124, 137
Sino-Pak friendship, 146-56
　China has been one of Pakistan's main suppliers of military equipment, 151
　China-Pakistan Military Committee, 152
　Chinese acceptance of Kashmir dispute, 150
　Chinese participation in Pakistan's nuclear programme, 152
　comprehensive nuclear cooperation agreement, 153
　considerable nuclear collaboration between China and Pakistan, 151
　defence cooperation of China with Pakistan, 112
　fundamental strategic proposition, 146
　military strategy and tactics, 149
　nuclear understanding against India, 153
　Pakistan's objectives of acquiring political and military superiority over India, 150
　Sino-Pak boundary agreement, 151
　testing of Indian political leadership's practical sense, 156
Sino-Pakistan Agreement of 1963, 115
Sino-Russian relationship, 148–49, 167
Sino-Russian trade, 149
Sino-Soviet border, 46
Sino-Soviet dispute, 98
Sino-Soviet hostility, 104
Sino-Soviet rivalry, 146
Sino-Tibetan frontier, 53, 56
Sino-US relations, tensions in, 148

Six-Point Agreement of the PMs, 80
Soft measures in stitching, 123
South Asian Association for Regional Cooperation (SAARC), 154
Southeast Asia Treaty Organization (SEATO), 150
Soviet Union
  invasion of Czechoslovakia (1968), 45
  reverted to neutrality on the Sino-Indian dispute, 100
Stockholm International Peace Research Institute (SIPRI), 132-133
Strachey, John, 47
Strategic realignment of forces in Asia, 166
Suez Crisis (1956), 45
Sumdorong Chu Valley, clash of Indian-Chinese armed forces, 108
Survey of India, 52, 57, 60-61, 71, 75, 78, 119
  Aksai Chin area as 'boundary undefined', 57
  showed the McMahon Line as 'undemarcated', 57
Suslov, Mikhail A., 99
Suspicions and hopes, 29-32

Tactical action to persuade China, 122
Tantric Buddhism, 14
Tantric variety, 15
Tashkent Declaration (1966), 155
Tawang Tract, 40, 52-53
Tawang, India's seizure of, 60
Terrorism in Kashmir, 154
Thapliyal, Sheru, 138
Thimayya, Kodendera Subayya, 84
Thirteenth Dalai Lama, 25, 52
'Three Treatise' school of Buddhism, 13
Tian Shan Mountains, 9

Tibet
  autonomy of, 25, 31
  Chinese Suzerainty over, 24-25, 52
  Communist Chinese intentions on, 2
  India's extra-territorial rights in, 66
  invasion of Sikkim, 40
  refugees in India, 31
Tibet Autonomous Region (TAR), 25, 40
Tibet Human Rights Centre, 41
Trade-off between China's relations with Pakistan, 167
Trade Protocol agreement (1983), 110
Transcending geographies, 8-11
Treaty of Lhasa, 24
Trump, Donald, 146

UN Charter and Resolutions, 41
Unearthing British perfidy, 47-59
  tripartite conference in Simla, 47
Union of Soviet Socialist Republics (USSR), 1
United Progressive Alliance (UPA) government, 116
UNSC veto-holding seat, 26
Upgradation of China's logistic capabilities, 112
US 'strategic relationship' with China, 38
USSR's 'ideological error' to support 'bourgeois' India, 98

Vajpayee, Atal Bihari, 32-34, 37-38, 40-41, 111-14, 116, 131
  clarificatory statement to parliament in September 1998, 113
  crystalizing effect of letter, 113
  'secret' letter to Clinton, 131
  travelled to Beijing, 37
Vajrabodhi, 14
Vedic Indian music, 19
Veto-holding seat of China in the UNSC, 95

Vikramaditya or Chandragupta II, 6

Walton, John, 54
Westernization, 104
World Bank, 132
World War I, 53, 164
World War II, 2, 44–45, 58, 85
'Wrong maps', question of, 72

Xiaoping, Deng, 30, 46, 80, 102, 104, 106–8, 113, 123, 139–40, 166
Xilian, Huang, 122
Xin dynasty, 10
Xing, Yao, 13
Xinhai Revolution (1911), 51
Xinhua News Agency, 96, 104
Xinjiang-Aksai Chin-Tibet Road, 88
Xinjiang province, Islamic fundamentalism in, 168

Yangtze Valley, 16

Yaobang, Hu, 30
Yeltsin, Boris, 146
Yi, Chen, 89
Yi, Wang, 115
Yijing, 12
Yingfu, Lei, 101
Younghusband, Colonel Sir Francis, 24
Yuan dynasty, 15, 23
Yumen (Jade Gate), 8
Yung-Hsi, Li, 5–6

Zedong, Mao, 26, 30
Zemin, Jiang, 114–16
   visit to India (1996), 110, 116
Zero-sum game, 92-102
Zhou dynasty, 4
Zia-ul-Haq, 152
Zili, Pan, 88
Zoroastrian Iran, 9
Zoroastrians, 11